I0033810

Financial Sector Development in Africa

Financial Sector Development in Africa

Opportunities and Challenges

Thorsten Beck and Samuel Munzele Maimbo,
Editors

THE WORLD BANK
Washington, D.C.

© 2013 International Bank for Reconstruction and Development / The World Bank
1818 H Street NW
Washington, DC 20433
Telephone: 202-473-1000
Internet: www.worldbank.org

Some rights reserved

1 2 3 4 15 14 13 12

This work is a product of the staff of The World Bank with external contributions. Note that The World Bank does not necessarily own each component of the content included in the work. The World Bank therefore does not warrant that the use of the content contained in the work will not infringe on the rights of third parties. The risk of claims resulting from such infringement rests solely with you.

The findings, interpretations, and conclusions expressed in this work do not necessarily reflect the views of The World Bank, its Board of Executive Directors, or the governments they represent. The World Bank does not guarantee the accuracy of the data included in this work. The boundaries, colors, denominations, and other information shown on any map in this work do not imply any judgment on the part of The World Bank concerning the legal status of any territory or the endorsement or acceptance of such boundaries.

Nothing herein shall constitute or be considered to be a limitation upon or waiver of the privileges and immunities of The World Bank, all of which are specifically reserved.

Rights and Permissions

This work is available under the Creative Commons Attribution 3.0 Unported license (CC BY 3.0) http://creativecommons.org/licenses/by/3.0. Under the Creative Commons Attribution license, you are free to copy, distribute, transmit, and adapt this work, including for commercial purposes, under the following conditions:

Attribution—Please cite the work as follows: Beck, Thorsten, and Samuel Munzele Maimbo, eds. 2012. *Financial Sector Development in Africa: Opportunities and Challenges*. Directions in Development. Washington, DC: World Bank. doi: 10.1596/978-0-8213-9628-5. License: Creative Commons Attribution CC BY 3.0

Translations—If you create a translation of this work, please add the following disclaimer along with the attribution: *This translation was not created by The World Bank and should not be considered an official World Bank translation. The World Bank shall not be liable for any content or error in this translation.*

All queries on rights and licenses should be addressed to the Office of the Publisher, The World Bank, 1818 H Street NW, Washington, DC 20433, USA; fax: 202-522-2625; e-mail: pubrights@worldbank.org.

ISBN (paper): 978-0-8213-9628-5
ISBN (electronic): 978-0-8213-9629-2
DOI: 10.1596/978-0-8213-9628-5

Cover design: Naylor Design, Inc.

Library of Congress Cataloging-in-Publication Data
Financial sector development in Africa : opportunities and challenges / editors, Thorsten Beck, Samuel Munzele Maimbo.
    p. cm.
    Includes bibliographical references.
    ISBN 978-0-8213-9628-5 — ISBN 978-0-8213-9629-2 (electronic)
    1. Finance—Africa. 2. Finance—Government policy—Africa. 3. Financial services industry—Africa. 4. Africa—Economic conditions—21st century. I. Beck, Thorsten. II. Maimbo, Samuel Munzele.
    HG187.5.A2F558 2012
    332.1096—dc23

                                                                                    2012029611

Contents

Figures

Tables

Foreword

The environment for African financial systems has changed considerably over the past years. Notwithstanding the recent global crisis that has impacted our perceptions of financial sector development generally, Africa retains a strong sense of optimism for the future. I am among many who feel that Africa has an unprecedented opportunity for sustained economic growth and poverty reduction. African financial sectors have a key role in leveraging that opportunity.

The challenge of our time remains, however, translating this optimism into jobs for millions of Africans who enter the workforce every year. To create jobs and increase competitiveness, the private sector in Africa needs a dynamic and robust domestic financial sector that mobilizes savings, finances firms' and households' investments into productive capacity, and provides them with the payment and other financial services they need to expand their business activity and reach new markets.

It is for this reason that I particularly welcome the papers contained in this edited volume. Each systematically addresses many of the areas in which specific challenges need to be addressed and opportunities captured if we are to accomplish Africa's jobs agenda. By taking a fresh look at microfinance, mobile banking, housing finance, agricultural finance, and the regulatory and supervisory agenda in Africa, this publication sets us on the right path.

In their own way, each paper points to the need to address Africa's financial sector challenges with domestic solutions. *Financing Africa: Through the Crisis and Beyond*, published in 2011—for which the papers in this volume were commissioned as background papers—rightly adopted the mantra "best fit" rather than "best practice." The papers in this publication reinforce this position. For example, when I speak with investors and bankers in Africa, many of them emphasize that banks are highly liquid, both from resources within and outside Africa. Remittances sent back by the African diaspora have become an important element of these resources. Our collective challenge is to pay attention to the growth of Africa's domestic funding base—that is, better mobilizing domestic savings, especially from the informal sectors, and improving the intermediation capacity of formal finance to ensure that Africa's growth is sustainably funded over the long term. Hence, a focus on strengthening the local financial sector and deepening local financial markets is central.

By digging deeper into some of the critical themes presented in *Financing Africa*, this current book will help policy makers concentrate on the critical issue of the effectiveness and efficiency of the financial intermediation function, in the midst of the unique political economy environment present in Africa, with realism and pragmatism. As the last paper reminds us, sustainable reforms require a willingness to work with second-best policies. Some political environments, for example, may make it difficult to rely on efficient courts to promote financial inclusion. In such countries a focus on the low-hanging fruit, such as encouraging relationship-lending schemes or social entrepreneurship, might offer limited progress but also a more promising way forward.

I, therefore, look forward to the debate that this book will foster on the selected topics it covers. Each is exciting for Africa in its own right. I thank the editors and contributors for their work as it not only makes a critical contribution to our research and thinking about financial sector development in Africa, but also highlights areas where we do not yet know enough and need more thinking. I am hopeful that *Financial Sector Development in Africa: Opportunities and Challenges* will help us all in better implementing and supporting the financial sector agenda in Africa.

Gaiv Tata
Director
Africa Region and Financial Inclusion Global Practice
Financial and Private Sector Development
The World Bank

Acknowledgments

The editors of this book, Thorsten Beck and Samuel Munzele Maimbo, acknowledge with thanks the role of Issa Faye and Thouraya Triki, their co-authors for *Financing Africa: Through the Crisis and Beyond*, in the selection of background papers for that publication that have been included in this volume. We thank the contributors to this volume for their quality of work and their patience in the review and editing of this publication: Mike Coates, Florence Dafe, Michael Fuchs, Robin Hofmeister, Alexandra Jarotschkin, Thomas Losse-Mueller, David Porteous, Simon Walley, and Makaio Witte. We are grateful to Stephen McGroarty and Stephen Pazdan of the World Bank Office of the Publisher for coordinating the book design, editing, and production process, and to Hope Steele for the editing of the book.

The edited volume was published under the overall guidance of Shantayanan Deverajan (Chief Economist, Africa Region, World Bank) and Gaiv Tata, (Director, Africa Region & Financial Inclusion Global Practice, World Bank). It also benefited from the support and guidance from management: Irina Astrakhan (Sector Manager), Paul Noumba Um (Sector Manager), and Michael Fuchs (Advisor), all members of the Finance and Private Sector Development, Africa Region. This publication benefited additionally from the partnership the authors continue to enjoy with the Secretariat of the Making Finance Work for Africa Partnership led by Stefan Nalletamby (Coordinator) and his team including Alessandro Girola, (MFW4A Knowledge and Research Manager), Rim Nour (Research Officer), and Olivier Vidal (Assistant Research Officer).

The authors, on behalf of the World Bank and on their own behalf, are especially grateful to the Deutsche Gesellschaft für Internationale Zusammenarbeit GmbH (GIZ) for having provided financial support that was very helpful in the editing of this publication.

Editors and Contributors

Editors

Thorsten Beck, Professor of Economics and Chairman of the European Banking Center: Before joining Tilburg University and the Center, he worked at the Development Research Group of the World Bank. His research and policy work has focused on two main questions: What is the effect of financial sector development on economic growth and poverty alleviation? and What are the determinants of a sound and effective financial sector? Recently his research has focused on access to financial services by small and medium enterprises and households. Thorsten has a PhD in Economics from the University of Virginia (1999) and a Diploma (MA) from Universität Tübingen (1995).

Samuel Munzele Maimbo, Lead Financial Sector Specialist, Europe and Central Asia (ECA) Finance and Private Sector Department, World Bank: Prior to joining the ECA Department, Samuel was lead financial sector specialist in the Africa region for five years. Before joining the World Bank, he was a Senior Bank Inspector at the Bank of Zambia and an auditor at Price Waterhouse. A Rhodes Scholar, Samuel obtained a PhD in Public Administration from the University of Manchester, England (2001); an MBA from the University of Nottingham, England (1998); and a Bachelor of Accountancy from the Copperbelt University, Zambia (1994). He is also a Fellow of the Association of Chartered Certified Accountants, United Kingdom, and a Fellow of the Zambia Institute of Certified Accountants.

Contributors

Mike Coates, Director of GBRW Consulting: GBRW is a London-based consulting firm focused on the banking sector in emerging markets. He is a former professional banker with extensive international experience in both financial services and the consulting environment. Mike specializes in strategy and planning, strategic marketing, and risk management for commercial banks. He has developed and delivered successful financial sector assignments in markets including the Arab Republic of Egypt, Azerbaijan, Ethiopia, Ghana, Kenya, Russia, Saudi Arabia, Syria, Tajikistan, and Vietnam. He has a BSc in Financial Services awarded by the University of Manchester and is an Associate of the Chartered Institute of Bankers.

Florence Dafe, Researcher, World Economy and Development Finance Department, German Development Institute, Bonn: Florence is a political economist and researcher at the World Economy and Development Finance Department of the German Development Institute in Bonn. She holds an MSc in Development Studies with a specialization in Development Economics and an MA in Communications, Politics and Economics from the University of Munich.

Michael Fuchs, Advisor, Finance and Private Sector Department, Africa Region, World Bank: Michael has worked in the Africa Region since 2003, focusing on financial sector development issues across a broad spectrum of countries. He worked for eight years in the Bank's ECA Region, five of which were focused on Russia in the wake of the financial collapse in 1998. He has a PhD and an MA from the University of Copenhagen and a BA from the University of York (UK).

Robin Hofmeister, Financial Sector Specialist, World Bank, Nigeria, and GIZ's Pro-Poor Growth and Promotion of Employment Program: Before being seconded to the World Bank, he worked in GIZ's program Promoting Financial Sector Dialogue in Africa: Making Finance Work for Africa, where he led the multidonor working group on agricultural finance.

Robin studied at the Universities of Münster, Germany, and Stellenbosch, South Africa, where he received his MSc in Business Management.

Alexandra Jarotschkin, Consultant, Development Economics Research Group, Macroeconomics and Growth Team (DECMG), World Bank: Prior to joining DECMG, Alexandra was a Mercator Fellow, working in the Africa Finance and Private Sector Development Department in Washington, DC, as well as in the International Monetary Fund's Resident Representative Office in Tanzania. A German National Academic Foundation and Friedrich Ebert Stiftung Scholar, Alexandra holds an MA in International Economics, Finance, and Development from the School of Advanced International Studies, Johns Hopkins University, and a BA from the Free University of Berlin.

Thomas Losse-Mueller, Financial Sector Specialist, World Bank: Thomas joined the World Bank in 2004, where he has worked on financial and private sector development projects in a variety of African and Eastern European countries. From 2008 to 2010, he led work on behalf of the German government in supporting the establishment of the Partnership for Making Finance Work for Africa. Prior to joining the World Bank, he worked in risk management for an international investment bank. He holds degrees in Economics from the School of Oriental and African Studies and the University of Cologne.

David Porteous, Managing Director, Bankable Frontier Associates: David has been involved in development finance internationally for the past two decades. He has had executive roles in public and private financial institutions in Africa, and is the founder and managing director of Bankable Frontier Associates, a consulting firm based in Boston. The firm specializes in advising on policy and strategy that promote financial inclusion, serving financial regulators and policy makers, private financial providers, bilateral and multilateral donors, and private foundations around the world. The firm seeks to optimize the return on its triple bottom lines of financial return, a positive social impact on end-clients, and the building of the knowledge base in the sector.

Simon Walley, Housing Finance Program Coordinator, Financial and Private Sector Development, World Bank: Simon joined the World Bank in 2006, working on a range of countries from Central Asia, Eastern Europe, the Middle East, and Sub-Saharan Africa. In particular he has worked on the development of secondary mortgage markets through the creation of liquidity facilities, mortgage subsidy schemes, market analyses, and covered bond legislation. Prior to his move to Washington, DC, Simon worked in housing finance for almost 10 years with the European Mortgage Federation and the Nationwide Building Society, and served as a regulator for the Financial Services Authority in the United Kingdom.

Makaio Witte, Junior Professional Associate, Africa Finance and Private Sector Development Department, World Bank: Makaio is a Junior Professional Associate in the Africa region of the World Bank. In his current position, he focuses on banking regulation and supervision in Africa and the impact of the European debt crisis on African financial sectors. Before joining the World Bank, Makaio worked as a research associate at Re-Define, an international think tank, on postcrisis financial market reforms and at GIZ in the program Making Finance Work for Africa. Makaio obtained a Master of Public Policy at the Hertie School of Governance in Berlin, and a BA in International Relations at the TU Dresden, Germany.

Abbreviations

ABCDE	World Bank Annual Bank Conference of Development Economics
AFI	Alliance for Financial Inclusion
AML/CFT	Anti Money Laundering/Combating the Financing of Terrorism
API	application programming interface
ATMs	automated teller machines
BCBS	Basel Committee on Banking Supervision
BCPs	Basel Core Principles for Effective Banking Supervision
BDS	business development services
BOG	Bank of Ghana
CBK	Central Bank of Kenya
CBN	Central Bank of Nigeria
CFT	Combating the Financing of Terrorism
CGAP	Consultative Group to Assist the Poor
CDD	customer due diligence
DDR	Disarm, Demobilize and Reintegrate
EMFN	Egyptian Micro-Finance Network
EMV	Europay-Mastercard-Visa
FAI	Financial Access Initiative
FOGAPE	Fondo de Garantía para Pequeños Empresarios

FSB	Financial Stability Board
FSD	Financial Sector Deepening
FSDT	Financial Sector Deepening Trust
FSI	Financial Stability Institute
GhIPSS	Ghana Interbank Payment and Settlement Systems
GIZ	Deutsche Gesellschaft für Internationale Zusammenarbeit GmbH
GPFI	Global Partnership on Financial Inclusion
GSM	global system for mobile communications
KCB	Kenyan Commercial Bank
KWFT	Kenya Women's Finance Trust
KYC	know-your-customer
IFIs	international financial institutions
IFS	International Financial Statistics
IPO	initial public offering
IRB	internal ratings-based approach
IT	information technology
ITU	International Telecommunication Union
MFI	microfinance institution
MIX	Microfinance Information Exchange
MNO	mobile network operator
MRFC	Malawi Rural Finance Corporation
NGO	nongovernmental organization
NIBSS	Nigeria Inter-Bank Settlement System
OIBM	Opportunity International Bank Malawi
PAR	portfolio at risk
POS	point of sale
RIM	Research in Motion
RTGS	real-time gross settlement system
SMEP	Small and Micro Enterprise Programme
SME	small and medium enterprise
SMS	short message service
SACCOs	savings and credit cooperatives
SOE	state-owned enterprise
UCB	Uganda Commercial Bank
USSD	unstructured supplementary service data

Introduction

Thorsten Beck and Samuel Munzele Maimbo

Africa's financial systems face challenges across many dimensions, as discussed in the report *Financing Africa: Through the Crisis and Beyond*.[1] The analysis in that report was based partly on several detailed background papers that are included in this volume. The next six chapters are written by experts in their respective areas and provide an in-depth analysis of these challenges and present possible solutions. In this introduction, we provide an overview of the different chapters and how they are related to each other and the main volume.

Part I: Expanding Access

The three chapters in part I focus on key challenges concerned with access to financial services, including financial and operational deficiencies in the microfinance market, reaping the benefits from the technological revolution of retail banking, and deepening and broadening agricultural finance across Africa. The three chapters thus each cover different aspects with a different focus, ranging from an institutional approach to a focus on innovation as a driver of financial broadening to an important element of financial infrastructure to a specific sector.

Financing Africa advocates a broader approach to financial inclusion, including looking at a broad set of institutions to deliver financial services to the bottom of the pyramid. Notwithstanding this approach, however, we recognize that microfinance institutions will continue to play a decisive role in the expanding access agenda in the coming years.

In chapter 1, **Alexandra Jarotschkin** gauges the current state of microfinance institutions (MFIs) across Africa, both in comparison with other regions of the world and within different subregions in Africa. She documents the limited outreach of African MFIs into rural areas and the slowdown in their expansion in the wake of the global financial crisis. She then discusses several challenges that microfinance in Africa must confront, including cost constraints, deficiencies in understanding clients' needs, absent or inefficient prudential and nonprudential regulation, and the lack of financial infrastructure.

Technology can be a game changer in the economics of retail banking. This is especially important in Africa, where financial systems face high barriers to further outreach, including high transaction costs. **David Porteous** focuses in chapter 2 on one specific aspect: mobile financial services. In the past decade, Africa has incubated some of the earliest deployments of mobile payment services and now hosts some of its most successful providers. Porteous's chapter characterizes the development of mobile financial services across several models. He predicts the rise of a new model that is based on mobile Internet and can thus help overcome market segmentation and monopoly barriers, with a truly transformative impact on expanding access to finance in Africa. While the first generation of mobile payment services provided only an additional delivery channel for existing customers, second-generation models—such as Celpay in Zambia and M-Pesa in Kenya—reached out to new, previously unbanked clientele. The fragmented nature of the mobile phone market in many African countries, the lack of interconnectedness of mobile phone providers, and the dependence of the second-generation model on mobile phone companies, however, limit the growth of mobile financial services. Porteous points to the promise of third-generation, mobile Internet-driven models that will enable a whole new range of providers to offer payment services to the public. Finally, a host of regulatory and competition issues arise from the rapid expansion and development of mobile financial services.

One sector where expanding access is especially challenging is agricultural finance. In chapter 3, **Mike Coates** and **Robin Hoffmeister** describe the many challenges that financing agriculture in Africa poses, but they also describe possible solutions. The barriers to financial broadening—high costs, high volatility, high informality, and governance challenges—loom even more prominently in agricultural and rural finance than in other sectors. Fostering competition and the adoption of technology-driven financial innovation is thus even more important in agriculture than it is in other sectors. The authors show how agribusiness, rural banks and credit unions, and small agricultural producers can adopt tactical solutions to catalyze the power of big commercial banks and private investors. They provide several examples of successful innovation in the region that involved new products and new providers, new delivery channels, and new connections among different segments of the financial system and the agricultural sector. However, they also point out that finance is only part of the solution and note that other major challenges in the policy and business environments and supporting infrastructure still remain to be overcome.

Part II: Lengthening Contracts

The challenges in long-term finance loom as large as those involved in expanding the outreach of the financial system. Africa faces many long-term investment needs, but lacks the necessary resources, markets, and products to satisfy these needs. This part of the book takes a detailed look at one of the areas where long-term finance is needed—housing finance.

In chapter 4, **Simon Walley** takes stock of housing finance in Africa. He documents the sizable need for additional housing in many African countries, based on these countries' continuous population growth and an ongoing urbanization trend. The current lack of housing finance has contributed to the urban sprawl with largely informal, poor-quality housing. He describes different housing finance regimes across Africa, their funding structure, and their refinancing schemes. He points to the major constraints for expanding housing finance in Africa: the lack of affordable housing, the lack of capacity and the high risk aversion of lenders, the adverse macroeconomic environment, and the lack of land titling.

Part III: Safeguarding Finance

As African financial systems deepen and broaden, new challenges arise for regulators and supervisors across Africa. In chapter 5, **Michael Fuchs, Thomas Losse-Mueller,** and **Mikaio Witte** discuss the repercussions of regulatory reforms in Europe and North America for African regulators as well as local challenges. They compare and contrast key elements of the international reform discussion with the priorities for reform in Africa and advocate a "building block" approach to defining reform roadmaps for regulatory and supervisory reform. Although Africa has escaped the direct impact of the global financial crisis, the authors point to several weaknesses in local financial systems that must be addressed, including gaps in regulatory frameworks and governance deficiencies. While many countries have committed to moving from Basel I to Basel II in spite of limited implementation capacity, most of the measures proposed under Basel III are of limited immediate relevance to African banking sectors, since the weaknesses they address are largely a result of regulatory philosophies and market practice in developed markets. An increasingly important challenge will be the regulation and supervision of cross-border banks and the cooperation that this requires across the continent.

Part IV: Financial Sector Reform: Activism and Local Political Conditions

Finance in Africa does not suffer from a lack of solutions, but from a lack of implementation. In *Financing Africa*, we advocate replacing the best practice with the best-fit approach. In chapter 6, the final chapter of this volume, **Florence Dafe** discusses the politics of financial sector reform in Africa and, more specifically, the space needed for an activist role for government to help create the markets and coordination mechanisms necessary for financial markets to deepen and broaden. How can governments in the political and economic environments typical of Africa intervene to increase the financial resources available for productive investment? The author describes the development that has occurred over the past decades, from market-replacing activist policies through the abandonment of government intervention in favor of modernist strategies toward a pro-market activist role of government. She points to politics as a key determinant of the effectiveness of government interventions and stresses critical differences between East Asia and Africa that can explain why government was more successful in its interventions in the former than the latter. Finally, she provides a framework for evaluating the conditions under which activist policies can work without being captured by incumbent elites for their own socioeconomic interests.

Note

1. Beck, T., S. Munzele Maimbo, I. Faye, and T. Triki. 2011. *Financing Africa: Through the Crisis and Beyond*. Washington, DC: International Bank for Reconstruction and Development/World Bank.

PART I

Expanding Access

CHAPTER 1

Microfinance in Africa

Alexandra Jarotschkin

Microfinance has been frequently celebrated as a panacea to help remedy poverty in a financially sustainable way among those who could not be reached previously: those without collateral and, very prominently, women. Hence, it is understandable that after the outreach success of microfinance institutions (MFIs) in South Asia, they were soon to be spotted in other regions, including Africa. Since their appearance, MFIs have been credited with the promise of decreasing the levels of financially excluded people on the continent. A decrease is necessary as currently countries on the continent display levels of exclusion ranging from 23.5 percent in South Africa (FinScope 2010a) to as high as 78 percent in Mozambique (FinScope 2009a), with many other countries somewhere in between. But have MFIs delivered on this inherent promise of financial inclusion? This chapter will first provide a quick reality check, pinning down precisely the efficacy of microfinance on the African continent in terms of growth and outreach in the previously excluded groups. Building on that clear understanding of the actual situation, the second part of the chapter will outline current obstacles to the microfinance mission on the continent, as well as some selected industry and regulatory best-practice solutions to these obstacles.

The chapter starts with an examination of some key outreach indicators, comparing across world regions and African subregions. Indicators that provide information on outreach are (1) MFI's financial penetration;[1] (2) the percentage of borrowers who are female; (3) average loan balances; and (4) the percentage of rural clients, rural automated teller machines (ATMs), and points of sale (POS). The next section will focus on the impediments to implementing this outreach and, where possible, some best-practice suggestions from across Africa. While impediments in this context are numerous, this chapter chooses to focus on four prominent ones: (1) cost constraints, (2) deficiencies in understanding clients' needs, (3) lack of or inefficient prudential and nonprudential regulation, and (4) the absence of financial infrastructure. In an effort to keep the depiction of impediments and some best-practice solutions close to each other, each obstacle description will begin with a summary recommendation, and, where possible, provide examples of pioneering MFIs and progressive regulation or financial infrastructure in Africa. A more detailed illustration of the same will follow.

Microfinance Outreach

Africa's microfinance industry has been growing. The continent's total asset increase over the last five years has been in line with a worldwide trend of a growing industry. On the whole, MFIs apparently weathered the financial crisis better than most industries until 2010, looking at asset growth rates. Yet, in 2010 asset growth rates not only slumped but also contracted and have yet to return to their precrisis growth levels (figure 1.1; MIX and CGAP 2009).

Banks, such as Equity Bank in Kenya and Capitec in South Africa, have garnered special attention over the last years, holding roughly US$1.7 billion and US$2.1 billion, respectively, in 2010. Both banks grew notably even throughout the crisis, even though Equity Bank could not sustain the gigantic precrisis growth rates of 190 percent per annum that it recorded in 2007 (up from roughly 82 percent growth per annum in 2006) after listing on the Nairobi Stock Exchange.

Outreach to Clients below National Poverty Lines

While the total assets of microfinance institutions have been growing, the overall reach of the industry has remained minor. In the overall picture of finance, MFIs in Africa make up only a small part of total assets compared with the MFIs in other world regions (table 1.1). In 2010 MFIs in Africa reported reaching nearly 7 million borrowers and a significantly larger

Figure 1.1   Total Asset Growth across Regions, 2005–10

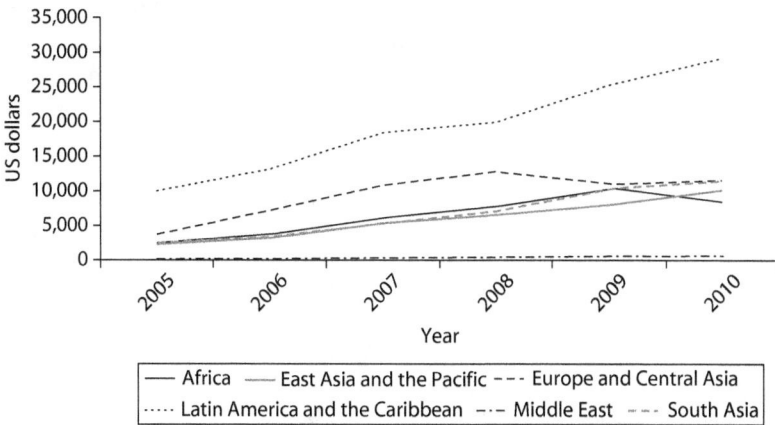

Source: MIX Market database 2012, http://www.themix.org/publications/mix-microfinance-world.
Note: All figures provided by MIX Market represent trends only because not all MFIs in a country report to the database.

Table 1.1   Total Borrowers, Depositors, and Penetration Rates, 2010

Measure	Africa	North Africa	East Africa	Southern Africa	Central Africa	West Africa
Population below national poverty line (millions)	437.9	31	91.3	73.6	65.8	176
Total borrowers (millions)	7.1	1.8	2.5	0.6	0.3	1.8
Penetration rate for borrowers (%)	1.6	5.7	2.8	0.8	0.5	1.0
Total depositors (millions)	17.5	0.03	10.5	0.6	1.1	5.3
Penetration rate for depositors (%)	4.0	0.1	11.5	0.8	1.6	3.0

Sources: Author's calculations based on the World Bank's World Development Indicators (database), http://data.worldbank.org/indicator; the CIA World Factbook, https://www.cia.gov/library/publications/the-world-factbook/; MIX Market database 2012, http://www.themix.org/publications/mix-microfinance-world.
Note: All figures provided by MIX Market represent trends because not all MFIs in a country report to the database.

17 million depositors. With considerably more borrowers than Eastern Europe, Central Asia, and the Middle East, these figures still bring Africa's borrower penetration rate to just 1.6 percent[2]—significantly lower than all other regions globally, aside from Eastern Europe and Central Asia. The savings penetration rate is somewhat higher at 4.0 percent.

Although total borrower and depositor growth rates were recorded at 11 percent and nearly 20 percent, respectively, in 2009, these rates contracted by 31 percent and 15 percent, respectively, in 2010. Breaking the number of borrowers and depositors down further into subregions, a very diversified picture unfolds: MFIs in East and North Africa take the lead by delivering loans to 2.5 million and 1.8 million borrowers, respectively, while MFIs in Southern (0.59 million borrowers), Central (0.31 million), and West Africa (1.82 million) are lagging behind (figure 1.2a). And yet all regions remain far below the 10 percent penetration rate. MFIs in North and East Africa have a penetration rate of only 5.7 percent and 2.8 percent, respectively, while MFIs in Southern, Central, and West Africa deliver loans to only 0.8 percent, 0.5 percent, and 1 percent of borrowers living below the national poverty line. As for depositors, MFIs in East Africa count nearly 10.5 million (11.5 percent penetration rate). MFIs in West and Central Africa account for 5.3 million and 0.5 million depositors, respectively—still, these numbers mean that only 3 percent and 1.6 percent of the poor are reached. Way behind are MFIs in Southern and North Africa, with only 0.6 million and 0.03 million depositors in 2010, which means only 0.8 percent of Central Africa's poor and even fewer— 0.1 percent—of the poor in North Africa have access to deposits. This range is remarkable since all regions started out with a similar level of depositors in 2000 (see figure 1.2b). MFIs in East Africa did not experience depositor growth spurts until 2002 but grew significantly afterwards, through the crisis and beyond, though to finally slump in 2010.

Figure 1.2   Total Borrowers and Depositors across Africa, 2000–10

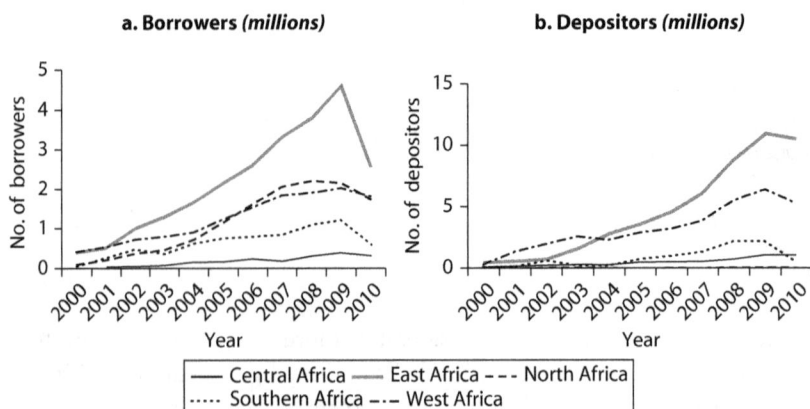

a. Borrowers *(millions)*   b. Depositors *(millions)*

— Central Africa — East Africa - - - North Africa
····· Southern Africa —·— West Africa

Source: MIX Market database 2012, http://www.themix.org/publications/mix-microfinance-world.
Note: All figures provided by MIX Market represent trends because not all MFIs in a country report to the database.

A Special Focus on Female Borrowers in Africa

One of the most obvious reasons why microfinance has focused on women, especially in its infancy, is the disproportionate effect of poverty on them. In Africa overall, the median ratio of women to total borrowers has been constantly above 50 percent and peaked around 78 percent, both in 2005 and in 2010 (figure 1.3). While these ratios were lower in Latin America and the Caribbean (65 percent) and the Middle East (46 percent) in 2010, they were higher in South Asia and in Europe and Central Asia, at 80 percent and 99 percent, respectively. On the subregional level, only North and Southern African MFIs cater to more women than the continent-wide median MFI.

Urban versus Rural Supply of Microfinance

Microfinance has been applauded for reaching into areas and providing access to customers that other financial services have left out. All across Africa, the rural population is vastly underserved by financial institutions. Unfortunately, thus far microfinance has not been the exception to this trend. According to data from the Consultative Group to Assist the Poor (CGAP) and World Bank (2010) on branches across Africa, the distribution of rural microfinance services—such as ATMs and POS locations—is rather slim compared with urban ones (see figure 1.4).

Figure 1.3   Ratio of Women to Total Borrowers, 2005–10

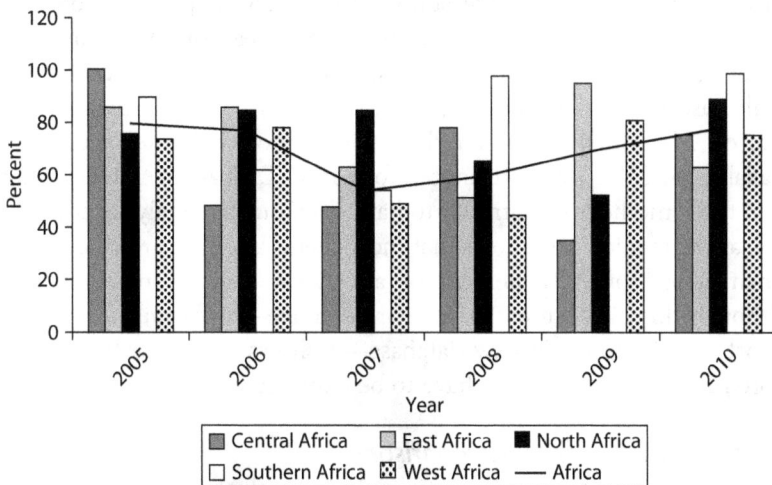

Source: MIX Market database 2012, http://www.themix.org/publications/mix-microfinance-world.
Note: All figures provided by MIX Market represent trends because not all MFIs in a country report to the database. Data represent subregional medians.

Figure 1.4   Rural and Urban Distribution of ATMs and POS, 2010

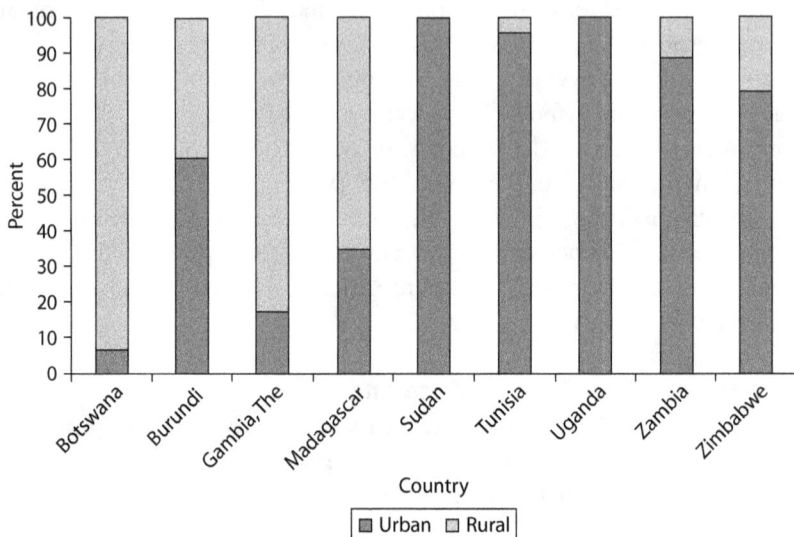

Source: CGAP and World Bank 2010.

Reaching out, MFIs face the same costs as banks, and infrastructure deficiencies make this effort costlier than in other world regions. Undoubtedly, MFIs have various ways to reach out to their rural clients—not only through extending their branch networks. Loan officers can travel to disburse loans or at least make trips to collect payments on loans, hence improving access for rural customers. Measuring the number of rural clients rather than the rural branch network would thus capture the "real" distribution of MFI services to those areas. Unfortunately, the data on MFI rural and urban client distribution, collected and openly available on MIX (Microfinance Information Exchange),[3] do not show even these methods of outreach to have been outstandingly successful. A look at the median MFI shows that most clients are from urban and semi-urban areas;[4] only 37 percent of all clients come from rural areas. Although this distribution is not representative—so far only a few MFIs report to this relatively new database—it shows that in order to reach more rural clients, new ways have to be explored.

Borrower and Depositor Comparisons

Comparing depositor growth rates in Africa with those of other regions in the world shows that Africa occupies a special position. Depositor growth rates have been accelerating—they decreased and contracted only

Figure 1.5   Depositor Growth Rates and Average Balances, 2005–10

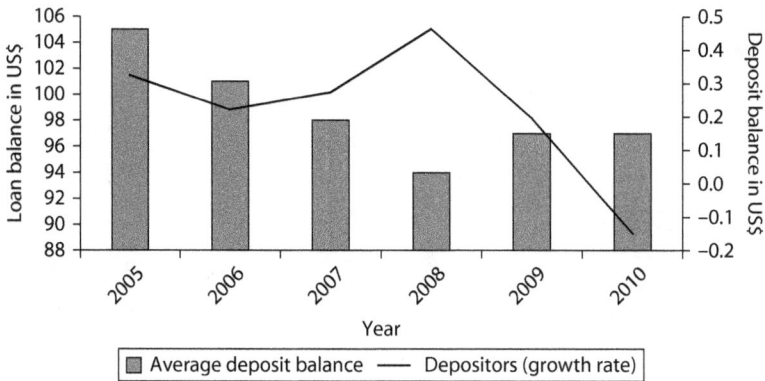

Source: MIX Market database 2012, http://www.themix.org/publications/mix-microfinance-world.
Note: All figures provided by MIX Market represent trends because not all MFIs in a country report to the database.

in 2009 and 2010 (figure 1.5). Regional comparison shows that Africa's depositor growth rates were matched only by the Middle East for 2009, leaving all other regions far behind, with some—such as East Asia and the Pacific—even experiencing negative growth rates. Yet this trend reversed in 2010, when East Asia and the Pacific and Europe and Central Asia experienced positive growth rates while the number of African depositors contracted.

Borrower growth rates have behaved very differently in Africa: falling continually for the past five years, they dropped to 8 percent in 2009, only to fall further in 2010 (figure 1.6). The further contraction in the borrower growth rate in the latter year has been paralleled only by Europe and Central Asia, while all other regions recovered and grew again after contracting during the height of the financial crisis.

Average loan balances are frequently used to explain a further dimension of outreach. If balances are decreasing, MFIs are going downmarket, serving poorer clients and vice versa (Cull, Demirgüç-Kunt, and Morduch 2006). The same can be assumed for average deposit balances in general, because poorer clients can save only smaller amounts in absolute terms.

Looking at Africa, the regional median of average deposit balances has been decreasing but increased again in 2009 and 2010. Although this indicates that outreach has been stepped up, it may also be a sign of MFI clients being able to save less because of inflationary pressures in the economy. Some support for this theory can be found in the increase in average loan balances—potentially, these are funds used for consumption

Figure 1.6   Loan Growth Rates and Averages Balances, 2005–10
(regional median)

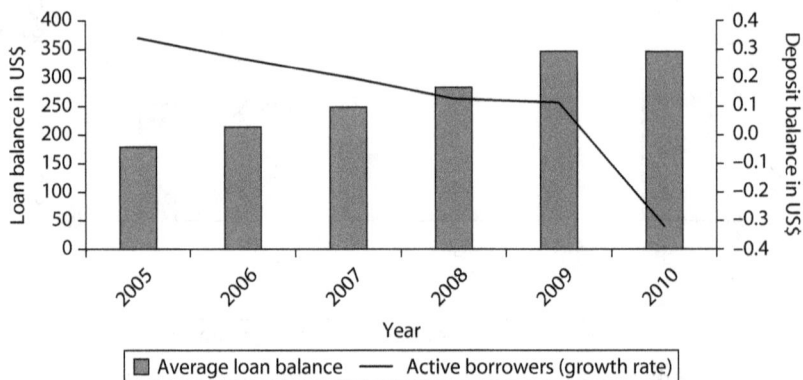

Source: MIX Market database 2012, http://www.themix.org/publications/mix-microfinance-world.
Note: All figures provided by MIX Market represent trends because not all MFIs in a country report to the database.

smoothing (MIX and CGAP 2009). Simultaneously, higher average loan balances illustrate MFIs rendering services to marginally richer clients over the past years. Although the regional average of loan balances has been notably larger than the regional median, the latter has been growing faster over the years. This illustrates an upmarket movement not only for the upper spectrum of MFIs but also for the median MFI.

On a disaggregate level, the business decision has been evident for Equity Bank (in Kenya) and Capitec (in South Africa), which have continually increased their average loan balances over the last years until 2010, up by 100 percent (2007) and 82 percent (2009), respectively. Increasing average loan balances and average deposit balances are certainly not required—some MFIs have illustrated otherwise. For example, Compartamos, the Mexican MFI, after issuing an initial public offering (IPO) in 2007, expanded its client base in the same market segment—as strong borrower growth post-IPO and constant average loan balances indicate. Yet, for existing Compartamos customers, the equity influx did not come with the advantage of lower interest rates; Equity Bank, however, did decrease interest rates. Indeed, Equity halved its median yield on portfolio, from roughly 40 percent (2006) to 20 percent (2007) after publicly listing on the Nairobi Stock Exchange on August 7, 2006, and was at 17 percent in 2010. Although Capitec did not publicly list, the bank also decreased its median yield to portfolio from 188 percent (2005) to 47 percent (2010).

Impediments to the Microfinance Industry and Best Practice Solutions

If MFIs in Africa are to expand their outreach—without a significant increase in external funding—they need to become more efficient and productive by decreasing the cost of due diligence.

Cost Constraints and the Application of Technology

In general, lending out $1 million in $100 increments will require higher staff costs than lending out the sum to only one person because of the due diligence involved. One way to decrease costs is to lend the sum to fewer customers—to go upmarket. To remain serving the same market segment or go even further downmarket, MFIs need to find other ways to jump the cost barrier: m-banking and biometric technology can be the game changers necessary. Another beneficial effect of m-banking especially is that it can also assist MFIs reach into rural areas by helping overcome infrastructure deficiencies and thus the costs involved in physically reaching out. Every MFI will have to conduct a cost-benefit analysis to understand the viability of technology application with respect to its scale, methodology, and the state of regulation in its country of operation.

Cost savings needed to expand MFIs' outreach. To extend their outreach, MFIs need to improve their performance. In 2010, MFIs in Africa performed the worst in a cross-regional comparison, with a return on assets of 1.02 percent, while the return on assets performance in the Middle East was strongest, at 3.99 percent. Although operating at lower levels, a closer look at the overall performance of MFIs in Africa over time shows that median returns on assets have slumped only in 2009 in comparison with the returns of previous years, and have already increased in 2010 (figure 1.7).

The comparatively lower return on asset performance by MFIs in Africa coincides with their cost structure (figures 1.8a,b and 1.9a,b). While financial costs are kept low because of successful deposit mobilization,[5] high overall expenses stem from operating costs (MIX and CGAP 2009). Overall, the cost per borrower for MFIs in Africa has increased steadily over the last several years. Although this could be seen as a sign of decreasing efficiency in nominal terms, it might also be the result of MFI's double-bottom line that includes reaching out to poorer clients. Somewhat surprisingly, the cost per borrower ratio has been only a third that of the ratios of East Asia and the Pacific and South Asia.

Figure 1.7   Median Return on Assets across Africa, 2005–10

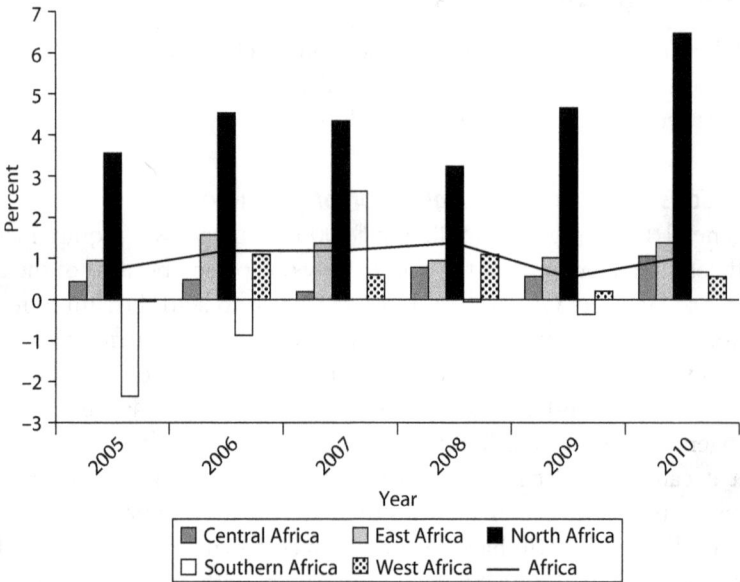

Source: MIX Market database 2012, http://www.themix.org/publications/mix-microfinance-world.

Figure 1.8   Costs and Borrowers, World Regional Medians, 2005–10

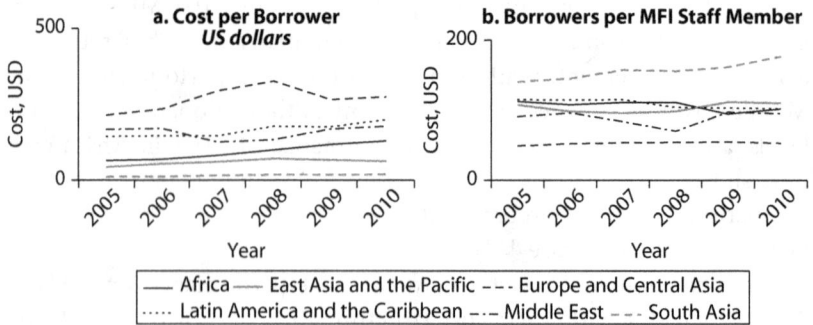

Source: MIX Market database 2012, http://www.themix.org/publications/mix-microfinance-world.

However, this cost does not take into account the lower per capita gross domestic product (GDP) terms because most African countries have a much lower gross national income (GNI) than countries in other regions. Hence, the ratio per capita would display these costs at an astronomically higher level than other regions. In terms of productivity, Africa has been performing slightly better in international comparison. Although return

Figure 1.9   Costs and Borrowers, African Subregional Median, 2005–10

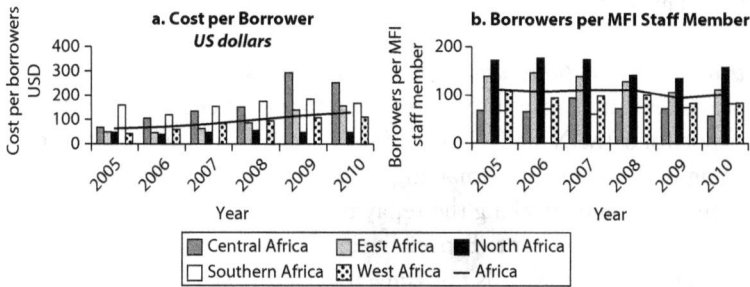

Source: MIX Market database 2012, http://www.themix.org/publications/mix-microfinance-world.

Figure 1.10   Median Yields on Gross Portfolio across African Subregions

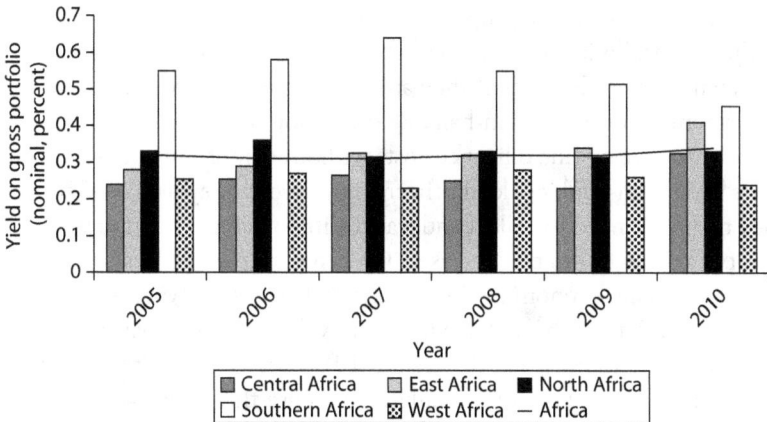

Source: MIX Market database 2012, http://www.themix.org/publications/mix-microfinance-world.

on asset performance does not depend only on efficiency and productivity, it would coincide with the efficiency and productivity of better-performing regions within Africa. The weakest-performing regions in terms of productivity and efficiency—Central and Southern Africa—also have the lowest returns on assets, while North Africa in particular, followed by East Africa, is on the opposite side of the spectrum.

High costs also show up in the interest rates that MFIs in Africa charge: only MFIs in the Middle East had a higher yield on portfolio than those in Africa. Overall in Africa, the median yield portfolio rose from 2009 to 2010 (figure 1.10). On the subregional level, median yields to portfolio decreased for MFIs operating in Southern and West Africa, whereas those for MFIs in East and Central Africa increased. While financial sustainability is crucial, it would be more welcome to see this development happen through increased efficiency and productivity in the near future rather than through increases in the yield to portfolio.

Improving productivity and efficiency for MFIs. MFIs in Africa need to improve their cost structure to allocate more of their funds toward their loan portfolio (MIX and CGAP 2009). For MFIs, due diligence means meeting with the client; explaining the loan procedure; and following up on, collecting, and checking the repayment. In some cases it also involves travel time to the client. Especially in the African context, where an abundant supply of labor is not a given, resulting staff salaries are high—magnifying already-high operating costs. In fact, MFI staff salaries on the African continent have been roughly three times higher than they are in the continent's peer regions (MIX and CGAP 2009).

If MFIs decide not to go upmarket, or if they want to sustain a large part of their portfolio in the same market segment, their due diligence obligations will remain the same if they are to avoid risking lower levels of loan repayment. However, the m-banking revolution might hold some answers for how to save on due diligence costs without compromising credit discipline.[6] Using m-banking, loan officers may save money and time because they no longer need to collect and travel with loan repayments. Hence, the cost per borrower can be decreased. Costs for the client will also decrease. Customers can economize by incurring less risk, saving money and (opportunity) time, by not having to travel with their loan repayment either (Kumar, McKay, and Rotman 2010). Various MFIs already in place have started making use of m-banking to secure these advantages.

After the rollout of M-Pesa, the mobile phone–based money transfer service, various MFIs in Kenya and Tanzania have started using the service for loan repayment. The MFI Tujijenge Tanzania, for example, has made the repayment of individual loans via M-Pesa below the threshold of US$1,800 mandatory. In Kenya, various MFIs offer the repayment via M-Pesa for both individual and group loans—that is, the Small and Micro Enterprise Programme (SMEP) and Kenya Women's Finance Trust (KWFT). As the SMEP, Tujijenge, and the KWFT only started using M-Pesa in 2009 for loan repayments, it is too early to tell whether the application of this technology and potential cost-savings will also be realized in lower interest rates. Moreover, deposit-taking MFIs allow their customers to save with them through M-Pesa. The most prominent example of such an arrangement is Equity Bank's product M-Kesho. In this fashion, MFIs can save further on transaction costs and arguably increase the savings propensity of most clients, because they do not have to physically travel to deposit their money. Studies looking at developed countries show that reminders encourage people to save more (Karlan et al. 2010). Using text messages to remind people to save, for example, might increase this propensity even further. More access to deposits for MFIs, in turn, drives down the cost of funds and thus lowers financial expenses.

One of the reasons for the longer time spent with the customer is the absence of client information, not only in regard to credit history but also formal identification. To save on screening time, biometric technology can be one innovative way to go. Opportunity International Bank Malawi (OIBM) was one of the first to pilot this technology in Africa. The bank captures clients' biometric information to provide convenient and secure access to finances for clients without means of formal identification. When a client opens an account, his or her fingerprint is scanned and stored in the bank's system, enabling electronic transactions at retail and ATM locations (OIBM 2011). A randomized control trial with the Malawi Rural Finance Corporation (MRFC) has illustrated how this can be instrumentalized to ensure higher loan repayment rates.[7] Every borrower in the test group had to leave his or her fingerprints with the MRFC and participate in a training session. In the training session, the MRFC demonstrated to its clients how the machinery would identify the client correctly, would not lend in case of nonrepayment, and would share this information with other banks, such as the OIBM. The results showed that fingerprinting can help increase repayment rates, especially among borrowers with ex ante higher risk profiles (Giné, Goldberg, and Yang 2010).

Cost-benefit analysis. Whether the application of m-banking and other technologies will generate cost savings or not will greatly depend both on a given MFI's methodology and scale, and on whether the regulatory provisions for the new technology are already envisioned.

Although cutting costs is one of the main ways to grow in most businesses, this correlation is not as simple for MFIs. Lower borrower per staff member ratios have been associated with higher returns on assets when looking at individual lending MFIs, because more time is necessary for due diligence (Cull, Demirgüç-Kunt, and Morduch 2007). In instances where MFIs rely significantly on loan officers and client interaction to build up credit discipline, m-banking might even have counterproductive effects. Faulu Kenya, for example, uses group repayment mechanisms and thus has declined to use m-banking for repayments, making use of the m-banking service for deposits only (Kumar, McKay, and Rotman 2010). Some studies have shown that it is possible to transition from group to individual repayment mechanisms without incurring more defaults.[8] When this move was successful, group meetings were still held despite the transition to individual liability. It is worth considering these findings when thinking about a transition to individual liability and m-banking and the use of frequent mobile reminders about client repayment rates.

Next in importance to methodology considerations is the scale of the MFI. Implementing m-banking solutions in a small MFI might be cost-intensive and thus will require that the initial application costs and the resulting profits be carefully evaluated accordingly. Consequently, particularly for smaller MFIs, it will be necessary to find ways to save costs when trying to access m-banking or biometric technology. Doing so early in the process will be crucial for success. From getting permission from m-banking operators to receive training sessions to exchanging knowledge and information about common problems, costs could potentially be saved if MFIs teamed up. In the Kenyan example, MFIs approached M-Pesa separately to receive the allowance for using the service.

The opportunities presented above apply to MFIs operating in countries where this type of technology already exists and is sufficiently well regulated. If MFIs wish to pilot this technology, they can jump into a difficult and tedious technological process, concurrently having to gain permission to launch the services. Lessons learned by the OIBM might prove useful for other MFIs on the continent as well.[9] On the technological side, Aleksandr-Alain Kalanda, Chief Executive Officer (CEO) of the OIBM, admits that the process took "longer and was more expensive and complicated to implement" than expected. He points to some of the pre-requisites necessary prior to rolling out a comparable service. Among these are the following:

1. A proven track record to implement complex technology-based projects
2. A strong core banking IT infrastructure that is able to handle large volumes of data flow
3. Substantial financial resources available to pay not only for the technological solution but also for the human resources, the agent network, and a significant marketing campaign.

Cost hurdles, as suggested by the OIMB's CEO, can also be overcome by teaming up with other MFIs.[10] In the case of the OIBM, which is equipped with a commercial bank license, the Central Bank of Malawi was in favor of the idea and granted permission.[11]

Understanding clients' needs and putting them into practice

Decreasing costs is not the only way to increase outreach. A good understanding of low-income clients' needs and respective product delivery is also necessary. Unfortunately, as a practitioner describes in the most recent *Banana Skins* report (CSFI 2011), MFIs that offer a comprehensive suite of financial services to their clients are "as common as unicorns." To increase outreach, MFIs need to carry out their own market research as well as utilize publicly available research. They must understand what different products are needed in their area and deliver those products modified to meet the needs of their respective clients. Both elements can help not only to better service current clients but also reach new ones. Furthermore, to increase the utility that current but also future clients can derive from an MFI's financial services, financial literacy training will be key.

Understanding clients. It is not only poor entrepreneurs who need access to financial services, nor are all poor people entrepreneurs. This holds true everywhere in the world, including Africa: various studies have shown how the poor use access to credit. The initial focus of MFIs on microcredit has been questioned in the literature, illustrating that the poor and underserved are as much in need of appropriate savings, payment, and insurance instruments as they are in need of microcredit. The influential book *Portfolios of the Poor* by Collins et al. (2009) has shown that in the minds of the poor, savings and credit are frequently interchangeable: the poor use credit to smooth consumption because they lack appropriate instruments to save safely.

The need for savings is reflected in the use of M-Pesa for storing money. The service had 13,341,387 customers and 23,397 agents as of December 2010 (Safaricom 2011). M-Pesa revolutionized the payment space but also our knowledge about the savings needs of a lot of Kenyans. The third-most-important use of M-Pesa—after sending and receiving money—has been storing it for everyday use. Savings, even at a zero interest rate, helps people protect their funds from being stolen on a journey or at home. Earning interest is the number one priority of customers for possible M-Pesa improvements (FSD Kenya and CGAP 2009). This idea was realized by M-Kesho, the partnership between M-Pesa and Equity Bank. M-Pesa illustrated not only the need for savings products but also the need for payment services that had been, thus far, vastly underrepresented and expensive in Africa. Nearly 28 percent of people using M-Pesa did not have a prior bank account. Next to offering the right product suite, MFIs need to understand how to deliver these suites conveniently to customers (FSD Kenya and CGAP 2009).

How to improve and use client knowledge. To better determine which product customers demand most, MFIs need to enhance their understanding of their customers' needs. They need to find out whether MFIs lack credit, insurance, payment services, and/or deposits through market research. Research is costly, however, and—as with all other improvements—needs to be done in a cost-efficient way. Thus far, 84 percent of MFIs in Africa have "used market research to identify client needs."[12] Together with MFIs in East Asia and the Pacific (84 percent) and Latin America and the Caribbean (85 percent), this is the lowest percentage of MFIs—in all other regions, 91 to 100 percent of reporting MFIs carry out market research to identify clients' needs. Moreover, only 43 percent of MFIs in Africa commission market research occasionally and 14 percent claim to order these services on a biannual basis; only 12 percent commission research regularly. In terms of regularly commissioned market research, this is the weakest performance across all regions: in East Asia and the Pacific it is 22 percent; in Europe and Central Asia, 40 percent; in Latin America and the Caribbean, 25 percent; in the Middle East, 42 percent; and in South Asia, 28 percent.

Although it is difficult to replace one's own market research, such research is frequently expensive. Yet research results that are already available can also be used to good advantage. In recent years, publicly available information on demand constraints has increased. For various African countries, FinScope delivers a report every two years that deals with financial access questions about what kind of access customers have (that is, whether their access is formal, semi-formal, or even informal); on which grounds customers make their financial decisions; and which constraints frame their choices and in some cases make it impossible for them to be financially included in any way. These studies are also broken down along areas within a country. Other in-depth studies, frequently in the form of randomized control trials, have been provided by the World Bank and J-PAL–affiliated professors.[13] More information about specific questions and countries has been provided by Gallup, Financial Sector Deepening (FSD) Kenya, and Financial Sector Deepening Trust (FSDT) Tanzania. Even if not directly applicable to very specific areas, this information may help to frame knowledge that MFIs have in hand about an area, and can help cut down on market research design costs.

Some examples of how to deliver the right services in the right way have been pioneered by Equity Bank and Capitec. According to Napier (2011), these two banks understood that customers who had thus far been excluded needed to be treated very differently from those familiar with financial services, and products and processes needed to be designed accordingly but, importantly, "without ever compromising on operating performance." Equity Bank initially delivered services to the "urban, non-salaried and collateral-less population" that had not caught the eye of existing banks. An important aspect of Equity's program was its attention to making customers feel accepted through high-quality service delivery—that is, by disbursing loans quickly. Much the same was true for Capitec Bank in South Africa. Capitec concentrated on poorer neighborhoods and former homelands. The bank provided flexible opening hours so that commuters could get to the bank after work.[14] Another example of investing in research and delivering the right product the right way has been M-Kesho. With M-Kesho, customers can save with Equity Bank without having to walk into the physical bank by depositing through m-banking services. Customers who normally lack a safe savings device gain access without incurring high extra costs because they can complete their transaction at any of the multiple outlets that allow M-Pesa. Furthermore, customers do not face requirements of a minimum balance or account opening fees or monthly charges to save (FAI 2010).

Equity Bank has served different excluded groups: women have been one of them. Female clients are generally less likely than men to have a formal bank account (Gallup 2010). Recent research has shown that women are less likely to have access to financial services in Africa than their male counterparts not because of their gender but because of other factors such as lower levels of education, the lack of a steady source of income, and not being the head of the household (Aterido, Beck, and Iacovone 2011). Thus, women may be less likely to access financial services because they might lack the necessary collateral or because they might not be legally privileged to the ownership of family belongings that could be used as collateral.[15] Loans that incorporate this information are more likely to increase loans to women.

In partnership with the United Nations Development Programme, Equity launched the Fanikisha project,[16] which provides access to financial services, information, and financial literacy training to women entrepreneurs (Business.UN.Org 2009). Through this project, Equity Bank provides loans without the traditional and inhibitive security requirement that used to lock out potential women entrepreneurs.

In six different loan facilities, Equity Bank offers loans from K Sh 1,000 to over K Sh 10 million with competitive interest rates and flexible repayment rates. A special feature of Equity Bank loans is that it also provides other discounted services, such as access to business improvement training and the chance to network with other business start-ups (Equity Bank 2010; for more details, see table 1.2).

Being proactive: financial literacy training. Providing market research and product suites that have been modified to reflect the results of that research is not yet the end of the story. Being proactive and trying to remedy demand constraints with financial literacy training might help bring down barriers to banking one step further. Recently derived evidence shows that, in the case of Tanzania, 25.8 percent of people do not bank because of knowledge barriers (FinScope 2010b). In Zambia at least 5.1 percent do not use banks, claiming they "do not understand how a bank works" (FinScope 2009b). This is likely to be correlated with people who cannot afford formal bank accounts, but it might also have to do with financial literacy issues. At least a percentage of people will not know about the possibility that they can access or be denied finance because they have insufficient knowledge about the potential benefits of accessing financial services.

Financial literacy training is costly, but it helps MFIs to strengthen their current client base, as well as build up a future one by increasing banking knowledge and trust in financial services among their customers, going against a "banking-is-not-for-me" sentiment that many people now hold. In particular, this is true for women for the reasons mentioned above. Women in Africa are less likely to make financial decisions because these decisions are mainly the province of their husbands. Of course, this is a very general statement, and the actual situation varies by the country and tribal context. Through financial literacy training, women might gain a different self-understanding with respect to finance. Furthermore, current clients are more likely to make sound financial decisions when they learn how to factor in their economic possibilities; thus, they are more likely to understand the consequences of overindebtedness. Looking at the current situation and the concerns expressed by the industry (credit quality concerns rank number one in the 2011 *Banana Skins* report), financial literacy training might have the power to improve credit discipline, thus paying out not only in the longterm but in the short-term as well.

Data compiled from surveys by the Social Performance Task Force database (by MIX and CGAP) show that—when compared with other

Table 1.2 Fanikisha Project

Type of loan facility	Fanikisha Shaba	Fanikisha Fedha	Fanikisha Imara	Fanikisha Dhababu	Fanikisha Almasi	Fanikisha Platini
Target group	For women in start-up process and microenterprises who would like to borrow through group approach Targets women who lack conventional securities Targets those in merry-go-round market	Targets women who have overcome challenges of business start-up Targets women who lack conventional securities to secure their loans and would borrow through group approach	Targets women in micro level who would want to borrow individually It is designed to support the growth and development of women micro-enterprises/small-scale businesses who lack conventional collateral to secure loans	Targets women in SME level who would want to borrow individually It is designed to support the growth and development of women small and medium businesses	Targets women in SME level who would want to borrow individually It is designed to support the growth and development of women small and medium businesses	Targets women in medium and large enterprises who would want to borrow individually It is designed to support the growth and development of women small and medium businesses
Features	Lending to groups (15–30 members) Access to loans from K Sh 1,000 to 300,000 Repayment period of 6–12 months Interest rate 1.25% per month	Lending to groups (7–10 members) Access to loans from K Sh 300,000 to 1,000,000 Repayment period of up to 18 months Interest rate 1.25% per month	Lending to individuals Access to loans from K Sh 30,000 to 500,000 Repayment period of up to 18 months Interest rate 1.25% per month	Lending to individuals Access to loans from K Sh 500,000 to 3,000,000 Repayment period of up to 24 months Interest rate 1.25% per month reducing	Lending to individuals Access to loans from K Sh 3,000,000 to 10,000,000 Repayment period of up to 36 months Interest rate 1.25% per month reducing	Lending to individuals Access to loans from K Sh 10,000,000 and above Repayment period of up to 5 years. Interest rate 1.25% per month reducing (negotiable)

(continued next page)

Table 1.2 *(continued)*

Type of loan facility	Fanikisha Shaba	Fanikisha Fedha	Fanikisha Imara	Fanikisha Dhababu	Fanikisha Almasi	Fanikisha Platini
Benefits	Access to business improvement training at very good discounts	Access to business improvement training at discounted rates	Access to discounted business improvement training	Access to discounted business improvement training	Access to discounted business improvement training	Access to discounted business improvement training
	Access to business advisory services	Access to business advisory services	Access to advisory services	Access to advisory services	Access to advisory services	Access to advisory services
	Chance to network and interact with other business people	Chance to network and interact with other business people	Flexible collaterals	Flexible collateral requirement	Flexible collateral requirement	Collateral flexibility up to 15% above normal
	Flexible repayment period	Flexible repayment period	Good repayment period	Good repayment period	Good repayment period	Good repayment period
	Very competitive interest rates	Speedy loan processing	Very competitive interest rates	Speedy loan processing	Speedy loan processing	Speedy loan processing
	Ability to borrow 10 times your savings	Very competitive interest rates	Opportunity to graduate to the next level with relaxed security requirements	Very competitive interest rates	Very competitive interest rates	Very competitive interest rates
	Opportunity to graduate to the next level (fanikisha fedha)	Ability to borrow 5 times your savings		Opportunity to attend motivational talks and trade fairs	Opportunity to attend motivational talks and trade fairs	Opportunity to attend international trade fairs and motivational talks
		Opportunity to graduate to other levels				

Source: Equity Bank loan offerings, available at http://www.equitybank.co.ke/loans.php?subcat=107 (accessed April 2012).
Note: SME = small and medium enterprise.

world regions—together with South Asian MFIs (20 percent), Africa (21 percent) has the smallest percentage of MFIs that responded to the survey option "yet to carry out financial literacy training," thus illustrating that at least the MFIs that took part in the survey understood the importance of financial literacy and invested in it.[17] A very large-scale example of a financial literacy campaign is currently being carried out by the Equity Group Foundation and the MasterCard Foundation. The project is supposed to cost more than K Sh 1 billion and target women and youth in particular by engaging 619,500 entrepreneurs over the next three years (Equity Bank 2010). By 2011, the program has already trained 57,000 people across Kenya (Kass Media Group).

Prudential Regulation

In order to increase the variety of products to include savings, prudential regulation has to become more viable for both the MFI and the regulator by being risk-based and incurring less costs. To ensure that the client is protected from deceptive financial practices, the equilibrium between more financial access and stability will have to include consumer protection as well. Particularly for MFI services, this has not yet been the case.

Deposit-taking MFIs. A look at the current funding structure of reporting MFIs in Africa shows that deposits are the main contributor to funding (figure 1.11). Equity—both commercial and donated—remains small overall (21 percent for 2010). MFIs in Africa, in an international comparison, have been generally successful in mobilizing deposits and have maintained slightly increasing levels of around 60 percent as a share of total funding in 2010. Predominantly, these deposits across different MFIs are voluntary deposit accounts. According to MIX and CGAP (2009), the funding structure composition strongly varies by organizational form. Deposits are an important funding base for credit unions and bank MFIs, while NGOs are a lot more dependent on borrowing as a source of funding. During the financial crisis, those institutions that relied more on deposits as their main funding source fared better (MIX and CGAP 2009). A comparison between deposit-taking institutions that were able to mobilize more deposits—those with more than 20 percent voluntary savings[18]—and those that were below this threshold shows that institutions in the first group, despite the crisis, were able to expand their number of borrowers from 12,000 to 15,500 in 2009. One reason was certainly the cheaper cost of funds. Another reason was the ability to offer loans at lower interest rates: the median yield on portfolio was 11 percent

Figure 1.11   Funding Structure of MFIs in Africa, 2005–10

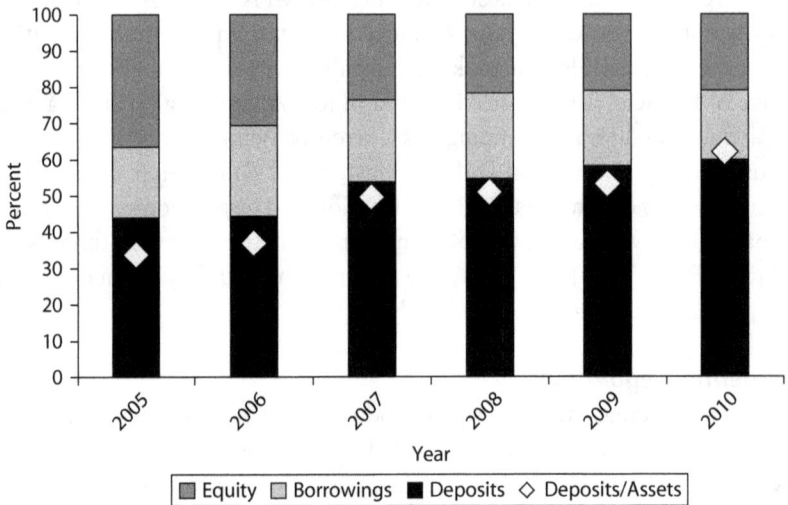

Source: MIX Market database 2012, http://www.themix.org/publications/mix-microfinance-world.

compared to 14 percent. Non-deposit-taking institutions drop out of the picture if they rely heavily on grants, as they can charge comparably lower interest rates because of their external funding.

Understandably, the industry's drive to become deposit-taking has been strong throughout the continent. According to Ehrbeck (2011), CGAP's new CEO, regulators should also have an interest in creating frameworks that endorse deposit-taking MFIs, as these are "inherently more attuned to their customers and thus likely to be more stable." It is good from an outreach perspective for the industry; it is also good from a stability point of view. Yet, what is witnessed on the continent is either the absence of clear regulation or what MIX and CGAP (2009) call a "worrisome gap between the adoption and enforcement of new regulation."

Twenty nine countries already have specialized microfinance laws in place and another five are drafting them (CGAP 2009). In some of these countries, MFIs—deposit- and non-deposit-taking—are supervised by the central bank fully, or responsibilities are shared with the ministry of finance. It is important to ensure that these bodies are not overburdened so that the scarce resources they do have can be allocated "risk efficiently." Three countries in Africa (Eritrea, the Seychelles, and Swaziland) have no form of legislation or framework for microfinance.[19] Another 15 countries have no specialized microfinance laws.[20] In these countries, MFIs fall implicitly or explicitly under the broader framework of the banking or nonbanking financial institutions legislation. It can be argued that this does not, in fact, create a level playing field between MFIs and banks, because MFIs are smaller in size and less complex in their financial transactions.

To help guide developing-countries' regulation, the Basel Committee on Banking Supervision (2010) has published its guidelines for deposit-taking MFIs. The very existence of this report is an acknowledgment of the increasing importance of microfinance. The report emphasizes the need for risk-based supervision that both tries not to overburden the industry and takes into account its differences. This way the supervisor, too, is less weighed down by regulatory activities.

The essence of risk-based prudential regulation and application. Apart from a few principles that are supposed to apply equally to banks and deposit-taking institutions,[21] the Basel Committee's guidelines suggest a tailored application of the Banking Core Principles to deposit-taking MFIs, taking into account the scope and size of their transactions and their limited complexity. For example, this means trade-offs in permissible activities and licensing criteria. While capital requirements might be lower than those of banks because of the smaller scope and simpler nature of their transactions, this same size and limited complexity might impose greater restriction on permissible activities. Further, different MFI activities will need to be ensured against shocks differently—that is, capital adequacy ratios need to be higher when MFIs are geographically concentrated and large and have few options for raising capital, and lower for the opposite, larger type of institution. As previously discussed in this chapter, MFIs need to find ways to save costs and become more efficient and productive. Regulation that takes this need seriously and incorporates it into regulatory realities will help the industry increase its outreach.

Simultaneously, scarce regulatory resources need to be allocated according to risk. The suggestions in the Basel Committee report emphasize the call for regulation that incorporates the need for specialized knowledge to identify and measure risks specific to microfinance. Across Africa, there is a need to build up specialized microfinance knowledge and (electronic) systems that can permanently track and respond to changing risks such as the risks involved with m-banking and using agents. To appropriately mitigate credit risk, the Basel Committee suggests setting loan documentation standards across the industry that reflect the distinct characteristics of MFIs: loans are the main asset and there is only one line of business.

Consumer protection. Beyond considerations of risk management, the trade-off between stability and access to finance will also have to be balanced with appropriate consumer protection. Effective disclosure and deceptive advertising have not been singular to banks during the financial crisis; they are widespread and widely dispersed among MFIs as well (CGAP and World Bank 2010). Better consumer protection regulation is costly for the regulator, but it certainly can help the industry increase its outreach by building trust between MFIs and its customers. The level of importance of these concerns is illustrated in the *Banana Skins* report (CSFI 2011), where "unfair competition" has been strongly lamented.

Disclosure at opening—defined as "the requirement to notify consumers in writing of pricing, terms, and conditions of a financial product prior to signing an agreement"—exists only in 40 percent of all African economies. In most cases, it is only commercial banks that are subjected to this regulation and not the whole array of financial institutions (CGAP and World Bank 2010). Even though an increasing number of countries have introduced or are about to introduce some form of disclosure requirement, only a few countries include specific language requiring MFIs to be covered also (CGAP and World Bank 2010).

Financial Infrastructure and Microcredit Rating Agencies

The Basel Banking Committee report is specifically geared toward deposit-taking MFIs, leaving out considerations on non-deposit-taking institutions. The regulation of deposit-taking institutions is to protect the depositor. Institutions that focus solely on microcredit have yet to reach the size at which they are systemically important, hence making prudential regulation unnecessary thus far (Christen, Lyman, and Rosenberg 2003). At the same time, increased competition in the absence of information has fueled imprudent lending practices that led to credit quality erosion. Thus, although credit-only MFIs might not require prudential regulation, financial infrastructure that is accessible to MFIs—such as credit bureaus—will be crucial to put an end to credit quality erosion. For this purpose, the infrastructure needs to encompass most of the MFIs in a country and to be competitively priced. The same is true for another mechanism that can help reinstate market discipline and sound competition: MFI credit rating agencies. Furthermore, these agencies also need to take in social ratings—that is, the assessment of the social performance of an MFI in terms of its ability to put its mission into practice and achieve social goals—to ensure competition along the double bottom line of MFIs: financial and social.

Financial infrastructure: A necessity. Concerns about credit quality erosion have become very real for Africa, as the 2011 *Banana Skins* report (CSFI 2011) illustrates. Although only at the back of the mind in previous surveys, credit risk now ranks as the number one concern worldwide, including in Africa. During the financial crisis, low repayment might have been fueled mainly by the dire economic situation of borrowers, along with unsustainable competition and the lack of credit information (MIX and CGAP 2009). In the absence of available information through credit bureaus and rating agencies and the "weakness of internal controls of MFIs," institutions oversupplied the same market segments and gave out loans to customers who were already overindebted (CSFI 2011). Moses Ochieng, CGAP/DFID regional representative, fears that overindebtedness might lead to the "implosion of some of the key players" in Southern and East Africa.

Looking at write-off ratios and portfolio at risk (PAR) data (> 30 days), this concern is justified (figure 1.12). Write-off ratios in Southern Africa for 2010 are nearly 1.2 percent, while East Africa slightly improved in terms of write-off ratios, PAR (> 30 days) increased sharply to 8.1 percent—above the African median. An even more pronounced deterioration in credit quality has been witnessed in North and Central Africa. North Africa started out with a low write-off ratio (2008, 0.05 percent) and ended up at 2.4 percent in 2010. Whereas Central Africa experienced a

Figure 1.12   Write-Off Ratios and Portfolio at Risk (PAR) (> 30 days)

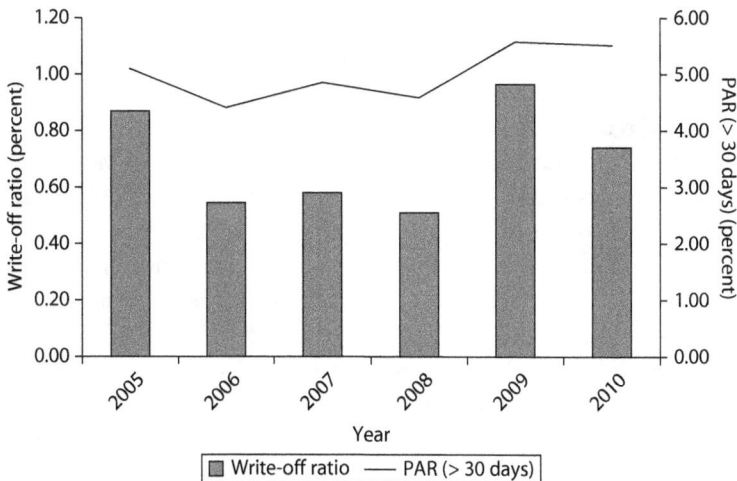

Source: MIX Market database2012, http://www.themix.org/publications/mix-microfinance-world.

decrease in write-off ratio to 1.1 percent in 2010, its PAR went up to 9.2 percent in the same year. Confirming the trend, West Africa's PAR went up to 8 percent and write-offs dropped to 0.2 percent. The overall African median was at a five-year high in 2009 in terms of write-offs, at around 0.96 percent; its PAR was 5.6 percent in 2009 and came down slightly in 2010. Compared with other regions, Africa has fared better than Latin America and the Caribbean (1.4 percent) in terms of its write-off ratio, but it is still high above the figures for the Middle East (0.06 percent), East Asia and the Pacific (0.35 percent), and South Asia (0.0 percent). As for PAR, Africa is again somewhat comparable to Latin America and the Caribbean's 4.81 percent but is above the ratios seen in East Asia and the Pacific (3.31 percent), South Asia (2.43 percent), and Europe and Central Asia (3.8 percent).

Credit bureaus. A great deal can be done in the form of financial infra-structure to relieve credit quality erosion. MFIs will require better credit information-sharing mechanisms and practical early-warning indicators to prevent unsustainable overlending. Credit registries and bureaus help provide a healthier environment for fairer competition for those clients with the best credit histories and raise incentives for borrowers to repay their loans. It can be argued that the use of credit history might be even more important for MFIs than it is for banks: the poorer the clients, the more important it is to replace the requirement for physical collateral with other means.

Despite the extent of credit quality erosion, overall only a few MFIs in Africa have been integrated into the continent's credit bureaus. In Sub-Saharan Africa, only in Burundi, Mozambique, Rwanda, South Africa, Tanzania, and Uganda are MFIs (and even there, only for deposit-taking institutions) required to participate in existing credit bureaus, even though 26 countries have public registries and 13 countries have private ones.[22]

A couple of lessons learned from a few African countries help illustrate the importance of cost-efficient set-ups and a full coverage of the MFI universe in a country. The more that MFIs that are concentrated in one geographic location share credit information, the more benefit can be gained for all. In Morocco, the four largest MFIs have started sharing credit information with each other through the informal service provided by one of them, Al Amana. Clearly, this puts these four MFIs at an information advantage. To bridge this gap, Morocco's Central Bank has been working on a registry that all MFIs are expected to provide information to and request it from. To ensure that all MFIs can afford to request information, competitive pricing will be necessary. The Arab Republic of Egypt's situation illustrates the type of problems that might arise with its credit information system I-Score. The high costs per inquiry relative to loan size made it impossible for NGO-MFIs to participate in the scheme. In response, the Egyptian Micro-Finance Network (EMFN), with financial support provided by the Social Fund for Development, contracted PlaNet Finance Egypt to establish an Information Sharing System for its network members. But because of an insufficient geographic overlap, the pilot was unsuccessful. Currently, the EMFN is negotiating integration into the I-Score registry at competitive costs.[23]

Microcredit rating agencies. Microcredit rating agencies have the potential to instate market discipline onto MFIs by publishing reports on their efficiency, growth, and outreach. The more MFIs these agencies rate, the more comparability, competition, and market discipline can be introduced. To ensure broad coverage, MFIs will need to be able to afford to buy a rating. Further, to make sure that microcredit ratings are installing market discipline but not at the cost of the social mission of the MFIs, social ratings should also be included in the report.

Currently, the universe of credit rating agencies that focus on MFIs is rather small. The two largest microcredit agencies—MicroRate and MCril, established in 1996 and 1998, respectively—have covered institutions across the globe.[24] Yet the number of institutions in a given country rated by these or other agencies is insufficient to ensure comparability and coverage of the set of all MFIs operating in that country. Furthermore, different rating grades and reporting formats among microcredit rating agencies have led MCril to criticize other agencies as being too liberal with MFIs, giving them "one to two notches above" what MCril itself assigned, and thus fueling the crisis of insufficient information about credit-worthiness.[25] Certainly, microcredit rating agencies are important and can help increase competition and market discipline in theory, but in practice they currently lack the coverage and standardization of assessment methods to do so.

The benefit of MicroRate is that it offers services for free to MFIs since it is fully funded by its own management. Commercial rating agencies have started moving into the microfinance space, also rather cautiously, as the partnership between Moody's and Kiva illustrates. Moody's has created a rating methodology for microfinance institutions and provided a pro bono credit rating to the 20 largest Kiva partners (Kiva.org 2009). Whether Moody's and other commercial credit rating agencies, if they see a business case in the future, are to reach scale in the MFI sector will depend heavily on their pricing. Currently, this is rather unlikely because Moody's and other commercial credit ratings agencies' interest will most probably lie only with larger institutions that will have only marginal impacts, if any, on market discipline overall.

The impact of microcredit rating agencies might not only be positive. If ratings focus solely on financial goals, various MFIs might end up competing for scarce resources along profitability criteria only and lose their broader outreach. To ensure that MFIs continue to meet their double bottom line, microcredit agencies will need to look at both indicators: social and financial. For now, this is unlikely to happen with commercial credit rating agencies; however, MicroRate has already incorporated a social performance evaluation. In this part of its report, MicroRate rates an institution according to the following elements (MicroRate 2011):[26]

- Mission, communication, and management
- Strategic planning
- Monitoring
- Client protection
- Customer service
- Recruitment and training
- Incentive system.

Other promising attempts to meet social goals are currently promoted through the MIX Market Social Performance Task Force surveys. These have been carried out for 2008 and 2009 thus far. The indicators included in these surveys range from rural outreach and target groups to market research on clients' needs. Currently, fewer institutions report to the social indicators database than to the standard MIX indicators. With more data, this information could provide useful material for international MFI comparison. Looking forward, it would be valuable if organizations, such as Kiva, that help even small investors to make their decisions would digest and include this information for every MFI promoted on their website. In the long run, this information could also be used by the government for comparative performance evaluation, on both social and institutional grounds, to assert tax incentives. As of now, tax breaks are determined by the profit or nonprofit status of an organization.

Conclusion

The MFI industry in Africa has grown significantly over the last several years, but it remains relatively small, as illustrated by its limited penetration rates. Apart from a few examples such as Equity and Capitec, most MFIs have yet to capture scale economies or increase outreach to the point where economies of scale are viable. To expand outreach, one option for MFIs in Africa could be to make use of m-banking and biometric technology. However, although this new technology may be viable for some MFIs, at its current stage it is not a panacea for all MFIs. Only a realistic cost-benefit analysis regarding scale, available methodology, and whether regulatory provisions are available and advanced enough in the country of operation to make the investment worthwhile can provide a reliable answer.

Although technology is a game changer, it is not everything. Investing in market research according to the MFI's financial capacity to understand its changing client needs and to diversify its product suites accordingly are just as important. Successful attempts—such as Equity Bank and Capitec—have illustrated ways that tailored products and services can bring change. Conducting market research and using existing publicly available studies are central to deepening knowledge about clients' product needs and specific delivery preferences. Recent data illustrate that MFIs in Africa have thus far carried out such research less frequently, on a regular basis, than other regions. Further action is necessary. Moreover, to make sure that current clients make the most use of different products available to them and more new clients can be acquired, financial literacy campaigns are important. The same sources show that the importance of financial literacy training in Africa has been broadly understood because only a few MFIs claim to have never carried it out.

To diversify their product suites to focus on deposits, MFIs frequently face regulation that is cost- and time-intensive at best and nonexistent at worst. Hence, to improve the transition from credit-only to deposit-taking MFIs successfully, regulation needs to be shaped with the size, scope, and complexity of MFI operations in mind. A report by the Basel Banking Committee is leading the way. This balance between financial access and stability will also need to take consumer protection into account. Thus far, only a few countries include MFI-specific language.

Prudential regulation for deposit-taking institutions will not suffice, as recent credit-risk concerns, which rank first in the *Banana Skins* report (CSFI 2011) among the concerns of all types of MFIs, illustrate. Complementary financial infrastructure that encompasses most MFIs in a given country and is affordable enough to be within their reach will be crucial. Hitherto, various countries offer credit bureau information to banks but largely do not cover MFIs because of uncompetitive pricing schemes. The next avenue to enhance nonprudential regulation would be standardized microcredit rating schemes with increased coverage. While these are a lucrative option, at least in Africa, they have yet to reach the scale and standardized rating processes necessary to instate market discipline and foster sound competition. Furthermore, the future design of rating agencies will have to be careful to be competitively priced and also include social components to strengthen competition along the double bottom line of MFIs: social and financial.

Notes

1. In order to make this estimate, *the poor* are defined as the population below the national poverty line.

2. The *lending penetration rate* is defined as active borrowers as a percent of population living below the national poverty line; the *savings penetration rate* is defined as depositors as a percent of population living below the national poverty line. These two definitions are taken from MIX and CGAP (2009).

3. See http://www.mixmarket.org/social-performance-data.

4. This is true for a few MFIs in the Democratic Republic of Congo, Ghana, Morocco, Tunisia, Uganda, and Zambia.

5. This is true only for the countries in the sample. Frequently, it is the stronger performing MFIs that report to the MIX database.

6. Information on how customers and loan officers can save time with m-banking is taken from Kumar, McKay, and Rotman (2010) and the CGAP Virtual Conference on "What benefits can MFIs expect to gain by using m-banking technology," accessed at http://technology.cgap.org/2010/09/08/virtual-conference-day-1-session-1-what-benefits-can-mfis-expect-to-gain-by-using-m-banking/.

7. The Malawi Rural Finance Corporation (MRFC) is a government-owned microfinance institution and the largest provider of rural finance in Malawi. The MRFC was established in 1993 following the collapse of the Small Holder Agriculture Credit Administration (SACA). The MRFC began operations in October 1994 using SACA's rural extension services offices of the Ministry of Agriculture and Irrigation (Luboyeski, Bagchi, and Chawinga 2004, 39). While its performance has been significantly above that of comparable institutions in the region, collection on loans has been deteriorating, falling from 90 percent in 2004 to 74 percent in 2006. The use of technology is aimed at arresting this deterioration (Giné, Goldberg, and Yang 2010).

8. See, for example, Giné and Karlan 2009. For this study, group meetings were still held but joint liability was converted to individual liability.

9. This information is taken from an interview with Aleksandr-Alain Kalanda, accessible at: http://technology.cgap.org/category/africa/Malawi.

10. This option is also described in Kumar, McKay, and Rotman 2010.

11. This information is taken from subsequent responses by Aleksandr-Alain Kalanda, accessible at: http://technology.cgap.org/category/africa/Malawi.

12. This is based on a sample of 49 MFIs that participated in either the 2008 or the 2009 Social Performance Task Force Survey provided on the MIX website http://www.mixmarket.org/social-performance-data.

13. Abdul Latif Jameel Poverty Action Lab (J-PAL) is a network of professors around the world who are united by their use of Randomized Evaluations (REs) to answer questions critical to poverty alleviation. See http://www.povertyactionlab.org/about-j-pal for more information.

14. All information on Capitec's and Equity Bank's service delivery is taken from Napier (2011).

15. In most cases in Africa, house or land is not accepted as collateral.

16. *Fanikisha* in Swahili means "achieve."

17. Thus far, there are only 47 reporting MFIs in the MIX social indicators database, including those in North Africa.

18. Definition is taken from MIX and CGAP (2009) report and the MIX benchmarking database.

19. All information on legislation and current credit bureau inclusion of MFIs is taken from CGAP (2009), quoted from MIX and CGAP (2009).

20. These are Angola, Botswana, Ghana, Lesotho, Liberia, Malawi, Mauritius, Namibia, Nigeria, São Tome, Sierra Leone, Somalia, South Africa, Tanzania, and Zimbabwe.

21. These are principle 1 (objectives, independence, powers, transparency, and cooperation); principle 4 (transfer of significant ownership); and principle 5 (major acquisitions). Three other principles would also apply equally once the industry becomes more advanced: principle 12 (country and transfer risk); principle 24 (consolidated supervision); and principle 25 (home-host relationships).

22. All information on legislation and current credit bureau inclusion of MFIs is taken from CGAP 2009.

23. All information on current credit bureaus in Egypt and Morocco is taken from MIX 2010.

24. See http://microrate.com/ and http://www.m-cril.com/conflictInterest.aspx.

25. See http://www.m-cril.com/Backend/ModulesFiles/NewsEvents/11-09-05_Mint_Article_Ratings_firms_liberal_with_MFIs_%20-_%20M-CRIL.pdf.

26. MicroRate's rating methodology is available at http://microrate.com/home/ratings-methodology/microfinance-institution-methodology.

References

Aterido, Reyes, Thorsten Beck, and Leonardo Iacovone. 2011. "Gender and Finance in Sub-Saharan Africa: Are Women Disadvantaged?" Policy Research Working Paper 5571, World Bank, Washington, DC.

Basel Committee on Banking Supervision. 2010. *Microfinance Activities and the Core Principles for Effective Banking Supervision.* Bank for International Settlements.

Business.UN.Org. 2009. "UNDP Partner with Equity Bank to Reduce Poverty and Promote Entrepreneurship by Increasing Women's Access to Credit." http://business.un.org/en/documents/2302.

CGAP (Consultative Group to Assist the Poor). 2009. *Overview of Microfinance-Related Legal and Policy Reform in Sub-Saharan Africa.* Washington, DC: CGAP.

———. 2010a. Conversation with Aleksandr-Alain Kalanda, Chief Executive Officer of Opportunity Bank of Malawi. http://technology.cgap.org/category/africa/malawi/.

———. 2010b. Virtual Conference on "What Benefits Can MFIs Expect to Gain by Using M-Banking Technology?" http://technology.cgap.org/2010/09/08/virtual-conference-day-1-session-1-what-benefits-can-mfis-expect-to-gain-by-using-m-banking/.

CGAP (Consultative Group to Assist the Poor) and World Bank. 2010. *Financial Access 2010: The State of Financial Inclusion through the Crisis.* Washington, DC: CGAP and World Bank.

Christen, Robert Peck, Timothy R. Lyman, and Richard Rosenberg. 2003. *Microfinance Consensus Guidelines: Guiding Principles on Regulation and Supervision of Microfinance.* Washington, DC: CGAP.

Collins, Daryl, Jonathan Morduch, Stuart Rutherford, and Orlanda Ruthven. 2009. *Portfolios of the Poor: How the World's Poor Live on $2 a Day.* Princeton, NJ: Princeton University Press.

CSFI (Centre for the Study of Financial Innovation). 2011. *Microfinance Banana Skins Report: The CSFI Survey of Microfinance Risk.* http://www.citi.com/citi/microfinance/data/news110125b.pdf.

Cull, Robert, Asli Demirgüç-Kunt, and Jonathan Morduch. 2006. "Financial Performance and Outreach: A Global Analysis of Leading Microbanks." World Bank Research Working Paper 3827, World Bank, Washington, DC.

———. 2007. "Microfinance Meets the Market." Research Working Paper 4630, World Bank, Washington, DC.

———. 2009. "Does Regulatory Supervision Curtail Microfinance Profitability and Outreach?" Research Working Paper 4748, World Bank, Washington, DC.

Ehrbeck, Tilman. 2011. "Reflections on the State of Access to Finance," March 30. http://www.cgap.org/p/site/c/template.rc/1.26.15875/.

Equity Bank. 2010. "Equity Bank Targets Women, Youth in Countrywide Financial Training." http://www.equitybank.co.ke/index.php/blog/view/ equity-bank-targets-women-youth-in-countrywide-financial-training.

FAI (Financial Access Initiative). 2010. "M-Kesho in Kenya: A New Step for M-Pesa and Mobile Banking." Financial Access Initiative blog post, May 27. http://financialaccess.org/blog/2010/05/m-kesho-kenya-new-step-m-pesa-and-mobile-banking.

FinScope. 2009a. Mozambique Survey. FinMark Trust.

———. 2009b. Zambia Survey. FinMark Trust.

———. 2010a. South Africa. Small Business Survey. FinMark Trust.

———. 2010b. Tanzania Survey. FinMark Trust.

FSD Kenya and CGAP (Financial Sector Deepening Kenya and Consultative Group to Assist the Poor). 2009. *Mobile Payments in Kenya: Findings from a Survey of M-Pesa Users and Agents*. Nairobi: FSD Kenya.

Gallup. 2010. Household Survey in 18 African Countries.

Giné, Xavier, Jessica Goldberg, and Dean Yang. 2010. "Identification Strategy: A Field Experiment on Dynamic Incentives in Rural Credit Markets." Policy Research Working Paper 5438, World Bank, Washington, DC.

Giné, Xavier, and Dean Karlan. 2009. "Group versus Individual Liability: Long Term Evidence from Philippine Microcredit Lending Groups." Working Paper 970, Economic Growth Center, Yale University.

Karlan, Dean, Margaret McConnelly, Sendhil Mullainathan, and Jonathan Zinman. 2010. "Getting to the Top of Mind. How Reminders Increase Savings." http://karlan.yale.edu/p/Top-of-Mind-April2010.pdf.

Kass Media Group. 2012. "Equity Bank Gives 1 Billion to Boost Financial Literacy." http://www.kassfm.co.ke/news/business/1311-equity-bank-gives-1-billion-to-boost-financial-literacy.

Kiva.org. 2009. "Kiva.org Enhances Online Microfinance with Moody's Credit Risk Expertise." Kiva.org Press Release, September 28. http://www.kiva.org/ press/releases/release_20090928.

Kumar, Kabir, Claudia McKay, and Sarah Rotman. 2010. "Microfinance and Mobile Banking: The Story So Far." Focus Note 62 (July), CGAP, Washington, DC.

Luboyeski, V., D. Bagchi, and M. Chawinga. 2004. *Microfinance Sector Assessment in the Republic of Malawi*. USAID, Chemonics Consortium. http://pdf.usaid.gov/ pdf_docs/PNACX006.pdf.

MicroRate. 2011. Microfinance Performance Ratings. http://microrate.com/ home/ratings-methodology/microfinance-institution-methodology.

MIX (Microfinance Information Exchange). 2010. "Arab Microfinance Analysis and Benchmarking Report," accessed at: http://www.themix.org/publications/mix-microfinance-world/2011/03/2010-arab-microfinance-analysis-and-benchmarking-report.

MIX (Microfinance Information Exchange) and CGAP (Consultative Group to Assist the Poor). 2009. *Sub-Saharan Africa 2009: Microfinance Analysis and Benchmarking Report.* Washington, DC: MIX and CGAP.

Mix Market (database). 2012. http://www.themix.org/publications/mix-microfinance-world.

Napier, Mark. 2011. *Including Africa: Beyond Microfinance.* London: Centre for the Study of Financial Innovation.

OIBM (Opportunity International Bank Malawi). 2011. *Christian Science Monitor on Biometrics & Mobile Money at Opportunity Malawi.* http://www.opportunity.org/blog/the-christian-science-monitor-on-biometrics-mobile-money-at-opportunity-malawi/.

Oxford Policy Management. 2011. *M-Banking Regulation.* http://www.regulatingbranchlessbanking.com/bankbasedpermissibilitysearch.

Safaricom. 2011. *M-Pesa Key Performance Statistics.* http://www.safaricom.co.ke/fileadmin/M-PESA/Documents/statistics/M-PESA_Statistics_-_2.pdf.

CHAPTER 2

Mobile Financial Services in Africa: The Next Generation

David Porteous

In 2002, under the headline "Africa Is at Telecom Forefront," the *Wall Street Journal* called attention to the launch in Zambia of a platform allowing payments via mobile phones (WSJ Online). The service was offered by Celpay, a specialized payment provider linked, at that time, to the mobile network operator (MNO) Celtel (later Zain). Eight years after this early start, one of the world's most successful and widely discussed mobile payment services is to be found in Kenya: the M-PESA money transfer service, launched in 2007 by MNO Safaricom. In June 2010, M-PESA reported more than 10 million registered customers, who collectively transferred US$400 million that month alone (Safaricom 2010). The 2009 nationwide FinAccess survey found that close to half of all Kenyan adults had already become users of the service (FinAccess 2009, 16). Celpay, for its part, remained active in Zambia in 2010, but with a different business model, targeting business-to-business payments rather than the consumer transfer market.[1]

I acknowledge with thanks the research assistance of Matt Herbert in compiling data used in this chapter during an internship funded by The World Bank. Also very helpful were the comments of my colleague Johann Bezuidenhoudt, who has been personally involved in some of the second-generation rollouts described, as well as those of anonymous reviewers at The World Bank.

41

Celpay and M-PESA: these two world-leading examples frame a decade of rapid development and accelerated deployment of mobile financial services in Africa,[2] piggybacking on the extraordinary growth of mobile coverage and penetration on the continent over this time. These two models also mark, respectively, the beginning, and now the heyday, of what we characterize here as the second generation of mobile financial services. This name distinguishes these models from the first generation, which started earlier, and the third generation, which is only now starting.

Mobile telephony is no stranger to generational classification of its technology standards: so-called 1G (first generation) wireless networks, first launched in the 1980s, were the first commercially operating analogue wireless networks, but were soon overtaken in the 1990s by the rollout of "2G" networks, which had the advantage of digital switching. As demand for data communications soared, 2G networks that had initially offered only basic data channels such as short message service (SMS) and unstructured supplementary service data (USSD) developed greater capability to handle data through implementing 2.5G and 2.75G standards. Networks with these capabilities are pervasive throughout much of Africa today. However, the need for ever-faster transmission of data for Internet browsing led to the deployment of commercial 3G networks from 2001 onward. First launched in places like Japan and the Republic of Korea, 3G is now widely available in cities and major urban areas in a number of African countries. The leading edge of mobile technology has now moved on to 4G standards, with even faster streaming speeds, although it has been deployed so far only in limited places such as Korea and certain U.S. cities.[3]

The Generations of Mobile Payments

The technological evolution described earlier provides the context for the evolution of mobile financial services laid out in this chapter. While mobile financial services have grown up in the wake of the spread of mobile phones and the growth of their capabilities, the generations we describe here are primarily based on the business models of the providers rather than on technology. Hence, to maintain the distinction between technology and business model, we will use the conventional acronyms "2G" or "3G" where necessary only to refer to the technology standard, but we will specify "second generation" or "third generation" to refer to the evolution of mobile financial services. This lens provides the best way to understand the state of play in mobile financial services today, and it also helps to get a sense of the trajectory into the future for which policy makers must be prepared. Table 2.1 sets out distinguishing features that are explained below.

The first generation of mobile financial services was launched in the late 1990s, mainly in developed regions such as the Nordic countries and Korea. Because these countries already enjoyed widespread financial infrastructure (including Internet banking access), the mobile channel was largely an extension play for existing providers, offering a few niche applications such as micropayments (an early example is buying a Coke from a vending machine using a payment instruction sent from a mobile phone). The limitations of the handsets and data services at this time meant that, by and large, this service had little to offer customers who already used Internet banking, and take-up was consequently low. Several early movers failed to get a sufficient number of customers signed up, and they were closed down by 2005 (Mas and Rotman 2008). However, a few banks in developing countries where Internet banking was less pervasive

Table 2.1   The Generations of Mobile Financial Services

	First generation	Second generation	Third generation
Timing	1990s→	2001→	2008→
Geographic focus	• Developed countries	• Developing countries (Zambia and the Philippines as pioneers)	• Worldwide
Main providers	• Especially banks or mobile network operator (MNO) groups	• Mobile network operators and some 3rd parties	• Payment providers of diverse types
Technology requirement	• Low; 2G	• Basic handsets; 2G	• Enhanced and smart handsets; 2.5G and beyond
Business model focus	• Add-on to existing banking channels • Micropayment revenue model	• Focus on building new channels (agents) • Motivations from voice market, such as churn reduction	• E-commerce • 3rd parties can be more active as niche providers
Constraints for extending access	• Value proposition low to most banked customers • Few interfaces, "poor relative" to alternative	• MNO's control over access	• Handset cost
Examples	• Many banks	• Celpay, M-PESA in Africa	• Mxit (South Africa); PayPal Mobile

Source: Author.

concentrated, successfully, on using the mobile as a specialist extension channel. We will discuss one of these—the First National Bank of South Africa—in the second section of this chapter.

While first-generation players generally launched in developed-country environments with established financial infrastructure, the initial second-generation players launched in 2001 through 2002 in developing-country environments such as Zambia or the Philippines. They soon realized, if they had not before, that they could not assume that there were nearly enough locations at which customers could convert cash into electronic value. Models that depended on bank branches alone simply could not make headway. The second-generation models are therefore distinct in their focus of building a new physical channel of merchants or agents at which cash could be loaded or withdrawn. These models were designed with the assumption that most clients had a basic handset capable only of basic 2G data channels, which was the case for the overwhelming majority of people adopting mobile phones for the first time. A final distinguishing feature of the second generation is that the MNOs had been dominant players to date. We will argue that, in order to develop and protect their core voice business, MNOs had the strongest incentives and abilities to play—but we will also see that these very same motivations may limit the ultimate reach of this generation.

The third generation of mobile financial services started with the spread of handsets capable of Internet browsing and running Java-type applications. These capabilities do not require the expense of a "smartphone." (Smart handsets are spreading quickly but, because of a price tag of US$200 upward, are limited to the top end of the market in developing countries.) Third-generation services simply require an "enhanced" phone or "feature" phone that is Internet-capable: these are now available for as little as US$60 in some markets. For several years now, a greater number of enhanced handsets than basic handsets have been shipped to developing markets, as customers seek features such as e-mail and Internet access. While mobile Internet is in its infancy worldwide, it is already showing what investment analyst Morgan Stanley calls "unprecedented early stage growth."

Africa is no exception to the global trend. A major implication for financial services is that specialist payment providers other than mobile operators may now more easily offer payment services, both as e-commerce transactions and person-to-person payments. A key difference from the second generation is therefore that the arrival of the Internet on the handset has in a sense thrown the door wide open to a new range of providers.

These niche providers are already offering innovative financial products in areas such as savings and person-to-person lending, but along with these products come some risks since it is very difficult for regulators to oversee and supervise the large numbers of diverse approaches, sometimes from outside of their jurisdiction. The risks, as well as the potential to increase access under this generation, are therefore higher.

The generations described here have distinct characteristics but are not discrete in their timing—rather, they overlap in successive waves, as shown in figure 2.1. Policy makers in Africa today have to deal with all three generations and the differing challenges they bring simultaneously, albeit at differing levels of intensity—the second generation is most prevalent while third-generation models are only starting to emerge.

The above genealogy frames the analysis for this chapter. The second section describes the state of play in Africa today, which is primarily concerned with second-generation models. We seek especially to understand why Africa has provided such fertile ground for these models and what their limitations may be for achieving objectives such as greater financial inclusion. The third section characterizes the third-generation models, many of which are still in their infancy worldwide, though they are scaling fast. Here we ask how important this wave might become in Africa. This analysis serves as a basis for understanding the policy and regulatory implications of this new wave. The fourth section consolidates the policy lessons to date, asking what types of regulatory environments have led to the fastest rollout of mobile financial services. It then highlights new questions emerging as well as new opportunities for greater financial inclusion. The conclusion returns to the theme of how best to harness the potential for financial inclusion arising from the now likely outcome that,

Figure 2.1   Overlapping Generations of Mobile Payment

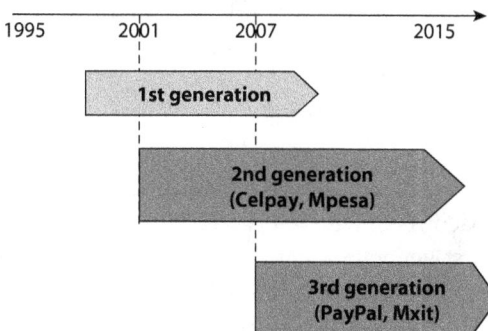

Source: Author.

over the next decade, Africa will become a continent with a critical mass of people "wired" for Internet access. While this may still seem unthinkable, it was unthinkable a decade ago that more than half of Africans would today have mobile phones.

The State of Play in Mobile Financial Services

In 2010, research group Gartner estimated that there were 100 million mobile payment users worldwide, with disproportionate representation in Africa and Asia (Gartner 2010). This is a small fraction of the 4 billion mobile subscribers, but the absolute number and the percentage are expected to increase rapidly over the next few years as services become better known and more widely accessible. There are now few countries, even in Africa, where basic mobile financial service is still not available. Equally, however, in Kenya and South Africa, the scale of usage exceeds a million active customers—a substantial fraction of the population—although recent deployments in countries such as Uganda, Tanzania, and Ghana make usage there likely to reach these same levels. Many more rollouts are planned or in their early stages: more than half (38) of the worldwide mobile money deployments tracked by the GSMA Deployment Tracker are in Africa.[4] Because the tracker focuses on telecommunication-linked deployments, this count is likely understated.

Early Models and How They Have Evolved

In this section, we will characterize the first- and second-generation models in Africa through the eyes of three successful models in three different African countries: first, a bank (First National Bank, or FNB, in South Africa); second, a third-party provider (Celpay's Zambia operation, which evolved out of a mobile network operator or MNO); and finally an MNO (M-PESA offered by Safaricom in Kenya), as shown in table 2.2. All three examples today report having a profitable and sustainable mobile channel, albeit all three are very different in scale, scope, and focus. New players have been spurred to enter the sector because of these players' success, so these three have served as demonstration cases of their respective approaches.

Banks were first-generation early adopters of the mobile phone as an additional banking channel, but they seldom drove adoption of this new channel among customers. During the past decade, most African retail banks of any size have introduced a mobile channel, much as they all

Table 2.2   African First- and Second-Generation Models

Measure	First generation		Second generation
	First National Bank	Celpay	Safaricom
Country of origin	South Africa	Zambia	Kenya
Year started	2005	2001	2007
Number of registered clients (2010)	2 million	10,000	10.2 million
Type of entity	Licensed bank	Third-party payment provider	Mobile network operator
Mobile financial service regulated as	Channel of a regulated bank	Payment system business under the National Payment System Act	Not regulated—operates under no objection
Service offerings	Bank account with alerts, notifications, bill pay, airtime purchase and person-to-person notices to registered beneficiaries only; also debit card	Business-to-business, electronic transfers for small and medium enterprises and one-man businesses using mobile wallet	Mobile wallet offering person-to-person transfers to any cell number, bill payment, and bulk payment; Business-to-person offerings (such as salaries, microfinance institution loans, and charitable support)
Strategic drivers	Making marginal clients viable	Making payment processes work for logistical chains	Reduce churn; Increased average revenue per user; At least break even on costs

Source: Author.

offer an Internet channel. However, the functionality of mobile (and Internet) banking is often very restricted; for example, in many cases, customers can only obtain balance information or transactional alerts but cannot make payments. A few banks, however, chose a more aggressive path.

First National Bank (FNB), a large retail bank in South Africa, is widely recognized as having a successful and profitable mobile channel that was launched in 2005. By 2010, the bank reported some 2 million active mobile customers, a significant proportion of its retail customer base. FNB had adopted an explicit strategy of migrating marginal customers (whom it could not serve profitably using conventional bank channels such as branches or even automated teller machines, or ATMs) to the mobile as their main banking channel. FNB's profitability comes mainly from the commission that FNB receives from MNOs each time its clients buy prepaid airtime directly from their bank accounts. Other banks in South Africa have pursued similar strategies, resulting in twice as many South Africans (30 percent of the banked population) using mobile banking than use Internet banking. However, FNB's success came in the relatively well-developed retail banking environment of a middle-income country in which half the adult population was already banked. Also, access to cash-handling channels such as ATMs or points of sale was widespread in urban areas in that country, so FNB did not have to build new channels for mobile usage. While a number of banks entered mobile banking in this first generation, FNB stands out for its focus on this channel, and for its success.

Second-generation providers had to go further. They sought to provide electronic payment services in countries such as Zambia, which lacked electronic payment infrastructure. The need to find cheaper and more effective ways of selling prepaid airtime was an early driver for MNOs because distributing physical scratch cards was more expensive and risky than selling airtime as a digital good (digital airtime could be bought in smaller quantities, which made it more accessible for poorer customers). Distributing airtime in this way necessitated a cost-effective payment solution. An electronic wallet offered promise: it could be stocked with money deposited via agents, and then the money could easily be transferred at the push of a few buttons either to purchase digital goods (predominantly airtime) or to send remittances.

This latter usage, person-to-person transfers, was an important driver in the launch of mobile financial services in the Philippines in 2001. The Philippines is a large country with many rural and remote areas underserved by traditional financial service providers. In addition, the nation's large overseas workforce already remitted large earnings flows to family back home. Early financial services launched by local MNOs Smart (2004) and Globe (2005) focused on this opportunity. The subsequent launch of M-PESA by Safaricom in Kenya (2007) also built on the need for safe, convenient, and affordable money transfers from cities to rural areas: it was marketed as a way to "send money home," in the words of the award-winning slogan from one of M-PESA's first commercials.

These second-generation solutions, born in the context of developing countries, faced a different type of challenge than the first generation: because they could not rely on an already existing payment infrastructure, they had to build their own distributional ecosystems to accept cash in and pay cash out (CICO). Today, Safaricom's large, sustainable agent network is recognized as the heart of its much-hailed success with M-PESA. For example, M-PESA now has more than 19,000 CICO agents who are spread throughout the country. This extensive network of connections helps customers develop familiarity and trust in the otherwise mysterious process of buying and selling electronic money. Furthermore, MNOs were more likely than banks to have the competence to build and manage widespread agent networks. Apart from the usual systems challenges of adding a new channel to back-office systems, many regulatory restrictions limited banks' ability to allow agents to accept deposits on their behalf. These restrictions are now easing, as more countries see the benefits of allowing banks to have a lower-cost form of distribution.

Table 2.2 summarizes the salient features of these three distinct second-generation mobile financial service models: FNB's bank-led approach for underbanked customers; Safaricom's M-PESA mass market mobile money transfer service; and Celpay's payment service (which focused on larger businesses that distribute goods and collect payments). It is worth noting that Celpay also distributes government benefits (government-to-person or G2P benefits) to demobilized soldiers in the Democratic Republic of Congo under a World Bank donor-financed scheme called Disarm, Demobilize and Reintegrate (DDR). This started as a mobile payment service through which the soldiers received their cash from agents' mobile phones, but the lack of liquidity among agents in rural areas caused the DDR scheme to become a more conventional cash-payout scheme involving mobile vehicles that served as distribution centers.

Beyond Payments

So far, although some markets (such as Uganda and Ghana) are showing promise, only Kenya has seen the large-scale adoption and active usage of a second-generation model. Both adoption and usage are necessary: while large-scale adoption creates the potential for transformation, frequent usage makes the business case sustainable for both the provider and its agents in the delivery chain. So who are the users? A survey of M-PESA users as early as 2008 found that perhaps only one-third were unbanked; by 2009, when the number of registered users had already greatly exceeded the total number of banked people in the country, the proportion of unbanked users had risen to almost half.[5] The transformational impact of M-PESA on the financial system has already been felt at various levels: M-PESA (together with other operators' two active mobile finance offerings) has reduced the cost and risk of domestic remittances relative to previous options such as bus-company transfers. Furthermore, although the service was built around simple money transfers, the scale of the network has now enabled further rounds of innovation, adding more financial services for users, with cash handling conducted through the M-PESA agent network. In May 2010, Safaricom and Equity Bank (Kenya's largest retail bank) announced a product partnership to offer a bundle consisting of a savings account, insurance, and credit to M-PESA customers through a new co-branded service called M-Kesho (see box 2.1). This may be the equivalent of a 2.5G service—one that builds on the second-generation platform to offer something more while not substantially changing the underlying model.

Why Africa?

Africa has clearly offered fertile soil for the growth of mobile financial services over the past decade. What factors have caused that abundant growth?

A necessary condition for the growth of mobile financial services is a large enough number of people who subscribe to mobile services. Aker and Mbiti (2010) have chronicled the rapid increase in wireless coverage: from 10 percent of the African population in 1999 to around 66 percent a decade later. Similarly, the total number of African mobile subscribers has risen 30-fold, from 16 million in 2000 to more than 488 million in 2010. In contrast, while developing regions such as South Asia have also experienced rapidly rising mobile penetration, they have not seen an equivalent number of innovations in mobile money. This is not to deny, however, that certain other countries have also proven fertile for

Box 2.1

Offering Additional Services: M-Kesho in Kenya

M-Kesho is the brand name of Equity Bank's package of financial products issued to clients who use the M-PESA mobile payment system in Kenya. It was launched in May 2010 jointly by Equity Bank and Safaricom, the MNO that runs M-Pesa, under a one-year exclusive arrangement. The core product is an interest-bearing bank savings account, although credit and insurance options are also available.

M-Kesho accounts are opened either at an Equity Bank branch or at an M-PESA agent's office, where the bank has placed one of its representatives.

The M-Kesho account offers only electronic transaction functionality: money can flow into and out of the account either from the customer's M-PESA account or (optionally) from a normal Equity Bank account. To deposit cash, customers must first load their M-PESA account at an agent and then initiate a transfer to the M-Kesho account. This transaction is free to the consumer, although Equity Bank pays M-PESA a fee for each transfer. To withdraw cash, the process is reversed, with the customer paying for the transfer out of the account, as well as the standard M-PESA withdrawal fee.

M-Kesho is therefore part of a next generation of mobile-enabled financial services, adding savings, credit, and insurance to the mobile transactional offering already in place. It has created a new form of partnership between a bank and a telecommunications company.

Source: Rosenberg 2010.

mobile money—Japan and Korea were early movers among developed countries, and developing countries Malaysia and Thailand have also had active mobile money deployments. Therefore, the spread of mobile penetration alone is not sufficient to explain the growth phenomenon in Africa.

For this task, the "diamond" of reinforcing factors that create regional competitive advantage, proposed by Harvard Business School professor Michael Porter, is a helpful framework. It is depicted in figure 2.2.

Starting with the right hand of the diamond in figure 2.2, demand conditions in Africa have clearly helped: accelerating urbanization of people who retain strong links to family members in the countryside creates strong demand for safe and efficient money-transfer mechanisms. But, like rising mobile penetration, internal migration is not peculiar to Africa, and indeed varies across the continent. Thus, mere

Figure 2.2   Porter Framework for the Competitive Advantage of Nations

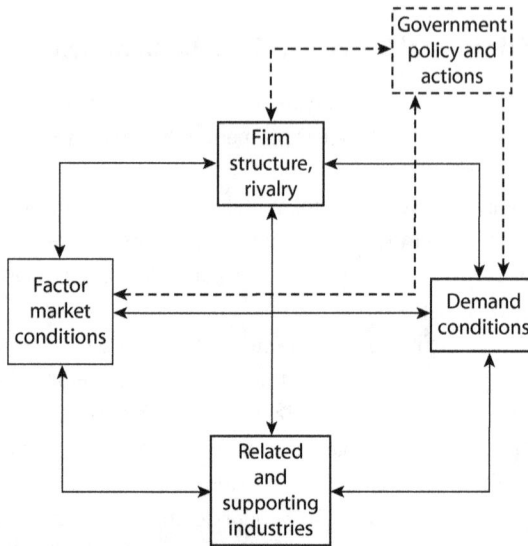

Source: Porter 1990.

urbanization is not a sufficient explanation. The lack of widespread formal electronic banking alternatives may also have helped new approaches such as mobile to gain traction more rapidly: African countries in general have low proportions of banked adults and low numbers of financial touch points such as ATMs or points of sale per capita.[6] But this distinction is associated more with national income level than with geography, so it would apply to low-income countries but not middle-income ones like South Africa or Botswana. While South Africa has been the birthplace of several second-generation models such as Wizzit and MTN Banking, these models have largely failed to take root in a financial system where two-thirds of adults are already banked and where card-acquiring infrastructure is widely available.[7] Thus, demand conditions in low-income countries in general, rather than in Africa specifically, may be favorable for second-generation mobile financial services.

Firm structure and rivalry, at the top of the diamond in figure 2.2, seem to have played an important role in the lucrative and booming mobile voice and data markets. The mobile telephony market in Africa is relatively concentrated: five large MNO groups controlled 62 percent of all African subscribers in 2010, whereas globally, 20 MNO groups controlled a similar proportion (70 percent) in 2009. This relatively high concentration means that operators had the scale and deep pockets needed to invest in the development of new products and then to roll them out more rapidly across the countries within a multinational group. All five of the large African MNO groups—MTN, Vodafone, Zain (now part of Bharti Group), Orange, and Orascom—have active mobile money strategies that have been or are being rolled out in multiple markets across the continent. Indeed, second-generation approaches have often been stimulated by rivalry in the core voice market: operators want to reduce the churn of prepaid voice subscribers, which is a significant feature of most MNOs and a big drag on their profitability.

The third box in the diamond shown in figure 2.2—the existence of key supporting industries—has also helped to promote movement. As with other technology-enabled services, leading software vendors have played important roles in promoting and supporting the adoption of mobile financial services. Africa, despite its generally low level of financial sophistication, is home to a disproportionately large number of indigenous suppliers of specialized payment technology and even patent holders of key technologies and processes. Among them is Fundamo, the Cape Town–based software house that was one of the earliest pioneers of secure mobile payment technology. Fundamo technology was first deployed in Celpay and is today one of the most widely deployed mobile financial service solutions globally.[8] While South Africa has been a hotspot for payment technology globally, it is not alone. Smaller technology firms from Kenya, Tanzania, Ghana, and Nigeria are all actively engaged in supporting mobile payments and mobile commerce across the continent today.

Finally, and perhaps most decisively, are government policy and actions. The common-law banking framework in Anglophone Africa has also helped to fertilize the soil for innovation in ways that countries with a civil code legal system—whether in Africa or elsewhere—could not or did not do in the early stages. Under a common-law framework, specific legal enablement was not required to launch mobile financial services; rather, it was necessary only to persuade regulators that planned innovations either did not fall under their purview or did not violate banking laws. In early-adopter countries such as Zambia and Kenya, regulators proved amenable to the view that the planned services were not deposit-taking businesses and therefore did not have to be regulated as such. Instead, they viewed the new services as being subject to differing intensities of informal oversight. This approach to regulating for innovation, ad hoc though it may have seemed at the time, is now considered to be in line with good practice for handling innovation, as we will discuss below. Hence, this factor—a regulatory environment that, if it did not promote mobile financial services, at least did not block them—may be the most important part of the explanation of "Why Africa?"

Emerging Limits of Second-Generation Models

In 2010, the climate appeared favorable for the continued rollout of second-generation models of mobile financial services. M-PESA, the poster child of this generation, continues to grow in Kenya, spurring others who aspire to emulate its remarkable success. The deployments of other major MNO groups, such as MTN in Uganda and Ghana, are now reaching scale, with a million or more registered users (Bold 2010; Rotman 2009). With more deployments planned in countries that still lack a major mobile financial service, it is almost certain that the number of active users of mobile money in Africa will continue to grow over the next decade.

However, it is not certain, or even likely, that future growth will follow Kenya's trajectory. Various authors have mused over the "perfect storm" of the country-level and firm-level characteristics that have led to such success there, and they have sought to explain why the rollout of similar models in other places—for example, across the border in Tanzania—has been much slower (Heyer and Mas 2009). Amid all the idiosyncratic reasons advanced, one in particular stands out: when it launched M-PESA, Safaricom already had a dominant market share (around 75 percent) in the prepaid voice market, and it has grown slightly since then. Except in monopoly mobile markets (such as Ethiopia), it is rare—not just in Africa but globally—for one MNO to have such a degree of market dominance. Market dominance means that the benefits of launching mobile money are not only larger for the MNO but, even more important, much larger for the customer base. If most transactions among subscribers happen on the same network, there are no risks and costs associated with connecting with other payment networks.

But just as African telecommunications regulators have liberalized mobile markets to increase competition and bring down the cost of airtime, so market shares have fragmented. Even in small markets, it is not uncommon to find four or even five mobile providers today, with the market leader having no more than a third of the market. One implication of this increasing fragmentation is that, in the absence of an interconnected solution, successive second-generation market entrants entering the market face diminishing returns—and, as mentioned above, clients face this risk as well. These risks highlight an inherent structural limitation of second-generation models: they depend on approaches that are, to a greater or lesser extent, mobile-operator controlled. This control is apparent for those deployments that use SIM Toolkit features on the SIM card, access to which is usually (although not always)[9] jealously guarded by the operator—indeed, this control is part of the proposition that models using this approach offer better security than most Internet banking applications. But operators may also exercise control to a lesser extent with USSD channels, since using these channels also requires negotiating an interface that is not standardized in many places, and requires agreeing on pricing and security features. However, because USSD approaches are less subject to operator control than the SIM Toolkit is, USSD has become the bearer channel of choice for network-independent provider models such as Wizzit or FNB.

More fragmented subscriber bases would not be such a problem if interconnection were possible or likely. However, the same incentives that brought mobile operators into second-generation mobile payment markets—the desire to hold onto existing mobile subscribers and stop them churning—also makes it less likely that these MNOs will willingly yield on this issue, since it erodes one of the fundamental drivers for entry.

The dependence on telecommunications-controlled or -influenced channels, and hence the dependence on telecommunications business drivers, is endogenous to many, though not all, second-generation models. In addition, certain exogenous factors are starting to exert increasing drag on rollout. For example, more countries are implementing the requirement that the identity (and address) of each mobile subscriber be recorded and verified at the time of sale. So-called SIM registration is a big departure from previous approaches that made getting a new SIM card easy and anonymous. Registration increases the MNO's cost of acquiring new prepaid customers and rules out as potential customers those who lack the necessary documentation. For example, SIM registration was fully implemented in South Africa in 2009, and it has drastically reduced new registrations. It has also affected mobile banking models that required the issuance of new SIM cards, since these are now subject to additional checks and procedures. Not only must the bank now conduct customer due diligence (CDD) in line with Anti Money Laundering/ Combating the Financing of Terrorism (AML/CFT) laws on new bank accounts, but the MNO must do so for new mobile subscribers as well. In theory, the requirements for financial and telephony registration could be harmonized: as Cenfri (2010) shows, the CDD requirements for basic bank accounts and prepaid SIMs are quite similar, although not the same. While a harmonized SIM registration process could create a customer base that is prequalified for basic financial services, the result at present is simply extra cost and difficulty in acquiring low-end customers. This is, at the very least, a lost opportunity for financial inclusion.

A View into the Emerging Third Generation

In 2009, the International Telecommunication Union (ITU) estimated that Africa had only 65 million Internet users in total—less than 10 percent of the population and by far the lowest proportion of all the continents (ITU 2010). However, of these 65 million, users with broadband access—those able to browse and download content from the Web at high speed—represent the hard core. In Africa, the proportion of broadband users who access the Internet via mobile channels is 17 times the fixed-line broadband base, by far the highest ratio of any continent.[10] Across Africa, the number of mobile broadband subscribers who can access the Internet via their phone or wireless modem ("dongle") has soared from less than a million in 2006 to 17 million in 2009. These continent-wide numbers are even more striking when seen at a country level: the Communications Commission of Kenya has reported that mobile Internet subscriptions had risen 74 percent in the year to September 2009 and, by then, constituted almost 99 percent of all Internet subscriptions in the country (Communications Commission of Kenya 2010, 15). The same report also showed that international Internet bandwidth had increased more than 600 percent in the same year, the result of the connection of two new submarine cables (which have also connected many parts of East, West, and Southern Africa in the past year).

The growth rates of bandwidth and mobile Internet connections in Kenya are, as with mobile financial services, outliers at present. But Kenya provides a foretaste of what the continent is starting to experience: a massive ramp-up in access to the Internet via mobile phones. This has been enabled by falling costs and rising connection speeds (also a result of the new submarine cable infrastructure) as well as by falling prices on Internet-capable handsets. These factors have generated a global groundswell, leading Morgan Stanley to the twin conclusions that mobile Internet was not only "bigger than most think" but also highly disruptive to established business models—from Microsoft to MNOs (Morgan Stanley Research 2009).

Even if mobile Internet usage is increasing rapidly, does it have any relevance for poor or less well-educated consumers? Here too, early evidence suggests that the take-up of mobile Internet may surprise, just as the adoption of mobile voice services stunned forecasters in the previous decade. For example, Gitau, Marsden, and Donner (2009) report on a focus group in Cape Town, South Africa, of unemployed women of limited educational background. These women had never previously used the Internet but, with some initial guidance, rapidly adapted to doing so using only a mobile phone. They found services like employment listings especially helpful, but they also actively used social networking platforms to connect with friends.

The massive growth of these social networks is itself a global phenomenon. The largest, Facebook, reported some 500 million members across the world in 2010.[11] Other networks tend to have regional followings—such as TenCent (China), Orkut (Brazil), and Friendster (Asia). Mxit is an African-based, mobile-focused example that now claims some 20 million registered users worldwide, the bulk of whom are young South Africans (see box 2.2). Mxit users exchange instant messages with one another using general packet radio service (GPRS) at a fraction of the cost of SMSs. Like the other platforms, Mxit has expanded its service offering to allow users who do not have bank accounts or credit cards to buy electronic money (called *Mxit Moola*) with which they can buy digital goods and entertainment, as box 2.2 explains more fully.

Implications for Mobile Financial Services

Mobile financial services will not be exempt from the disruptive effect of mobile Internet. In developed countries, the arrival of feature-laden smartphones such as Apple's iPhone or the Research in Motion (RIM) Blackberry has ignited demand for a range of new payment applications, since smartphones have the capability of offering user-friendly secure interfaces for banking or payments independent of the mobile operator. In 2010, smartphones made up 14–17 percent of worldwide mobile phone sales, according to research groups Nielsen and Gartner, and this proportion is rising very fast; Morgan Stanley forecasts that sales of smartphones will exceed sales of PCs by 2012. However, the high price of smartphones (typically $400–$600 without a subsidy from the MNO) makes them inaccessible to all but the wealthy in developing countries.

However, it is not necessary that a phone be "smart" to access the Internet: "enhanced phones" with browsing and Java capabilities will do. As Pickens, Porteous, and Rotman (2009) show, sales of enhanced phones

Box 2.2

The Growth of Mobile Data-Enabled Social Network Platforms: Mxit in South Africa

While SMS (the 2G message-exchange standard for the global system for mobile communications, or GSM) has attracted much attention, other forms of text-based communication via a mobile phone have also grown rapidly. At the forefront of this non-SMS revolution is the South African company Mxit. Originally an acronym for "Message Exchange," Mxit is a mobile social networking site that allows its customers to send messages of up to 2,000 characters. The service connects users via GPRS/3G, which allows users to message at a significantly lower cost than that of SMS. The low cost and versatility of the system have led to an explosive growth in clients, especially among teenagers and young adults. Started in 2005, by 2010 the company had 20 million registered users worldwide.

A more recent feature of Mxit is its mobile money service. "Mxit Moola" is a virtual currency that can be bought on the Mxit website and then used to purchase a variety of goods and services. Via partnerships with two large South African banks, Mxit users can purchase Mxit Moola without the need for a credit card or bank account. Rather, customers buy Mxit Moola vouchers to fund their accounts from either street-level vendors or self-service kiosks; "funds" from the account are then used to purchase airtime or entertainment products, such as music, games, and books. While the system is currently offered only in South Africa, Mxit has indicated that it plans to introduce the service into 26 countries worldwide.

Mxit's push into the payment space has been motivated by several factors. Many of its users are teenagers and young adults who do not have access to a bank account. To cater to these users' needs, and to increase the Mxit platform's utility, the company needed to create a value-transfer system that did not require a credit card or a bank account. This tool, in turn, increased the product's attractiveness to other potential consumers, growing the service into areas where Internet-based social networking sites do not (yet) compete. Finally, Mxit claims a competitive pricing advantage because of its delivery of service via GPRS/3G. The company has indicated that its low data costs—a fraction of that paid for traditional SMS service—allow it to deliver mobile-money options to consumers at a fraction of the cost of other mobile money services.

Mxit's status as a provider of social networking, entertainment, and emerging financial services makes it an intriguing example of rising African mobile commerce firms of the third generation.

Sources: http://site.mxit.com/; author.

now make up the largest share of mobile phone sales worldwide; the cheapest phones of this sort, made in China or Korea, can cost less than US$100. These phones have the capability of downloading applications that can, among other things, secure data transmission end-to-end around a payment or banking-type of transaction, addressing a concern often raised by regulators. There are a number of implications for mobile financial services.

First, mobile Internet is likely to boost the demand for mobile payments. For one thing, it should reduce the cost significantly for providers and customers. Mobile data may cost 1/50th of the price of an SMS for an equivalent message size. Furthermore, by opening access to a new world of digital goods ranging from music to e-books, which can be downloaded regardless of location, the mobile Internet is more likely to stimulate demand for remote payment—at present, payees may be limited to other people on the same network or else defined bill-payment recipients such as power companies.

Second, the convergence of mobile with the Internet means that mobile banking users will be exposed to the same threats as Internet banking customers. The number, spread, and type of viruses infecting mobile phones are growing rapidly, exposing clients to the same vulnerabilities, from phishing for credentials to more sophisticated forms of attack that would lead to unauthorized access to client accounts or data. Since the phones are connected to the World Wide Web, unauthorized access could come from almost anywhere. Since many of the mobile Internet consumers in Africa will be entirely new to the world of banking, let alone Internet banking, the level of threat will be elevated for these users. Inevitable schemes and scandals will result in calls for special vigilance on the part of regulators and providers who are already hard-pressed in some places to deal with issues arising from the far smaller numbers using PC-based Internet banking.

Third, on the supply side, the use of Internet channels will enable a whole new range of providers to offer payment services to the public. This proliferation of new entrants may cause customers to favor providers with trusted and established brands like banks—banks that may, until now, have been restricted from offering mobile services by the cost or terms of access offered by mobile operators. But it will also enable new forms of competition for retail-payment space. As an example, with over 225 million registered users in a large number of countries, in 10 years, PayPal has built from scratch one of the largest global retail electronics payments businesses independent of the international card associations Visa and

MasterCard. PayPal's growth was originally driven by e-commerce on the Internet, but its capability has been extended to include payments by mobile phones as well. The number of PayPal mobile users is currently doubling annually. As a global electronic payments engine, PayPal's core competence lies in risk analytics, so it can manage the risk of fraud while still speeding up payments. In 2009, PayPal opened the application programming interface (API) to its payments engine so that outside developers could incorporate it into their own solutions. Roth (2010) describes how this move has unleashed a number of creative new businesses, such as Twitpay, a payment service for users of the popular microblogging site Twitter, which uses PayPal's engine. For Roth, the increased competition to provide forms of electronic payment between the large established providers such as MasterCard and Visa (which have their own mobile offerings) and newer competitors such as PayPal presages an era in which money becomes "flexible, frictionless and (almost) free."

Even as MasterCard and Visa have significantly expanded their presence in Africa through licensee banks in the past decade, PayPal has also expanded its international network to include some developing countries, such as Mexico and Brazil, in its full-service offering. To date, users in just one African country (South Africa)[12] have the ability to send, receive, and withdraw funds to a bank account or card account, although users in a number of African countries are listed as being able to receive payments.[13]

Internet social networks have a larger reach than PayPal and are now starting to add financial services to their offerings. In September 2010, Facebook joined Mxit and some other social networks with the rollout of its own virtual currency system. Called "Facebook Credits" and available for purchase in mass retailers, the currency will enable users to pay for games and purchase digital goods on the Facebook network. In rolling out its virtual currency program, Facebook is responding to a need for a micro-payments system for the increasingly diverse entertainment offerings on its site, such as Farmville, as well as generating alternative forms of revenue from its client base.

The introduction of person-to-person transfers of value on these Internet-based social platforms may even result in some platforms becoming the "Western Unions" of the third-generation era—able not only to connect people for information (as Western Union originally did via its telegraph service) but adding a convenient, easy payment service for remittances to be sent between already identified and linked friends.

Other niche financial services providers can thrive in an environment of widespread Internet access that reduces transaction costs for them and their clients. This is the promise that follows the development of an e-payment infrastructure: that other desirable financial services—savings, credit, and insurance—will follow.

Examples of independent third-generation services in Africa are limited at this early stage. But we see elsewhere examples of Internet-based financial service models that focus on optimizing user experience for niche services. Some of these are likely to arrive soon in Africa in some form—not necessarily under their own brands, but as their service concept is copied.

For example, Smartypig (http://www.smartypig.com/) is a U.S.-based niche savings service launched in 2008 which is only offered via the Internet (mobile and PC). Registered users in the United States and now Australia can open a bank account online in a federally insured partner bank. The Smartypig Web interface enables clients to set flexible savings goals (in terms of the amount and period of savings) about which they can be automatically reminded via e-mail, which prompts them to save more. Describing itself as the leader in "social banking," Smartypig also enables its members to publish their savings goals on their social network pages, enabling friends and family to contribute by clicking on an icon that authorizes a debit from their bank account to the relevant SmartyPig account.

Similarly, the rise of peer lending sites such as Prosper.com in the United States or Zopa in the United Kingdom creates an opportunity for new forms of personal and even small-business lending to emerge outside of regulated banks. However, the success of these sites depends on the existence of other elements of financial infrastructure, such as credit bureaus to standardize risk assessment, payment systems to disburse loans and collect repayments, and specialized debt collection houses that handle defaults on an outsourced basis.

There is little doubt about the significance of mobile Internet for mobile financial services, although there is disagreement about the pace at which it will happen. Fundamo's founder Hannes van Rensburg, for example, acknowledges that the future lies in smartphones, but not in just any smartphone: he draws on research that shows that only iPhone customers are really active mobile Internet browsers in the United States so far, suggesting that it will take longer than people think to see widespread mobile browsing (van Rensburg 2010). For the argument in this chapter, the rate of take-up of mobile Internet services is less important than the inevitability of that take-up. Based on early trends, it is possible that adoption could take place faster than many people, including van Rensburg, expect. Some payment providers already offer Java-enabled applications and use of the Internet that let their consumers access services, but the second generation of mobile financial services is currently dominant and will remain so in Africa for a while. However, third-generation models based on mobile Internet will increasingly supplant the second generation within the next 5 to 10 years.

Actions for Policy Makers and Regulators

The application of any technology inevitably brings new questions as well as unintended and unforeseen consequences. When the take-up of the technology—in this case mobile communications—happens at historically unprecedented rates, though, finding answers to the inevitable questions is even more important. Over the past five years of sector analysis, clear policy lessons about enabling first- and second-generation deployments have emerged in some areas, while questions remain in others. Some questions have been sharpened while others—particularly those attached to the regulation of third-generation models—are not yet clear.

Learning from First and Second Generations

The allure of using mobile technology to enable greater financial inclusion is stronger than ever, and it is now within reach in most places. Kenya provides us with the first picture of what the large-scale adoption of electronic payments looks like in a developing country, by accelerating it into an environment of safe, fast, and cheaper remote payments. On the backbone of pervasive channels for converting cash into electronic value, a whole range of new financial services can be offered.

Countries that wish to enjoy these benefits need to learn the lessons of the second generation. Chief among the clear lessons so far is that countries that adopted "a test and see" approach to innovation (now enshrined as good practice by the G20—see GPFI 2010, 5) have witnessed rapid progress, whereas countries that adopted an approach restricting available models have seen limited progress. But this lesson is no surprise, because it is inherently impossible to predict all the models and consequences of a new technology: countries that have attempted to do this by overregulating prematurely have arrested, or at least retarded, development in their markets.

In this respect, the difference between Kenya and Nigeria is striking. Kenya chose early on to allow early deployments to go ahead without a clear regulatory framework—not just M-PESA but three others currently operate under the same reporting and oversight regime from the central bank in that country. In 2010, three years after the launch of M-PESA, The Central Bank of Kenya is consulting on draft e-money and e-payment guidelines that may be implemented in 2011. The Central Bank of Nigeria (CBN) licensed one early mobile payment provider (which has yet to launch on scale) and then published detailed mobile payment guidelines in 2009. The CBN not only required that all providers adhere to the guidelines, but also suggested that it would limit licenses to restrict mobile payments to a given number of chosen applicants from a large pool of interested parties—banks, telecommunication companies, and others. The CBN issued the first full approvals of 15 mobile payment services in 2011.

To be clear, allowing piloting and experimentation is accepted good practice, but it is not good practice for regulators to stand back for too long. Good practice goes further, requiring that regulators declare their intent (or a roadmap—see Porteous 2006) to prepare appropriate market-wide guidance or regulation at necessary development thresholds. Kenya has clearly passed the thresholds at which "test and learn" applies: by most measures, M-PESA has become so large that, if it failed, there would be systemwide consequences—a large number of people would be affected, even if the values exchanged were not enough to cause systemic failure in the larger financial system. Therefore, providing greater certainty is now a priority of regulators in Kenya as well as in other markets where a number of schemes are emerging (for example, Tanzania and Uganda).

Second, the success of second-generation models focuses attention on a key issue that is beyond mobile only: the need to have a pervasive, efficient cash-handling channel that would enable electronic payments to take off and that would enable citizens to open electronic stores of value—whether in the form of bank accounts or mobile wallets. This issue raises the question of whether and on what basis regulators should allow financial providers to use agents to take and disburse cash. In a world where real-time communication substantially reduces the risks of agent fraud to both provider and client, there is a clear case for regulators to allow banks to appoint agents. A majority of developing countries now do so. However, agent regulations often restrict the type of merchant who can be an agent or the type of service that can be provided—and they do so in ways that unnecessarily reduce the reach of this important channel. Fears that agents would replace bank branches have so far proved groundless: in countries such as Brazil (which now has 160,000 bank "correspondents," or agents—quadruple the number a decade ago), the number of bank branches has not declined markedly. In Brazil, as in Kenya, bank branches play a key role in the chain of cash distribution, providing liquidity services to agents without which the agents would not be able to play their role of cash handlers. Hence, regulators must look beyond merely enabling agents to the wider question of the efficiency of the distribution structure of financial services in general. Apart from merely licensing agents, there may also be a case for reviewing the often onerous and unclear requirements that regulate the creation of new bank branches (BFA 2010a).

Third, enabling mobile financial services requires inter-agency coordination, since at least two regulators are always involved in some form: the financial regulator and the telecommunications regulator. Indeed, the G20 Principles for Innovative Financial Inclusion call for cooperation and coordination across government agencies,[14] so that reforms in one area are not bottlenecked by contrary policies emanating from another regulator. Even if the MNO's role is "simply" to be the data channel, communications regulators will oversee the quality and robustness of the channel (such as uptime) and will also have the purview to consider competition issues such as terms of access to mobile data services.

Coordination also brings the hope of taking advantage of regulatory requirements in one sector to create benefit in another—which does not happen automatically. One current example of a large potential gain from closer coordination may arise from the requirement that prepaid customers register and prove their identity in order to have continuing access to the service. Of 44 African countries surveyed (see annex 2.A), only 9 countries currently require registration of SIM cards with some process for verifying identity. This requirement is new. But more countries are actively following suit. The requirements for SIM registration are very similar to those typically required for customer due diligence on basic bank accounts. This means that a SIM registration process could be designed so as to also satisfy banking know-your-customer (KYC) requirements, at least for a basic account on a tiered approach to KYC. If this happened, everyone with a registered SIM would not only have a unique electronic ID number (the phone number) but would also be pre-verified for a basic account as well. One of the largest hurdles to great banked access—that is, the high costs of opening an account—could be greatly mitigated. However, as a recent Cenfri report (2010) shows in the case of South Africa,[15] a lack of explicit and deliberate coordination between the telecommunication authorities and the financial authorities overseeing AML/CFT requirements may lead to uncertainty, and possibly to the loss of this great opportunity to advance access to formal financial services into the next generation in Africa.

These three issues at least seem clear in their implications for policy makers. But a further issue is emerging, with questions being sharpened although clear answers do not yet exist. Financial regulators have not traditionally had to deal directly with competition policies, even though this may have been among their mandates (possibly in concert with a national competition authority). By contrast, telecommunication regulators are usually explicitly mandated to deal with competitive issues—such as discriminatory access to telecommunication channels or a large incumbent's unwillingness to allow a new competitor to interconnect calls to its network—to promote the efficiency and competitiveness of the network as a whole. Communications legislation in some countries (such as Kenya) even explicitly recognizes the all-too-common situation of one player holding a dominant market position, and therefore endows the regulator with enhanced powers to scrutinize and intervene in such cases. However, financial regulators usually lack such explicit powers. Indeed, relatively few countries have granted payment regulators explicit mandates and corresponding powers to consider competition in payment markets, although these markets are subject to similar network considerations—Australia and the United Kingdom are relatively recent examples.

The competition issues around mobile financial services manifest at several levels. First, the way that MNOs provide third parties with access (and pricing) to channels such as SMS and USSD (whether the third parties are banks or payment service providers) can affect the viability of a mobile financial service. Complaints have arisen in some markets that mobile operators have used pricing to block or impede access, making it harder to compete. In theory, if not in practice, these telecommunication channel issues are the province of the telecommunications regulator, although it would help if coordination with the financial regulator sharpened the issues around which forms of discriminatory practice are unhelpful. Similarly, MNOs in some markets allege that banks impede access to existing payment systems in ways that slow interconnection to these systems. Financial regulators would have to take note of the latter, as part of overall policy for the development of national payment systems.

Second, and even more important for mobile financial services, acquiring and managing the large networks of cash-handling merchants or agents that are so crucial to success are subject to economies of scale. Fragmented networks with small numbers of agents exclusive to one provider are unlikely to be able to reduce cost to the extent required. Requiring that agents be nonexclusive, as is the practice in countries such as Nigeria and Kenya (for banks at least), may avoid locking in groups of agents, but it does not necessarily address the core business model question of whether there are high fixed costs to acquiring these agents. Merely *allowing* agents to be multiply acquired by providers does not mean that they *will* be, since the business case for the acquirer is diminished. The issue then becomes the basis on which financial providers can interconnect across agent networks, so that a customer of Zap's mobile financial service could withdraw cash from an M-PESA agent, for example. Technologically, there is little barrier to this, at least for agents using mobile phones; mobile networks operate using standards that are, by definition, interoperable (that is, capable of talking to each other). But enabling interconnection is a step beyond this. Networks may well have commercial incentives to negotiate mutually acceptable interconnect fees, and this often happens among groups of financial institutions that create private switches, but this does not necessarily connect all elements of the national retail payment infrastructure. However, an incumbent with a large, established agent network may, in fact, be reluctant to connect with a national payment infrastructure. The interconnection issues with mobile agents are no different from those with card payment systems, where banks with large ATM networks may be reluctant to interconnect except on terms that make it unfavorable for others to do so.

If this is the case, regulators have several options beyond the default position of encouraging greater interconnection through moral suasion. One solution may be to drive the establishment of a national switch, and require that all retail payment networks connect to it. The regulator may even participate in the governance structure of a new national switch in order to ensure that it operates in the national interest. One country, Ghana, has gone further: after finding initially that banks were not willing or able to support the development of a national switch, the Bank of Ghana set up a wholly owned subsidiary company, the Ghana Interbank Payment and Settlement Systems (GhIPSS), with the mandate of establishing and operating a national switch. As box 2.3 explains, GhIPSS went further to create a new payment instrument based on a smart card, e-Zwich, which was also designed to bring unbanked people into the financial system.

Box 2.3

Regulators Drive Interconnection: The Bank of Ghana and a National Payments Switch

Starting in 2000, Ghana initiated various reforms of its payment system, resulting in the passage of a Payment System Act and in setting up a real-time gross settlement system at the Bank of Ghana (BOG). BOG then encouraged banks to establish a national switch that would interconnect retail devices such as ATMs and point-of-sale (POS) devices. However, early discussions resulted in little progress, so BOG decided to go ahead anyway creating, in 2007, a separate subsidiary named Ghana Interbank Payment and Settlement Systems (GhIPSS). GhIPSS has the mandate of providing and managing infrastructure for electronic payments systems in the country.

While procuring the technology for a national switch, GhIPSS was drawn to a solution that offered additional features, including the issuance of smart cards that would allow biometric authentication of clients (thought to be useful for illiterate clients) as well as the capability to operate offline, which was useful in areas without mobile coverage (at that time, only a third of the population were mobile subscribers). This new retail payment system, called eZwich, was seen as a means of enabling banks to bank unbanked people and people in areas beyond the reach of mobile coverage. Launched in 2008, eZwich was not fully interoperable with existing ATMs or Europay-Mastercard-Visa (EMV)-compatible devices, which banks have subsequently rolled out.

Drawing on its powers as a regulator, BOG mandated that all deposit-taking institutions had to issue eZwich cards to their personal customers and had to deploy eZwich POS devices at all branches and agencies. All existing bank switches had to integrate to eZwich, and all future switches had to be eZwich-compliant. The Bank of Ghana, therefore, adopted a much stronger approach to interconnection than do most central banks, not only funding and operating a retail payment switch but also mandating that banks connect to that switch.

Two years after launch, the record of eZwich was mixed. All Ghanaian banks had connected to the eZwich, but not all had issued smart cards by early 2010. Despite GhIPSS's high-profile marketing and promoting eZwich to the public, only 323,000 cards had been issued at the end of 2009 (an estimated 3.5 million people were banked), and banks had deployed eZwich POS devices at 2,425 merchant locations. Banks' lack of enthusiasm about deploying the cards and devices reflected the lack of a business case: the cards and devices were more expensive

(continued next page)

Box 2.3 *(continued)*

than magstripe cards and standard POS devices, so established banks' participation was grudging. Conversely, some smaller banks saw the advantage of being able to offer customers access to the larger eZwich network. However, usage of cards (at 1.5 deposits and 1 withdrawal per card per year in 2009) has been very low, prompting concerns that merchants had little reason to maintain the device since few customers sought to use it.

Over the same period as the rollout of eZwich, mobile penetration in Ghana had doubled to 67 percent. Under branchless banking guidelines, three nonbank mobile payment systems received BOG's approval to launch in 2009. This enabled nonbanks to offer real-time, person-to-person payment and bill payment capabilities. One of these systems, offered by MTN (the largest network operator) in conjunction with seven banks, reported 160,000 customers and 2,300 agents within five months after the launch.

The speed of growth in mobile coverage and penetration was not foreseen at the time BOG selected an offline solution. While the more expensive offline eZwich solution struggles to gain traction in a market with increasing options for electronic payments, the central switching capability that GhIPSS offers remains attractive to banks and especially new payment providers. In 2010, GhIPSS is considering implementing additional switching solutions, which may enable interconnection of other devices, including mobile.

Source: BFA 2010b.

New Questions Raised by the Third Generation

The arrival of third-generation models accelerates and intensifies some of the issues raised by the previous generations, since third-generation reach may be much wider; the risks to vulnerable consumers may also be higher.

In particular, since MNOs are no longer the gatekeepers for financial solutions (as they were in many second-generation models), there are new risks as well as new opportunities. On the positive side, third-generation providers face fewer barriers to entry in building on the use of the Internet channel. The entry of a new generation of small providers earlier may entice incumbents to provide more affordable and appropriate solutions for different population segments. On the other hand, the new entrants will likely lack the financial substance and large brands of MNOs—strong financial substance and brands have ensured that the risk of insolvency was low and that there were external incentives to provide good customer care for mobile financial services. Third-generation entrants may also not be subject to any regulatory framework in their role as retail payment providers—while even if second-generation financial services were unregulated, their MNO providers were accountable to a sectoral telecommunications regulator that had broad influence over their market conduct. New entrants may also cross borders as PayPal has, further eroding national regulators' oversight and influence.

The third-generation model, therefore, raises the question of whether and how to provide for a new class of payment service provider that *is* subject to authorization and oversight. These questions go to the heart of the vision of retail electronic payments and the institutional infrastructure necessary to support its sound development. Few countries have yet answered them. For most African countries, much of the past decade's focus has been placing the basic pillars for electronic payments, such as payment system legislation (which provides the legal certainty necessary especially for systemically important payment systems) and a functional real-time gross settlement system (RTGS) for large inter-bank payments. (In African countries, the RTGS is usually operated by the central bank, which can offer final settlement via accounts it holds for regulated banks.) On the latter front, there has been much progress: most African countries now have operating RTGSs (Kenya has had a functional RTGS since 2005, for example), although a few outliers, such as Ethiopia, were still—in 2010—in the process of implementing one.[16] However, the overwhelming majority of African countries still lack the pillar of payment system legislation; among these are Kenya and Tanzania, which have been the site of so much innovation in mobile payments to date.[17] Indeed, the traditional paradigm of payment systems is changing in these very countries: while overseeing the systemically important payment systems remains vital, regulators are focusing more on the oversight and consumer protection issues raised by pervasive retail electronic payment systems. Some countries that have pioneered second-generation models (Zambia and Ghana, for instance) have now adopted legal frameworks that give regulators authority over various forms of payment. Celpay, for example, started as an unregulated service provider and is now authorized as a designated payment system business under Zambia's 2007 National Payment System legislation.

Designing appropriate policy and regulation and implementing supervision or oversight in the fast-evolving world of electronic payments are no easy tasks. Payment system departments with central banks, which are largely entrusted with this effort, generally have very limited capacity. Many African central banks often have at most two or three individuals charged with addressing these issues (these people are separate from the payment system staff, who deal with the operations of the national gross settlement system). Traditionally, central banks gave resource priority to the banking supervision department, with good reason: the biggest losses have traditionally arisen from the poor supervision of banks. However, the growth of new payment providers and new payment systems that are not operated by banks, and therefore not subject to traditional models of supervision, questions this resource imbalance going forward. As the new payment instruments start to be widely useful, the risks and consequences of fraud and failure—to both the financial system and the economy as a whole—are greatly increased. These mounting risks, aside from the opportunities for economic development and financial inclusion from well-functioning systems, justify a much greater emphasis on equipping these departments.

Conclusions

In their 2007 book, Honohan and Beck called attention to the role of government in making finance work for Africa. They highlighted in particular the need for fair competition, for adequate infrastructure (including payment systems and credit bureaus), and for coordination among different policy makers and regulators. This chapter has focused on one fast-evolving part of the financial sector in Africa—mobile financial services—and has shown that these three issues remain relevant priorities for policy makers. The need for coordination is clear and growing, and the definition of what constitutes essential infrastructure is now extending to include the mobile network and national payment switches, which enable more efficient connection of channels. The questions associated with competition around distribution channels—whether these channels are ATMs or agents—are more pointed today than they were even three years ago.

Meanwhile, the ongoing rollout of mobile networks continues apace. This makes it possible, even likely, that almost every person in Africa will be within mobile coverage within 10 years, up from two-thirds in 2009. It is also quite likely that a considerable majority will have and use mobile phones—not only for voice calls, but also for data services including some form of Internet browsing. Second-generation mobile financial services in

Africa have demonstrated both to Africa and to the world the potential that can be unlocked when financial services piggyback effectively on this seemingly inexorable expansion. But they have also shown that the acceleration of financial service provision via mobile is not inevitable: it can be greatly retarded or greatly aided through enabling policy and regulatory environments. Fertile environments allow for a test-and-learn approach to new technology, but will also have to publish roadmaps indicating what the "tests" are and how and when the "learning" will be applied to inform the next rounds of actions at the appropriate stages.

If enough policy makers in Africa adopt this approach to enablement, then it is entirely feasible that, along with their mobile subscriptions, most adults on the continent could also have an electronic store of value. This e-value will serve as the lynchpin of their access to the formal financial sector within a decade. Whether this will be contained in a bank account, in an e-money account issued by an MNO, or by a third-party provider will vary by country. In each case, the provider will be subject to risk-appropriate oversight. Government payments to individuals can then be electronic transfers, saving cost for governments and reducing the risk of fraud and theft. Remittances will be easy and cheap.

To speak of the imminent arrival of a cashless society still seems highly speculative in developed countries, and almost incredible in Africa, a continent deeply locked into cash-based local economies. After all, developed societies such as Singapore have tried to force a transition to cashlessness with limited success, or at least a delayed timetable.[18] While the end-state of cashlessness is perhaps indeed far in the future anywhere in the world, the transition to a "cash-lite" society is more plausible. This will happen when electronic payment is pervasive enough that the need for cash is reduced and the stock of cash in circulation is declining, at least in relative terms. On the back of an enabled, accelerated mobile financial services rollout, African countries may be among the global leaders moving toward that "cash-lite" future. Further generations of provider models may have risen up by then, but in this sector at least, Africa will remain a cradle for ongoing innovation.

Notes

1. Celpay's approach was also described in the previous work by Honohan and Beck (2007).
2. We use the phrase *mobile financial services* as the umbrella term covering both traditionally distinguished categories of mobile banking (where mobile is

a channel to a bank account) and mobile payments (where mobile is used to effect payment, whether or not a bank or bank account is involved)—see AFI (2010).

3. 4G technology has also been deployed in Africa: in April 2010, Kenya's Safaricom announced plans to begin testing a 4G network in late 2010: see http://www.nation.co.ke/business/news/Kenyas%20Safaricom%20says%20 to%20test%204G%20later%20in%202010/-/1006/890190/-/j9u85pz/-/ index.html.

4. See http://www.wirelessintelligence.com/mobile-money, accessed August 20, 2010.

5. For more information, see FinAccess Kenya report 2009, available at http:// www.fsdkenya.org/finaccess/documents/09-06-10_FinAccess_FA09 _Report.pdf.

6. A recent cross-country survey in 18 African countries conducted by Gallup (Marlar 2010) showed that the percentage of adults with a bank account ranged from 1 percent in Niger to 49 percent in South Africa, although it was below 20 percent in 13 countries—this second figure is within the range that Honohan and Beck (2007) estimated for low-income countries. This is almost certainly lower than the percentage of people who have mobile subscriptions in these countries.

7. The lessons learned by MTN and Wizzit Banking have, however, been invaluable for informing rollouts elsewhere on the continent—whether by the MTN Group, by those using Wizzit technology, or by unconnected firms that have benefited by observing the experience of these early movers.

8. Ten of the 73 mobile money deployments list Fundamo as a technology partner. Note that the disproportionate influence on payment innovation extends to other niches too. South Africa–based Net1 is a leading proponent of smartcard-based payment systems, while South Africa–developed switching solutions such as Postilion are widely deployed in financial institutions worldwide.

9. In early South African deployments, this was apparently not the case, and MNOs shared keys with particular banks.

10. By comparison, the ratio in Europe and the Americas with an established fixed line infrastructure is more like 1:1.

11. As a promotion, Kenyan MNO Safaricom offered mobile data subscribers free access to Facebook for one weekend in September 2010. Clearly this type of social network has pulling power for potential clients.

12. PayPal announced its first deal with an African bank (First National Bank) in March 2010, enabling members in Africa to withdraw funds via the local bank. See FNB 2010.

13. See "Send and Receive Payments Securely Worldwide," https://www.paypal.com/us/cgi-bin/webscr?cmd=_display-approved-signup-countries-outside.

14. See http://www.gpfi.org/knowledge-bank/publications/g20-principles-innovative-financial-inclusion.

15. In South Africa, SIM registration was first required on all new subscriptions from July 1, 2009, and on all existing subscribers by the end of 2010.

16. Of the 15 African countries responding to this question in the World Bank 2008 Payment System Survey, all reported having an RTGS, most set up since 2005, with the central bank as the operator in all cases.

17. Although none of the 20 African countries in the World Bank 2008 Payment System Survey reported that they lacked any formal powers of payment system oversight, only 10 had oversight powers under a specific payment system law, and the balance relied more on "general empowerment" or powers in the general central bank law (World Bank 2008, table 1.5).

18. See the summary of experience in Pickens, Porteous, and Rotman 2009.

References

AFI (Alliance for Financial Inclusion). 2010. *Mobile Financial Services: Regulatory Approaches to Enable Access.* http://www.afi-global.org/library/publications/mobile-financial-services-regulatory-approaches-enable-access.

Aker, Jenny, and Isaac M. Mbiti. 2010. "Mobile Phones and Economic Development in Africa." CGD Working Paper 211, Center for Global Development, Washington, DC. www.cgdev.org/content/publications/detail/1424175.

BFA (Bankable Frontier Associates). 2009. *The Mzansi Bank Account Initiative in South Africa,* Report for FinMark Trust. http://www.finmarktrust.org.za/documents/R_Mzansi_BFA.pdf.

———. 2010a. *Regulation and Supervision of Bank Channels in Kenya.* Report for FSD Kenya. http://www.fsdkenya.org/pdf_documents/10-02-05_Regulation_supervision_of_bank_channels.pdf.

———. 2010b. *eZwich Case Study.* Report for Third Windsor Regulators Forum on Regulating Branchless Banking, Windsor, United Kingdom.

Bold, Chris. 2010. "MTN's Recipe for Mobile Banking Success." CGAP Technology Blog, March 3. http://technology.cgap.org/2010/03/03/mtn-recipe-for-mobile-banking-success/#more-2221.

Cenfri. 2010. "Will RICA Facilitate the Development of Transformational Mobile Banking in South Africa?" www.cenfri.org.

CGAP (Consultative Group to Assist the Poor). 2009. *Financial Access 2009: Measuring Access to Financial Services around the World.* http://www.cgap .org/p/site/c/template.rc/1.9.38735/.

Communications Commission of Kenya. 2010. *Quarterly Sector Statistics Report: 3rd Quarter Jan–Mar 2009/2010.* June 30.

Donner, Jonathan. 2009. "Mobile-Based Livelihood Services in Africa: Pilots and Early Deployments." In *Communication Technologies in Latin America and Africa: A Multidisciplinary Perspective,* ed. M. Fernández-Ardèvol and A. Ros, 37–58. Barcelona: IN3. http://in3.uoc.edu/web/PDF/communication-technologies-in-latin-america-and-africa/Chapter_01_Donner.pdf.

FinAccess. 2009. "FinAccess National Survey: Dynamics of Kenya's Changing Financial Landscape." June. http://www.fsdkenya.org/finaccess/.

FNB (First National Bank). 2010. "FNB and PayPal Bring Global eCommerce to South Africa." FNB. https://www.fnb.co.za/news/archive/2010/20100325 paypal.html.

Gartner. 2010. "Gartner Says Number of Worldwide Mobile Payment Users to Reach 108.6 Million in 2010." Press Release, June 21. http://www.gartner .com/it/page.jsp?id=1388914.

Gitau, Shikoh, Gary Marsden, and Jonathan Donner. 2009. "After Access: Challenges Facing Mobile-Only Internet Users in the Developing World." Paper presented at the 28th International Conference on Human Factors in Computing Systems, April 2010, Atlanta, GA.

GPFI (Global Partnership on Financial Inclusion). 2010. "Innovative Financial Inclusion: Principles and Report on Innovative Financial Inclusion from the Access through Innovation Sub-Group of the G20 Financial Inclusion Experts Group." May 25, 2010. http://www.gpfi.org/knowledge-bank/ publications/g20-principles-innovative-financial-inclusion.

Heyer, Amrik, and Ignacio Mas. 2009. "Seeking Fertile Grounds for Mobile Money." Mimeo. September 3. www.bankablefrontier.com/publications.

Honohan, Patrick, and Thorsten Beck. 2007. *Making Finance Work for Africa.* Washington, DC: World Bank.

Houpis, George, and James Bellis. 2007. "Competition Issues in the Development of M-Transaction Schemes." Vodafone SIM Panel Policy Paper No.6. http:// www.nokia.com/NOKIA_COM_1/Corporate_Responsibility/Sidebars_new_ concept/Transformational_Potential_of_M-Transactions/VOD833_Policy_ Paper_Series.pdf.

ITU (International Telecommunication Union). 2010. "Key Global Telecom Indicators for the World Telecommunication Service Sector." *ITU-D, ICT Data and Statistics,* available at http://www.itu.int/ITU-D/ict/statistics/at_ glance/KeyTelecom.html, accessed June 18, 2010.

Jenkins, Beth. 2008. *Developing Mobile Money Ecosystems.* Cambridge, MA: Harvard Kennedy School. http://www.hks.harvard.edu/m-rcbg/CSRI/publications/report_30_MOBILEMONEY.pdf.

Leishman, Paul. 2009. "Mobile Money: A US$5 Billion Market Opportunity: Initial Findings of the CGAP-GSMA Mobile Money Market Sizing Study." *MMU Quarterly Update* March.

Lyman, Timothy, Mark Pickens, and David Porteous. 2008. "Regulating Transformational Branchless Banking: Mobile Phones and Other Technology to Increase Access to Finance." Focus Note 43. CGAP/DFID, Washington, DC. http://www.cgap.org/p/site/c/template.rc/1.9.2583/.

Marlar, Jenny. 2010. "Few in Sub-Saharan Africa Have Money in a Bank." *Gallup World.* http://www.gallup.com/poll/127901/few-sub-saharan-africa-money-bank.aspx.

Mas, Ignacio. 2009. "The Economics of Branchless Banking." *Innovations: Technology, Governance, Globalization* 4 (2): 57–75.

Mas, Ignacio, and Kabir Kumar. 2008. "Banking on Mobiles: Why, How, for Whom?" CGAP Focus Note 48. CGAP, Washington, DC. http://www.cgap.org/p/site/c/template.rc/1.9.4400/.

Mas, Ignacio, and Sarah Rotman. 2008. "Going Cashless at the Point of Sale: Hits and Misses in Developed Countries." CGAP Focus Note 51. CGAP, Washington, DC.

MMU Deployment indicator. http://www.wirelessintelligence.com/mobile-money.

Morgan Stanley Research. 2009. *The Mobile Internet Report,* December 15. http://www.morganstanley.com/institutional/techresearch/mobile_internet_report122009.html.

Napier, Mark, ed. 2010. *Real Money, New Frontiers: Case Studies of Innovation in Africa.* Cape Town: Juta.

NIBSS (Nigeria Inter-Bank Settlement System). 2009. *Operational Rules and Regulations for the Nigeria Central Switch (NCS).* Nigeria Inter-Bank Settlement System.

Pickens, Mark, David Porteous, and Sarah Rotman. 2009. "Branchless Banking 2020." CGAP/DFID Focus Note 57. CGAP, Washington, DC. http://www.cgap.org/p/site/c/template.rc/1.9.40599/.

———. 2010. "Banking the Poor through G2P Payments." CGAP/DFID Focus Note No 59. CGAP, Washington, DC. www.cgap.org.

Porteous, David. 2006. "The Enabling Environment for Mobile Phone Banking in Africa." Report commissioned by DFID. Bankable Frontier Associates, Somerville MA, May 2006. http://www.bankablefrontier.com/assets/pdfs/ee.mobil.banking.report.v3.1.pdf.

———. 2008. "Is Mobile Banking Advancing Access to Basic Banking Services in South Africa?" Bankable Frontier Associates/Finmark Trust. http://www.finmark.org.za/new/pages/Focus-Areas/Payment-Systems.aspx?randomID=37df4fb1-05b8-46ad-aabe-4134b31e6dfe&linkPath=8&lID=8_10.

———. 2009. "Mobilizing Money through Enabling Regulation." *Innovations: Technology, Governance, Globalization* Winter: 75–90.

Porter, Michael. 1990. *The Competitive Advantage of Nations.* New York: Free Press.

Rosenberg, Jim. 2010. "M-PESA Meets Microsavings with Equity Bank Deal in Kenya." CGAP Technology Blog. http://technology.cgap.org/2010/05/18/m-pesa-meets-microsavings-with-equity-bank-deal-in-kenya/.

Roth, Daniel. 2010. "The Future of Money: It's Flexible, Frictionless and (Almost) Free." *Wired Magazine* February 22. http://www.wired.com/magazine/2010/02/ff_futureofmoney/.

Rotman, Sarah. 2009. "Mobile Payments in West Africa." CGAP Technology Blog, July 9. http://technology.cgap.org/2009/07/09/mobile-payments-in-west-africa/#more-1081.

Safaricom. 2010. "M-PESA Key Performance Statistics." July 8. http://www.safaricom.co.ke/fileadmin/template/main/downloads/M-PESA_Statistics.pdf.

Van Rensburg, Hannes. 2010. "What Will Smartphone Dominance Do to Mobile Banking?" Mobile Banking Blog, August 10. http://mbanking.blogspot.com/2010/08/what-will-smartphone-dominance-do-to.html.

Wachira, Nick. 2010. "How CCK Cut Off Safaricom's Fightback Options." *The East African,* August 23. http://www.theeastafrican.co.ke/news/How%20CCK%20cut%20off%20Safaricoms%20fightback%20options/-/2558/994264/-/klml8gz/-/index.html.

Wireless Intelligence (database). www.wirelessintelligence.com.

World Bank. 2008. *Payment Systems Survey 2008.* http://siteresources.worldbank.org/INTPAYMENTREMMITTANCE/Resources/Global_Survey_Appendix.pdf.

WSJ Online. 2002. "Africa Is at Telecom Forefront." *Wall Street Journal* (WSJ Online), December 2. http://business.highbeam.com/436100/article-1G1-94740253/dj-wsje-update-africa-telecom-forefront-msi.

Annex 2A   National ID and SIM Registration in Africa

Table 2A.1 lists the requirements for different types of ID and SIM registration in 44 African countries.

Table 2A.1 ID and SIM Registration Requirements

Country	National ID[a]	Source	SIM registration required[a]	Source
Angola	Yes, 2009	http://www.inmarsat.com/About/Newsroom/00028595.aspx?language=EN&textonl	No	
Benin	Yes	http://www.gouv.bj/spip.php?article381	No	
Botswana	Yes, 1987	www.laws.gov.bw/.../CHAPTER%6200102_%620NATIONAL%620_REGISTRATION_SUBSIDIARY_LEGISLATION.pdf	Yes, December 2009	https://www.communicationsdirectnews.com/do.php/140/39972?199
Burkina Faso	Yes, though in process	http://fr.allafrica.com/stories/201001181571.html	In process	https://www.communicationsdirectnews.com/do.php/140/39972?199
Burundi	Yes	http://fr.allafrica.com/stories/2009121801 49.html	No	
Cameroon	Yes	http://www.unhcr.org/refworld/country,,IRBC,,CMR,,4a704095c,0.html	Yes, February 2010	https://www.communicationsdirectnews.com/do.php/140/39972?199
Cape Verde	Yes	http://www.nosi.cv/index.php?option=com_content&view=article&id=90&Itemid=90&lang=en	No	
Central African Republic	No		No	
Chad	No		No	

(continued next page)

Table 2A.1 *(continued)*

Country	National ID[a]	Source	SIM registration required[a]	Source
Comoros	Yes	http://www.interieur-comores.com/index/index.php?option=com_content&view=article&id=72%3Ala-carte-nationale-didentite-&catid=40&Itemid=57	No	
Congo, Dem. Rep.	No, In process	http://fr.allafrica.com/stories/200911301565.html	No	
Congo, Rep.	Yes	http://1984.over-blog.com/article-642936.html	No	
Côte d'Ivoire	Yes	http://fr.allafrica.com/stories/200809250938.html	In process	https://www.communicationsdirectnews.com/do.php/140/399722199
Djibouti	Yes		No	
Equatorial Guinea	Yes	http://adoption.state.gov/country/equatorial%20guinea.html	No	
Eritrea	Yes	http://www.unhcr.org/refworld/country,,IRBC,,ERI,,49b92b4b0,0.html	No	
Ethiopia	Unclear		Yes	
Gabon	Yes	http://www.gabon-tourism.gaboneco.com/show_article.php?IDActu=14205	No	
Ghana	Yes	http://news.myjoyonline.com/features/201005/45891.asp	Yes, 1 July 2010	https://www.communicationsdirectnews.com/do.php/140/399722199
Gambia, The	Yes	http://allafrica.com/stories/200912230616.html	No	

Country		URL	
Guinea	Yes	http://fr.allafrica.com/stories/200809250938.html	No
Guinea-Bissau	Yes	http://www.datacard.com/case-study/guinea-bissau	No
Kenya	Yes	www.identity.go.ke	Considering it
		http://news.idg.no/cw/art.cfm?id=97BAE8AF-1A64-6A71-CE48938A5591ED4	
Lesotho	Yes	http://www.psc.org.ls/news/NATIONAL_ID_CARD.php	No
Liberia	Yes, In process	http://www.starradio.org.lr/content/view/13862/59/	No
Madagascar	Yes	http://french.peopledaily.com.cn/International/6795757.html	No
Malawi	In process	http://www.nyasatimes.com/national/malawi-to-start-issuing-national-id%E2%80%699s.html	No
Mali	Yes	http://www.migrationinformation.org/Profiles/display.cfm?ID=247	No
Mozambique	Yes	http://allafrica.com/stories/201006081151.html	No
Namibia	Yes	http://allafrica.com/stories/200811280807.html	No
Niger	Yes, but not common	http://mondeactu.com/monde/niger-la-classe-politique-remontee-contre-le-code-electoral-5709.html	No
Nigeria	Yes, 2007	http://www.thisdayonline.com/nview.php?id=169613	In process
		https://www.communicationsdirectnews.com/do.php/140/39972?199	

(continued next page)

Table 2A.1 *(continued)*

Country	National ID[a]	Source	SIM registration required[a]	Source
Rwanda	Yes	http://allafrica.com/stories/201006071299.html	No	
Senegal	Yes	http://www.nation.co.ke/News/africa/Senegal%20ID%20card%20delays%20cast%20doubt%20over%202012%20polls%20/-/1066/9128444/-/n08mlh/-/index.html	No	
Sierra Leone	Yes	http://freetown.usembassy.gov/pa012004.html	In process, 30 June 2010	https://www.communicationsdirectnews.com/do.php/140/399722199
Somalia	No		No	
South Africa	Yes	http://www.home-affairs.gov.za/Hannis_project.asp	Yes, 31 December 2010	https://www.communicationsdirectnews.com/do.php/140/399722199
Sudan	Yes, 1970s	http://www.unhcr.org/refworld/country,,IRBC,,SDN,456d621e2,3df4bea618,0.html	No	
Swaziland	Yes	http://www.gov.sz/home.asp?pid=2258	No	
Tanzania	No	Interview with Jacques Voogt	In process, 30 June 2010	https://www.communicationsdirectnews.com/do.php/140/399722199

Togo	Yes	http://www.mediaf.org/fr/themes/fiche.php?itm=1220&md=&thm=18	No	http://news.idg.no/cw/art.cfm?id=97BAE8AF-1A64-6A71-CE489938A5591ED4
Uganda	Yes	http://allafrica.com/stories/201004090006.htm	Considering it	http://news.idg.no/cw/art.cfm?id=97BAE8AF-1A64-6A71-CE489938A5591ED4
Zambia	Yes	http://news.idg.no/cw/art.cfm?id=071AF482-1A64-67EA-E4B297FCADCF3934	Considering it	http://news.idg.no/cw/art.cfm?id=97BAE8AF-1A64-6A71-CE489938A5591ED4
Zimbabwe	Yes	http://www.zimbabwe-embassy.us/subpage5.html	In process, August 31 2010	https://www.communicationsdirectnews.com/do.php/140/39972?199

Source: Author.

a "No" means that there is no publicly available evidence that this is in place, whereas "yes" or "considering it" refers to a specific source. It is therefore possible that this list may undercount the "considering it" group at least.

CHAPTER 3

Financing Agriculture: Selected Approaches for the Engagement of Commercial Finance

Mike Coates and Robin Hofmeister

Facilitating access to finance to fund the growth of African agriculture is one of the greatest challenges for stakeholders with an interest in both financial and agricultural sector development on the continent. Agriculture in most parts of the world has traditionally been a difficult sector for lenders and investors because it is often exposed to high systemic risks—both environmental risks (such as drought, flood, disease) and market risks (for example, price volatility, trade policy barriers, transport and logistics challenges). Nevertheless, many markets (in both developed and developing countries) have worked out practical agricultural finance systems that greatly enhance the competitiveness of domestic agricultural value chains. It is important to note that these systems, though usually market-led, are often underpinned by significant explicit or implicit government support and a pro-growth business environment that encourage innovation in financial intermediation. The hurdles to replicating these successes in Africa are significant, yet they need to be overcome if African countries are to improve food security and increase prosperity.

This background paper concentrates on the practical interface between the commercial financial sector and the growth of agricultural value chains. It pays particular attention to the themes of rural, savings-led financial service providers in the first section, Finance for All; to buyer and supplier finance in the next section, Finance for Markets; and to strong private sector players financed by commercial banks and private funds in the final section, Finance for Growth. The chapter argues that for African agriculture to grow, it will need access to the big balance sheet lending of the increasingly sophisticated and rapidly growing commercial banking system in many African markets.

This chapter draws heavily on conclusions, examples, and experiences from recently conducted studies on financing agricultural value chains in four African countries (Burkina Faso, Ethiopia, Ghana, and Kenya) commissioned by the Deutsche Gesellschaft für Internationale Zusammenarbeit GmbH (GIZ).

It is not an exhaustive or exclusive review, and if there is any lesson to be learned from the GTZ studies, it is that a wide range of parallel ideas, initiatives, and innovations to improve access to agricultural finance exists and is needed. These include proposals for the development of products such as leasing and other types of productive asset finance, invoice discounting and factoring, warehouse receipts and other types of stock finance, innovative insurance schemes, and many others. It also includes the development of financial sector infrastructure and other elements of the business environment such as the commercial legal system, credit rating agencies, collateral registries, and land reform, to name but a few. A wide range of technical assistance and capacity building to financial institutions not limited to savings and credit cooperatives, microfinance institutions (MFIs), commercial banks, insurers, capital markets, commodity markets, rating agencies, and regulators would qualify. Financial support through dedicated credit lines and credit enhancement tools, for example, as well as subsidized agricultural risk insurance and hedging instruments could also be considered. Initiatives aimed at improving the management and financial skills of agricultural businesses and/or to the financial literacy of small producers in particular would be well received. The development of transport infrastructure, power, and irrigation are just a few of the major infrastructure hurdles to be overcome to achieve greater competitiveness. Finally, any number of initiatives to strengthen the development and implementation of good policy in relation to the agriculture, financial, and commercial sectors, and in public finance reform, would have an indirect impact.

The urgency of the required improvement in agriculture can also tempt governments into politically motivated, activist policy decisions. Examples include measures such as interest rate caps, directed credit, or debt forgiveness. The findings of the study reinforced the importance of not reverting to approaches which have been seen to weaken the environment for agricultural finance in an unintended way. Direct market interventions in both the financial and agricultural sectors are generally to be avoided with a particular qualification. Well-run state-owned agribusinesses, such as national marketing boards or commodity exchanges, for example, seemed to be a positive example for an activist role of the government as they have a positive effect on the flow of finance to agriculture compared to more chaotic value chains where there was a complete absence of major market players, either private or public. In Africa the urge for the public sector to step into markets should be carefully observed and, wherever possible, efforts should continue to try to attract private sector players to replace public sector market participants.

Finance for All

The commercial banking system in major African cities is going through a boom. New branches are in evidence in previously underserved locations, automated teller machine (ATM) networks are expanding rapidly, wholesalers and retailers are increasingly using ATM/point-of-sale (POS) systems, and mobile banking is being adopted enthusiastically by consumers. These advances are symptomatic of the focus that commercial banks have on winning their share of increasingly lucrative urban mass and niche markets (for example, private banking). These markets are not only profitable by virtue of rising incomes, but they also benefit from the cost-effectiveness of a relatively concentrated distribution network.

Access to Finance in Rural Areas

While major provincial centers are also receiving their fair share of attention, small villages in remote areas do not. With a few notable exceptions, investment in rural branch networks by commercial banks will continue to be focused, for obvious reasons, on areas of high population density. Innovative approaches to bring financial services to more isolated rural areas involve branchless banking (including m-banking). Although such approaches are worthy additions, they are not a total substitute for a branch network and nothing seems to capture the full financial services needs of a community like a "bricks and mortar" branch.[1]

Rural Financial Services Providers

Commercial banks are largely absent from remote rural areas, even in developed markets. The development and massive growth of credit unions in Europe and the United States over the last 150 to 200 years was the response. Credit unions (often termed *savings and credit cooperatives* or SACCOs) are member-based financial institutions designed to capture and intermediate the savings of local communities or organized groups who feel they are underserved by the more mainstream financial sector.

Whereas credit unions provide an opportunity to expand the outreach of financial services, they also face many challenges. Governance issues and the over-politicization of some credit unions in Africa are affecting their ability to operate effectively and sustainably. This can be viewed to some extent in the light of the abuses of the nascent cooperative movement in Africa which have occurred in a number of instances, mainly during the last 25 years of the last century. The danger is that, because of their community-based ownership structure, some players in government are tempted to see them as some sort of extension of the public sector. Well meaning or not, some government efforts to catalyze the development of SACCOs, to use them to direct public sector credit, and to interfere in their governance and management are an anathema to the very principles that underpin the cooperative spirit. In their purest form, SACCOs are owned by their customers and savers, which means that members have a vested interest in actively ensuring that the SACCO is run along sound principles. Borrowers are generally well known to members, and the social pressure to conform by repaying loans is particularly strong. If members are not exposed to this risk, then the incentives to ensure good governance are broken down. To pull back from this position will require a substantial effort by policy makers, practitioners, apex organizations, and development partners.

Another important issue is the absence of any prudential regulation of credit unions in most countries in Africa, although the bigger ones are mobilizing substantial amounts of savings. It is all very well to argue that the principles of risk and reward should apply to savers in SACCOs, but it is also vital to ensure that the financial position and risk profile of a particular SACCO are well understood by the community. While it is important that well-managed SACCOs are able to expand and poor SACCOs to wither, it is simultaneously important that the sector not be exposed to systemic risks. Regulation of SACCOs has proved a challenge. Because they are usually small, their size means that thorough audits and intensive inspection are not cost-effective. This is a challenge to the sector, and one in which apex institutions (see below) can play a vital role. As well as cascading and embedding an effective system of monitoring and control, apex institutions are strong enough to provide financial support to struggling SACCOs and "rescue" failures by implementing changes to the management and governance structure.

Other rural financial services providers include MFIs and rural banks, which can face similar challenges in some markets.

Limitations of rural financial services providers. Even rural financial services providers tend to minimize agricultural lending and focus on the local salaried and merchant populations of the village or regional center. Although this may have some indirect benefit for agricultural producers in terms of establishing a deeper pool of local liquidity to facilitate trade, it is not comparable to the explicit and direct financing of specific productive agricultural activity.

Two major reasons that rural financial service providers minimize agricultural lending are discussed here: they perceive the risk to be high and they lack institutional capacity (internal skills, processes, technologies, and business culture).

When asked, managers of rural financial services providers point to the risks of agricultural lending and cite previous examples of poor repayment by farmers. However, this may change in time. Some credit unions in Kenya and rural banks in Ghana are showing promising signs of increased agricultural finance. It is clear that this model can work in the right circumstances, as exemplified by the relatively larger amounts of finance leveraged for production by cooperative banking systems in markets such as Latin America and South and East Asia. However, it should be noted that in the right circumstances over-politicization almost always is aligned to value chains that are much more "structured" and organized around a larger private sector agribusiness. The commercial environment in many of these markets is also much more developed, which gives lenders a greater degree of stability and comfort. This shows that the quality of the businesses to be financed is one key to improved access to agricultural finance.

The majority of the rural financial services providers have low institutional and human capacity and are small and isolated (though some have grown to have a more significant regional presence). SACCOs are often part of an apex structure, which offers some short-term liquidity support. Nevertheless, their balance sheets are usually independent and very limited. As a consequence of both balance sheet restrictions and their origins as "savings first" institutions, they are very conservative in their lending approach. Nor are they overly keen to access sources of wholesale finance even on generous long-term terms, which they perceive as a potential trap for the sustainability of their business. When they do access these sources (often donor funded), they tend to intermediate them into much safer and shorter-term lending than was originally intended by the providers of this finance. Though sometimes frustrating, they are to be lauded for their sensible approach.

Overcoming the limitations. Rural financial services providers need long-term support to build their balance sheets through a broad-based approach to asset and liability management. This entails a wide-ranging approach to improve management; to develop profitable strategies (and to improve capitalization through retained earnings); to develop and sell profitable products (including fee income); to boost the size of savings (provided adequate prudential regulations and a strong regulator are in place); to improve the information technology (IT) infrastructure and management information systems; and to develop the competence, professionalism, reward, and career opportunities for staff. Only if all these complementary initiatives are adopted will rural financial services providers be able to adopt a more aggressive and sophisticated risk strategy that includes a significantly greater proportion of finance for agricultural producers.

In addition, efforts need to be made to help rural banks and credit unions in particular to organize themselves into stronger networks, which can then help them to centralize and strip out costs, harmonize market and product development, share information and best practice, support each other's balance sheets, and provide opportunities for mobility and career progression for staff. Often this will result in the establishment of a shared commercial banking operation, often termed an *apex bank*. These apex banks, such as the Co-operative Bank in Kenya, can facilitate access to wholesale banking markets for their core cooperative or rural banking shareholders. They can also generate profits by competing with other commercial banks for lucrative retail or corporate customer bases.

Apex institutions can work with their rural or cooperative banking networks to sell products that are most profitably developed and managed from the center, utilizing the better economies of scale, improved cost of funds, and greater marketing strengths. Sometimes cooperation in marketing can extend to a shared brand and advertising costs, to further exploit efficiencies. Sharing customer metrics and default information can also improve product development and risk management approaches.

The success of apex banks varies in different markets. It is a generalization, but an experience founded in logic, that apex institutions in which rural and cooperative banks have an ownership and management stake will be more successful in meeting the needs of this market than apex institutions where rural and cooperative banks have no role in ownership or governance. For example, many of the most successful apex institutions were formed by, capitalized by, and in response to demand from rural and cooperative banks themselves. Institutions that have been "artificially" created by governments and/or development agencies tend not to be as responsive to the needs of financial institutions. Often these government- or agency-formed entities have wider economic development objectives that may not easily reconcile with the interests of the banks they purport to support.

It is not our view that cooperative or rural banks should necessarily be "captured" within a single network or structure. Other commercial banks should be free to collaborate with rural or cooperative banks, and compete with each other as well to offer the most competitive arrangements, depending on the needs of a specific institution. These arrangements could range from offering wholesale credit lines to rural financial services providers to applying private sector credit assessment skills to allocate finance to high-performing institutions. Cooperation with commercial banks (and other financial services organizations such as insurance, m-banking, and money transfer firms) in terms of strategic partnerships and agency arrangements should also be encouraged. It may also be that rural banks could be open to equity investments or even acquisition by commercial banks that value the rural banking business, but feel they can enhance profitability by adding balance sheet strength and cutting costs by centralizing some operations.

Finance for Markets

In relation to finance for markets, supplier and buyer finance with and without the involvement of commercial banks can be an extremely useful tool in helping address the severe lack of working capital hampering agricultural value chain actors. This section considers the need to expand and lower the costs of working capital, which, in turn, helps agribusiness and producers to retain earnings for investment and, in the long run, makes them more attractive for bank lending. The section also notes that there is more opportunity in shorter- to medium-term credit than long-term lending in this area.

Sources of Working Capital for Producers

Catalyzing private sector credit for small agricultural producers in Africa is one of the most vexing issues for policy makers and economic development professionals focused on livelihood development and poverty alleviation. By and large, financial institutions are very reluctant to lend to this group in particular. Quite aside from their sector-specific concerns in relation to agriculture, most financiers are unwilling to address this market because of a number of real or perceived concerns, including the following:

- Concern that much small-scale agriculture is not very profitable on the whole, and the opportunity cost of sacrificing market share in other fast-growing and profitable banking markets is not warranted
- Concern that the operating and distribution model required to cost-effectively reach small producers is a difficult, long-term, and large investment compared with the likely payoff
- Concern that small producers do not have the right values and behaviors in relation to financial services—specifically poor repayment records and a low propensity for other product purchases—to increase customer profitability for the banks.

The result, of course, is that most small agricultural producers have no access to formal financial services from the leading financial institutions of the country. Short-term working capital shortages are therefore often covered by credit from extremely expensive informal credit sources, further undermining producer profitability.

Currently producers in some of the better-structured value chains receive trade credit from larger private sector players such as input suppliers (for example, suppliers of fertilizers and pesticides) or buyers (including agriprocessors, exporters, and traders). By "better structured" we mean value chains that are short and efficient (for example, agribusiness tends to deal directly with producers or producer groups rather than being intermediated by layers of "middlemen"), value chains that are well organized (for example, those with strong and stable relationships between agribusiness and producers), and value chains that have good economies of scale (for example, those in the areas of purchasing, transport and logistics, and processing, which are often generated by bigger agribusinesses). The chapter suggests that building on the existing relationships between agribusiness and producers by adding buyer finance (also known as *buyer credit*) and supplier finance might constitute a vital structure in bridging this gap between the big balance sheets of the commercial banks and small producers. It is also a way of overcoming the fundamental information asymmetry that exists between large banks located in distant cities and small agricultural producers. This often leads to accusations that the banks fail to "understand" small producers and simultaneously that producers fail to be "transparent" to banks. In fact, there is an element of truth to both charges. By using the superior insight into the producer market held by many agribusinesses, this problem can be overcome.

Buyer and Supplier Finance

Buyer and supplier finance is a subset of trade finance, one of the oldest and simplest branches of finance and an umbrella term for a wide range of financial solutions (for example, factoring and forfeiting, invoice discounting, and letters of credit) which have underpinned the growth of value chains in developed markets for centuries. Specifically, in buyer and supplier finance, we are promoting the idea of using formal short-term credit lines to agricultural producers supplied by banks to prefinance agricultural production and intermediated by either input suppliers or agrifood buyers. In order to avoid confusion, in the terms *buyer* and *supplier finance*, the terms *buyer* and *supplier* refer to the status of the producer (in this case) in the transaction. For instance, either the producer is a buyer (for example, from an input supplier) or a supplier (for example, for an agrifood buyer).

This is a familiar concept to bankers, agribusinesses, and, to some extent, producers. It has been effectively applied by major African value chains such as cotton, coffee, and cocoa in some countries for years. Renewed efforts could be made to promote the outreach of this type of finance, which can be a practical and realistic solution to the working capital problems of producers.

Supplier and buyer finance works best when a value chain is well structured and served by a pool of well-managed companies with established banking relationships, who are instrumental in supplying inputs or in buying agricultural production. It is not particularly amenable to chaotic markets dominated by various layers of informal commodity trading.

Short-term trade credit. A signal that a value chain might be ready for supplier or buyer finance is the prevalence of trade credit for prefinancing agricultural production (box 3.1). In this case, we find that input suppliers or produce buyers are already using their own balance sheets to extend credit to customers or suppliers, respectively.

Box 3.1

Case Study: Buyer and Supplier Finance in Ghanaian Cocoa

Perhaps one of the best examples of short-term trade credit for agricultural producers is the cocoa value chain in Ghana. Cocoa is a huge industry in Ghana, and the purchase of produce from producers is dominated by a market of private sector buying companies (licensed buying companies or LBCs) with licenses to sell to the state-owned marketing monopoly.

These LBCs routinely provide significant amounts of short-term credit to producers for the purchase of the required inputs (for example, fertilizers and pesticides) before the growing season. In return, the cocoa growers agree to sell the resultant cocoa harvest to the LBCs at an agreed price. The capital and interest are repaid to the LBC through the proceeds of the sale and the balance goes to the farmer.

Similarly, credit can also be provided by the input supplier. In another example from Ghana, one of the country's largest suppliers of fertilizer and other agricultural inputs is providing supplies on credit to members of a major cocoa growers association, with repayment due following the harvest.

Source: Coates et al. 2011b.

Such trade relationships exist all over Africa, wherever there are strong private sector players involved in the value chain with robust relationships with producers. The depth of trade credit, however, is inherently limited by the size of the balance sheets of these firms. Trade credit devours working capital, and most firms will reach their limits sooner or later.

Building trade credit into buyer and supplier finance. Buyer and supplier finance is simply the leveraging of trade credit facilities with the involvement of a bank. The mechanism allows the extension of significant amounts of credit by using the combined balance sheets of both the firms and the bank.

The advantages of this type of finance are clear to the bank:

- The intermediary firm has close links with producers at a grassroots level, and it is not essential for the bank to replicate the costs of infrastructure to reach this market.
- The intermediary firm has already identified a pool of creditworthy borrowers who have developed a repayment record.

- The intermediary firms are much better placed to make sure that the finance is spent by the borrower on productive inputs rather than diverted into activities that may not realize repayment.
- The finance is a real trading advantage to the intermediary firm and can be used to solidify current banking relationships or to attract new customers from competitors.

Supplier versus buyer finance. There are subtle differences between the transactional structures, which present different risk profiles for each of the transactions. In supplier finance, the producer undertakes to sell produce to the buyer in return for the provision of credit to prefinance production. Assuming the producer fulfills this promise, the buyer is then in a very good condition to control repayment, which is a positive feature. Usually the buyer will deduct the costs of the loan directly from the payment due to the producer, who will receive the balance. However, this positive feature can be undermined by poor business relationships and behavior between the parties. *Side-selling* occurs where producers breach their promise to the buyer to sell an agreed amount and quality of produce at a predetermined rate in favor of other buyers who may be offering a better market rate at the time the produce is ready to sell. This behavior can be exacerbated by buyers who renege on price promises (or manipulate the overall amount due to the producer) and contribute to a breakdown in trust. In this circumstance, the buyers lose control of the source of repayment to the risk of both themselves and the financier.

Alternatively, input suppliers are in an excellent position to ensure that the funds advanced are spent on agricultural inputs rather than diverted to other, potentially nonproductive, activities. However, they have less control over the ultimate source of repayment. Both buyer and supplier finance arrangements rely on stable and professional relationships between producers and intermediary firms. To some extent it is beneficial if the intermediary firms are in a position of relative market power to the producer, and the practical sanctions for breach of loan covenants (for example, difficulty in sourcing alternative suppliers or buyers) for the producer are clear. This sort of sanction is usually more obvious to producers than the more ambiguous threats of legal action in costly and ineffective legal systems.

In some circumstances, intermediaries have the best of both worlds and are able to practically control repayment, as well as ensure that the credit is spent on the required input supplies. Contract farming operations and outgrower schemes—business relationships in which the buyer provides farm inputs such as credit or extension services to the supplier in return for the guaranteed supply of agricultural products—sometimes show these features. Such schemes also offer the producers economies of scale in bulk input purchasing and logistics, together with marketing power.

Buyer and supplier finance in practice. The bank must first identify suitable intermediary firms—either input suppliers or produce buyers. These firms would ideally be those with whom they already have solid banking relationships. For the purposes of reaching producers directly, the intermediary firm would have direct trading relationships with producers and/or producer groups; however, for the purposes of value chain finance this is not necessarily the case (box 3.2).

The bank needs to agree on an appropriate credit line and terms and conditions in line with the market risk profile and competitive conditions. It needs to develop a simple and streamlined credit process for the intermediary firm, ideally with a basic application form that the intermediary can use to "score" the proposed customer in line with the agreed credit policy. For example, criteria could include a specified minimum length of time that the producer/producer association has had a relationship with

---

Box 3.2

Case Study: Development of Supplier Finance in Ghana

A bank in Ghana had a large local supermarket as a customer. The supermarket was keen to expand its sales of horticultural produce from local producer groups, but supplies were unreliable and limited. It wanted to improve its supply chain by making formal arrangements with producer associations to supply an agreed quantity and quality of produce and price in return for helping prefinance production. Rather than relying entirely on its own balance sheet, it had approached the bank with a view to helping with a credit line of its own.

Although the bank would have been a reluctant lender directly to small agricultural producers, it was comfortable in banking a larger supermarket customer with formal management and accounting structures. The bank was willing to increase its working capital credit lines to the bank on the back of a clear explanation of the trading model. This expansion of working capital for the supermarket was used to help increase prefinance production and to improve the working capital arrangements of its key horticultural suppliers.

Source: Coates et al. 2011b.

the intermediary, their record of supply, the repayment history of any previous credit, the general reputation and professionalism of the producer/producer group, and other tangible and intangible factors. Ideally the intermediary firm would share a proportion of the credit risk presented, an arrangement that motivates compliance with the agreed policy and good lending discretion. In this case, it can be very useful for the bank to work collaboratively with the intermediary to develop a practical application process, as often the intermediary will be aware of the very specific factors that make a borrower a reliable source of repayment.

The intermediary firm can then process applications, passing the compliant ones on to the bank for checking and quick approval for the release of funds from the loan account. There are many systematic risk controls that a bank can put in place to control risks that may be gradually eased over time as intermediaries prove their reliability as "agents" of the bank and improve their own risk management controls.

One of the simplest of these controls is to mandate that producers receive payment for their produce in a dedicated account held with the bank (a particularly easy arrangement in the case of supplier finance) from which repayments can be automatically deducted. This also represents a "cross sell" opportunity for the bank and a way of increasing the formalization of producer financial activity. Studies have shown that where producers receive payment into a bank account, they are more likely to retain earnings over time.

Where it is more practical for the borrowing customer, it may be that the account is held with a cooperating rural bank or credit union. The rural bank or credit union may even be willing to underwrite a small proportion of the credit line for its own customers, further deepening understanding between producers and financial institutions. We believe it is this type of practical integration between the agricultural and financial sectors using what is essentially a very simple working capital product that could yield great long-term benefits.

Credit enhancement for buyer and supplier finance. There is an opportunity for the development community to catalyze or increase the growth rate of such facilities by providing a credit enhancement product (for example, a partial loan guarantee fund) that may improve the risk appetite and/or pricing of commercial banks. Clearly all the caveats that apply to such credit enhancements must apply—that is, it must be demand-driven, be sustainable, and not create market or competitive distortions. Moreover, the process of accessing the fund should be both simple and transparent.

Technical assistance in buyer and supplier finance. In some cases, technical assistance in developing and marketing a buyer/supplier finance product is recommended. The nature of the assistance needed depends very much on the market. For example, many commercial bankers will not need assistance with the concept of the product, but instead they will find challenges in the know-how required to commercialize the product. Consulting and assistance are likely to be more helpful in making the business case than practical implementation, with which they are well equipped to deal without outside assistance. This chapter advocates the identification of best-practice case studies of buyer and supplier agricultural finance in other markets (for example, Latin America or South and East Asia, Eastern Europe, or even OECD countries—those in the Organisation for Economic Co-operation and Development). It also advocates the promotion of field visits by senior banking executives to see how a product is working on the ground and to quiz senior-level counterparts on the value of the product to their banking offer.

Additionally, although most African bankers are capable of grasping the product, the banks themselves are often much less sophisticated. They may struggle with institutional problems and are likely to require more broad-based support to bring their institutions up to the basic levels required for this type of product.

Other Approaches to Release Working Capital

We have chosen to expand more fully on buyer and supplier finance arrangements both because they serve as useful examples to illustrate how the relationships among banks, agribusiness, and producers tend to work and because these products rarely need any further development of financial sector infrastructure or the legal and regulatory environment. However, other extremely viable and interesting alternatives can certainly be used to expand or release working capital for agricultural value chains if the circumstances are right.

One option currently being explored is the use of warehouse receipts, which are in relatively common use in some other markets. Under this arrangement, commoditized produce (for example, wheat, coffee, cocoa, maize) is deposited in a warehouse by the owner and a receipt is issued against it. This receipt stipulates the quantity, quality, and type of produce deposited. The warehouse receipt is generally negotiable, meaning ownership is transferable, making it quite suitable for collateral. Therefore, financial institutions have proved willing to extend loans against this security in the right environment.

From a financial perspective, this is a simple product, but it does require some fundamentals to be in place. It is essential that very good warehousing facilities be in place—so that both parties to the transaction can be confident that the produce is well protected and secure. There must also be high levels of trust among the players, and particularly the assurance that the warehouse operator will not release the produce to any party other than the true owner (that is, against the presentation of the warehouse receipt). Inspection and grading services must also be reliable to ensure that the produce is of the precise type, quantity, and quality stipulated. The legal environment must be supportive of the bank's right to quickly and unilaterally realize security in the event of default, usually by selling the warehouse receipt to a third party, and a vibrant secondary market for warehouse receipts must be in place. There is nothing particularly complex about these components, but they must all work together in a fairly flawless way.

Warehouse receipts tend to be a slightly awkward product for very small producers, who rarely have the volume of produce that makes such an operation cost-effective. However, these receipts are very suitable for higher levels of aggregation, perhaps in the trading environment or for agricultural cooperatives, which can certainly help release working capital for the benefit of the value chain as a whole. They are only suitable for certain types of produce, however—that is, for those that are highly commoditized (that can be reliably and consistently graded), for which there is a clear and open market price, and that are not highly perishable. Warehouse receipts are particularly useful for very short-term finance. A typical example might be to use a warehouse receipt to give a quick cash injection while a seller waits for a glut in the market (typically straight after harvest) to pass through the system before prices improve. For similar reasons of market volatility, of course, banks will typically extend only a relatively modest proportion of the market value of a warehouse receipt.

Assets such as equipment and machinery can also be financed through leasing, which can help release working capital over the medium term. Simply put, a lease is a series of contracted payments after which the asset passes from the lessor (the owner) to the lessee. Banks are often willing to finance such arrangements for the lessee if the lessor agrees to allow them to take a charge on the asset in the event of default. These arrangements usually work best when a bank works closely with a supplier of agricultural machinery and equipment. Banks find it difficult to value and realize such assets, so it is ideal to have a side contract with the supplier stipulating a buy-back clause. This means that the supplier will agree to buy back the asset from the bank at an agreed value in the event of default. Furthermore, the supplier may even be willing to undertake the asset recovery on the part of the bank, which means that this should essentially be a hands-off transaction for the bank. It usually works best with assets that have a vibrant secondary sales market.

Again, the legal environment has to be right, because it must be easy and quick for the bank to seize and realize collateral in the event of default. One of the reasons for the popularity of leases in developed markets has usually been their favorable tax treatment, and the possibility of treating them as off-balance sheet items for accounting purposes. Leasing and other asset finance solutions have huge potential for African agribusiness, and it is a product that should continue to be developed. It remains to be seen how much value it will offer directly to the smallest producers, but given the right circumstances it certainly has promise.

The Difficulty of Long-Term Lending

Appetite for long-term lending (over five years) by the private sector (and indeed the public sector) will probably be limited for some time. Agricultural value chain players will need to find investment capital from retained earnings and reserves rather than banks. Although many African banks were not as badly affected by the financial crisis as financial institutions with greater exposure to international markets, the subsequent economic downturn is having an effect on portfolio quality. This, when combined with the greater prudential emphasis by central banks, means that many banks are trying to improve capitalization. The effect is a generally more conservative lending approach, which often limits the growth of newer or more adventurous customer segments (such as agriculture), and a focus on restricting the term of lending. The bigger opportunity comes in smoothing and facilitating the flow of cash and reducing the crippling burden (in terms of business failure and the costs of emergency short-term finance) that a chronic lack of working capital presents to many agricultural value chains. It is perceived that this lack of capital can be met by buyer and supplier finance, which is something in which the commercial banks are interested.

Finance for Growth

Finally, with regard to finance for growth, medium-size African agribusinesses are critical to structuring agricultural value chains and enabling higher growth rates. This section considers equity finance, which is often required before or alongside debt to overcome perceived chronic under-capitalization. One way to link medium-size African agribusinesses and sources of international, regional, and domestic capital would be a continent-wide agribusiness investment pipeline. An improved equity base again facilitates access to debt finance. Finally, the section notes that promising agribusinesses are often likely to need access to high-quality and cost-effective business development services to facilitate this process.

Importance of Agribusiness

The GTZ studies on *Financing Agricultural Value Chains in Africa* (Coates et al. 2011a, 2011b, 2011c, 2011d) have shown that a major differentiator between value chains is the presence of a strong agribusiness player at some point in the value chain. Agribusiness thrives on competitive advantage, and the businesses often go to considerable efforts to build efficiency and predictability into their specific supply chains. They try to build stable working relationships with producers and closely monitor the quality of the product they receive.

It is important to realize that agribusiness does not just involve typical privately owned companies. It also encompasses agricultural cooperatives, state-owned enterprises (SOEs), and marketing franchises.[2] Although agricultural cooperatives and SOEs come with their pros and cons, the impact they have on value chain structure is evident. Perhaps this is because the remit of cooperatives and SOEs often involves material investment and effort in the organization of producers and the provision of extension services.

Agricultural cooperatives are an area of particular interest. Agricultural cooperatives had a promising start in some African markets in the 1950s and 1960s. In some cases, changes in political philosophy combined with blatant state-sanctioned corruption and asset seizure effectively destroyed the movement and its reputation in the eyes of producers. They now appear to be on the rebound, with examples of large agricultural cooperatives exhibiting many of the positive features of well-run commercial enterprises. They also have positive social features because producers, through their membership or "ownership" of the cooperative, benefit by sharing in the profits (box 3.3).

Size Matters in Agribusiness

The authors do not wish to denigrate the role that agricultural micro-enterprises can play in an economy, especially in relation to the development of increased off-farm income for producers. However, in terms of

Box 3.3

Case Study: Dairy Cooperatives in Kenya

A typical example might be the dairy industry in Kenya, and the case of a major local dairy cooperative. The cooperative had established a sophisticated supply chain involving collection centers distributed throughout the catchment area of the cooperative, the provision of a range of extension services, and operation of a mobile cooperative store that helped farmers access input supplies with the benefit of a bulk discount and sometimes with trade credit. Sometimes agricultural cooperatives had also catalyzed the creation of the local credit union in order to provide financial services for their underlying membership.

Source: Coates et al. 2011a.

overall value chain development, it seems that major value-addition businesses are especially capable of creating a true competitive advantage in terms of the marketing, quality, and cost of production.

Describing the types of agribusinesses with the most potential is difficult when using definitions based on financial metrics. It is often more useful to describe their characteristics. First, they should not be so large that they are listed or capable of listing on stock markets for the purposes of raising capital, nor should they already be targets for mergers and acquisitions or professional investment. However, they should be large enough to require a full-time professional management team that encompasses most of the usual functions of a professionalized company. For example, they should have dedicated functions for finance, marketing, human resources, and operations or similar departments, at the very least. They should exhibit at least some split between the ownership (even if it is concentrated within an individual or family) and the day-to-day management of the business. It is likely that there may be problems with this relationship (which can be resolved through good advice and assistance), but they are unlikely to be purely owner-managed businesses.

The evidence suggests that small and especially medium-size businesses are often quite capable of breaking out of their current business model and delivering high growth, increased profitability, and employment opportunities for the local population.

It is for this reason that we advocate a renewed focus on small and medium enterprises (SMEs) rather than the micro end of the market, and particularly a concentration on medium-size businesses. The question remains, however, of how best to fund long-term growth to help these businesses reach the scale and professionalism of management required to serve domestic needs, as well as potentially compete in international markets.

Undercapitalization of Agribusiness

A recurring worry of bankers in response to proposals to increase credit allocation to agriculture seems to be a perception of the "undercapitalization" of agribusiness. By this they mean businesses that are constantly having short-term cash flow issues as a result of having insufficient investment or access to longer-term capital.

These issues can be the result of a number of causes. Perhaps the business is growing too fast in relation to its longer-term capital (typically called *overtrading*), and is struggling to finance production while it awaits payment on previous sales. Perhaps the owners understand this problem but are unable or unwilling to make further investment in the company themselves. Typically they will then try to access expensive short-term credit (if it is available), which will compound the problem. Perhaps the owners do not understand the implications of expensive credit, or are stripping the company of cash for other purposes. After all, a profitable company should be able to retain earnings and build up its capital over time in line with growth.

These are some of the issues that bankers look at very carefully when assessing a credit proposition. Lack of cash is a business killer, and lending to an undercapitalized business is a dubious proposition. That is why, when bankers get a request from a customer for a major increase in long-term lending, they like to see a significant contribution of equity investment as well. It is difficult to generalize, and it varies from bank to bank and sector to sector, but for illustrative purposes many commercial bankers may start to take a close look at an SME if it has more debt than equity, as a general principle (that is, on the assumption that the debt-equity should be a 1:1 ratio or better).

Clearly, many business owners may take a different attitude. Some of them perceive that they have already risked a lot and expended much effort in building what they see as a profitable operation. They feel that it is now up to the banks to fund long-term growth while they begin to reap the profits. This gap in expectations is a feature of every market, particularly in emerging markets where business owners may have less commercial experience and poor access to good financial advice.

Attitudes of Owners to Financiers

The injection of outside equity capital is an enabler for access to increased debt capital, not just for reasons of improved solvency. Investors who take an equity capital stake become part owners and are able to take part in decision making. They often bring professional management skills with them that can dramatically improve the prospects of the business. Investors can be broadly grouped into private individuals (or "business angels") and professional investment funds or firms. The latter tend to focus on larger, established investments because their higher direct costs warrant larger investments (for example, working upwards from perhaps US$1 million, which would be considered quite a small investment) while the former can often be found sponsoring smaller businesses or even start-ups (maybe just injecting quite small amounts of capital, as little as a few tens of thousands of dollars).

However, the dilution of equity also means that the current owner(s) can lose control over the business (box 3.4). This includes losing control over money, but it also includes a loss of esteem and status that are derived from a position of complete control. Sometimes the business is a family concern, and the owners are reluctant to dilute the family's stake. Sometimes the owner just thinks that nobody else is really competent to make decisions for the business. Ultimately, however, many businesses become stifled by this type of governance, and they become stagnant and moribund.

Limited Equity Capital Investment in Agriculture

In Africa, the professional equity investment pool is limited but growing rapidly in economic sectors where growth levels are high. Equity investment can be a risky business, and tends to gravitate to sectors with rapid growth potential in order to offset high risks with potential high returns. Agribusiness is not typically seeing the same levels of attention as most other sectors in terms of equity investment, and can be a difficult sector to approach for professional investors.

First, professional equity investment is heterogeneous. Agriculture varies enormously between one subsector and another. This variety is complicated by a relatively diverse range of value chain participants. Compare this, for example, to telecommunications, or mining, or construction, or retail and wholesale trade, and the difference is obvious. Usually in these examples financiers can deal directly with a major private sector player who has a great deal more control over the supply chain and market than is the case with most agricultural value chain actors.

Box 3.4

Case Study: Equity Investment in a Fruit Juice Processing Plant in West Africa

The business was a relatively sizable fruit juice (pineapple, citrus) processor in West Africa with sales of several million dollars in both domestic and international markets. The business had been built from inception by the owner, who had now accepted the need to invite external investment and relinquish total management control.

The business had for some time been underperforming, and bankers were not responding positively for increased facilities. The situation came to a head, however, when the owner/manager had to take a substantial break from work for reasons of ill health.

Not untypically of businesses of this type, the owner/manager insisted on exerting ongoing control—to the extent of taking the company's checkbook home and insisting that any payments to suppliers (for example, local fruit growers) had to be authorized by him. Unsurprisingly, business began to grind to a halt because suppliers were not paid on time.

This appears to have been a cathartic moment for the owner/manager, who responded positively to the approach of a Nigerian private equity firm. As an interim measure prior to investment, a professional general manager, who is overseeing a restructuring of the business, has been appointed.

The latest news is that management expected the company to embark on a successful new growth phase as a result of the new investment.

Source: Coates et al. 2011b.

Second, at a subsector level in particular, information is scarce and the understanding of potential investors limited. Other sectors, such as those noted above, put a great deal of energy into business planning and financial analysis with a view to seeking investment. They publicize this information and lobby hard to make sure that investors are kept apprised about the growth potential of their sectors. It is difficult to find similar examples in African agricultural value chains aside from some of the most solidly structured.

Another possible inhibitor of potential investors is the lack of depth in the market to develop viable exit strategies for their investments. There are a range of approaches that can be considered. If firms have grown to an appropriate size, then the potential for listing on the rapidly developing local and regional stock markets can be considered. However, it is likely that for a large proportion of the target agribusinesses, the main exchange may be an inappropriate market because of the extensive listing requirements involved. Consideration can in some countries be given to the establishment of a "junior" exchange with a lighter regulatory regime that is suitable for smaller companies. Clearly investors are able to solicit private sales and placements, and one of the goals of such an initiative would be to bring firms to a point where they are suitable for vertical or horizontal integration into existing agribusinesses (domestic or international), or for other professional investors specializing in larger investments. Finally, it may be appropriate to explore with senior management the possibilities of management buyouts and, in appropriate circumstances, to approach commercial banks with specific proposals in mind.

Finally, there is a lack of readily prepared, sound investment opportunities, despite the enormous potential in processing, for example, or in new types of production such as aquaculture (as opposed to capture fisheries). The agribusiness sector in most countries in Africa is much smaller than it could be, which limits the number of available opportunities. Investors are going to focus on the easy-win sectors first. This chapter proposes two interventions that the public and economic development sectors can undertake to assist the private sector on its way: (1) the establishment of a continental agribusiness investment pipeline, and (2) the delivery of tailored enterprise development services to selected investment opportunities.

Intervention 1: Establishment of a Continental Agribusiness Investment Pipeline

The process of identifying and executing successful equity transactions is costly. Deals are difficult to structure, are prone to failure, and require time and effort by highly remunerated investment professionals. The agricultural sector needs support to compete with other economic sectors in this regard, perhaps by at least making the first part of the deal process—that of identifying opportunities with high potential—easier for investors.

Typically, in developed markets, small, medium, and large businesses have a range of advisory avenues open to them in raising equity capital. Large businesses generally retain the services of professional financial advisors or investment bankers to help them access capital markets. The largest agribusinesses in Africa have access to parallel services in the more sophisticated commercial centers. The situation diverges most dramatically at the SME end of the spectrum, where developed markets have a strong network of accountants and business advisors who are able to connect investable opportunities with sources of equity (whether institutional or perhaps business angels). Such services are rare in Africa.

One of the best ways of linking medium-size African agribusinesses and sources of international, regional, and domestic capital is to establish a continent-wide agribusiness investment pipeline. This would create a database of background information and data on "qualifying" firms that wished to register their interest in soliciting further investment. Financial data could be tracked over time, both prior to and following investment, thereby giving investors an insight into the financial structure of the businesses and comparative data. This could be overlaid on information relating to the investment climate in the country and some practical tips for success in the local investment environment. It could facilitate meetings between investors and registered companies, simply by providing up-to-date contact information. The information could be available online, but could also be promoted at investor roadshows and in the business press in order to catalyze interest.

Intervention 2: Business Development Services for Agribusiness

As well as collecting and distributing data on agribusiness, development agencies and governments could prioritize such firms for receipt of high-quality business development services (BDS). The costs of investment activity can be reduced substantially, and the chances of success materially improved, if an investable business is in a position to deal with investors on a professional level. Regardless, the receipt of high-quality advice should be of assistance to the firm concerned, even if an investor does not come forth.

Obviously, potential investees need to have their accounts in order, but investors will also be looking at other sources of financial management information for indications about the current marketing activity, sales potential, and underlying costs of the business. Investee firms should also have well-developed and realistic strategic and business plans, with clear and measurable parameters of success. They should understand the principles of good governance and professional management and be ready to adopt different approaches. They will need to understand the true implications of seeking investment in terms of negotiating the terms of management control, and also to understand how professional investors value a company so as not to have unrealistic expectations. These are just some of the many areas that BDS for agribusiness could cover, specifically in relation to the promotion of investment. Clearly there are other potential topics for development that would need to be discussed on a case-by-case basis with the firms involved and tailored to their precise needs.

Such highly customized services are expensive, and consideration will need to be given to making them sustainable. Perhaps a finder's fee could be levied in the event of successful introductions, or maybe some form of carrying interest considered. There may even be opportunities to assume management contracts to represent investor interests in the investee firm. BDS could be paid for by the investee firm, with only a partial subsidy to make them cost-effective. Some contribution by the beneficiary is vital in ensuring that services are effectively demand-led. Even in circumstances where a subsidy is vital, this can be structured through the provision of vouchers redeemable for qualifying services from preapproved private sector providers. This is at least a way of stimulating competition in the provision of high-quality, highly tailored services.

Conclusion

Agricultural value chains are underinvested in Africa; most need major injections of a mix of investment and working capital. Within the limited scope of this chapter, some potential areas of focus have been highlighted: first, where it is believed that the financial sector could have the greatest impact in promoting agricultural value chain development, and second, where priority has not hitherto been accorded to the extent warranted. The following principles should come into play when considering financial sector development policy for the agricultural sector:

- It is vital to engage the interest of the commercial banking system—commercial banks can leverage large balance sheets to support the levels of growth required.
- Diversity is a strength in a financial sector; front-line rural and cooperative banks, which are sufficiently strong and efficient, can expand the outreach of financial services to Africa's small producers, especially in collaboration with the commercial banking system.
- Supply chain finance and buyer credit are practical methods for expanding access to working capital for value chain actors, especially producers.
- Other promising approaches to release working capital include warehouse receipt financing and the leasing of machinery and equipment.

- Improving the working capital of agricultural value chains helps players retain earnings for investment by default.
- Equity investment has a major role to play in transforming medium-size agribusinesses in Africa and setting them on a renewed high-growth trajectory.
- Improved capitalization has the effect of improving access to bank lending as a result.
- Larger businesses tend to have greater growth potential than micro-enterprises; these should be the primary target group.
- Effort should be made to avoid too much focus on long-term lending, which is a very difficult objective—there is much more opportunity in shorter-term finance and medium-term credit for machinery and equipment financing if the legal environment is supportive.

Africa is a huge and growing market with a vast export potential for home-grown agrifood products. There is great promise for African agriprocessing in terms of input substitution, but the industry needs transformation in order to achieve this. Finance is only part of the solution. There are also major challenges in the policy and business environments and supporting infrastructure to overcome.

Notes

1. Developed markets learned this lesson in the 1990s when intense branch rationalization was halted and sometimes even reversed. To a certain extent, customers adopted much cheaper mobile and Internet banking channels. But when it came to perceptions of the bank as a brand, and when they needed to make major financial services purchases or transactions, the value of a convenient branch presence was deemed essential.

2. When considering what "qualifies" as an agricultural business, the definition should not be too narrow. Agricultural value chains depend on a wide range of ancillary services, so it is useful to expand the definition of the agricultural private sector to include these players.

References

Coates, Mike, Richard Kitchen, Geoffrey Kebbell, Catherine Vignon, Claude Guillemain, and Robin Hofmeister. 2011a. *Financing Agricultural Value Chains in Africa: Focus on Dairy and Mangos in Kenya.* Bonne, Germany: GIZ (Deutsche Gesellschaft für Internationale Zusammenarbeit). http://www2.gtz.de/wbf/library/detail.asp?number=9738.

————. 2011b. *Financing Agricultural Value Chains in Africa: Focus on Pineapples, Cashews and Cocoa in Ghana.* Bonne, Germany: GIZ (Deutsche Gesellschaft für Internationale Zusammenarbeit). http://www2.gtz.de/wbf/library/ detail.asp?number=9741.

————. 2011c. *Financing Agricultural Value Chains in Africa: Focus on Cotton and Cassava in Burkina Faso.* Bonne, Germany: GIZ (Deutsche Gesellschaft für Internationale Zusammenarbeit). http://www2.gtz.de/wbf/library/ detail.asp?number=9740.

————. 2011d. *Financing Agricultural Value Chains in Africa: Focus on Coffee and Sesame in Ethiopia.* Bonne, Germany: GIZ (Deutsche Gesellschaft für Internationale Zusammenarbeit). http://www2.gtz.de/wbf/library/ detail.asp?number=9739.

PART II

Lengthening Contracts

LearningLib.Com

CHAPTER 4

Housing Finance

Simon Walley

The aim of this chapter is to provide an assessment of where housing finance stands across the African continent in the aftermath of the world financial crisis. This is an ambitious task given the diversity of economies and housing finance systems that encompass the North African Maghreb countries, Sub-Saharan Africa, and the Indian Ocean countries, as well as the special case of South Africa, which stands out from many of its neighbors.

The world downturn brought on by the credit crunch was itself borne out of the failures in the housing finance mechanisms in the United States and other "mature" markets. These failures precipitated a wide-ranging review of how the financing of homes is best delivered. This review includes a reappraisal to determine which institutions may be the best placed to deliver housing finance and to which types of borrowers. The crisis has yet to fully run its course, but some salient policy lessons have nevertheless already been drawn. This chapter will consider to what extent these lessons are relevant and applicable to African markets.

This housing finance overview will also seek to describe and quantify some of the driving forces behind both the supply and demand for housing finance in Africa. The assessment of future demand can be based on population growth, income growth, and urbanization trends. Juxtaposing the current situation alongside future demand will allow for a gap analysis to be performed. Such an analysis will provide the basis for the final, forward-looking section of the chapter. It will attempt to set out a recommendations framework of ways the gap in housing and the financing of housing can be bridged.

Lessons and recommendations will be based on the data presented in this chapter, on experience working in African countries and other countries—both developed and emerging economies—and by highlighting some of the success stories that are already taking place in Africa. There are many positive developments that could be the spark for bigger movements and replication in new markets. Above all, however, this chapter aims to provide some enlightenment on the path out of the crisis and toward the longer-term financing of housing in Africa. As will be shown, housing finance systems are chains containing many links, each of which must be strong and play its part for the system as a whole to prosper. This chapter is therefore directed to lenders, developers, and policy makers as well as the myriad other stakeholders that, each individually, have a role to play in promoting an efficient housing finance system on the African continent.

Demand for Housing Finance

All housing is financed in some form or other. Housing can be financed through a mortgage, savings, housing microfinance, or investment capital or through the imputed value of one's own labor. Given the size of the expense that typically represents the largest purchase of any household, it makes sense to extend the financing period as long as possible to improve affordability. However, in Africa the absence of long-term funds has inhibited the growth of housing finance and other forms of financing requiring long-term money. This leaves many households with their only option: to build incrementally with the purchase of raw materials coming out of any surplus in each paycheck. This is typically a slow, inefficient way of constructing housing, and it eliminates any economies of scale that could be achieved from buying materials in bulk. It also means that the "housing good" can be consumed only right at the end of the financing period, rather than from the outset with a traditional mortgage loan.

Formal financing of housing in Africa has been limited to date. Figure 4.1 shows that—with the exception of South Africa, Namibia, and some of the North African countries—mortgage finance barely registers as an asset class in the African financial system. As a continent, mortgage debt outstanding to GDP is around 10 percent, which compares to

Figure 4.1   Mortgage Debt as a Percent of GDP

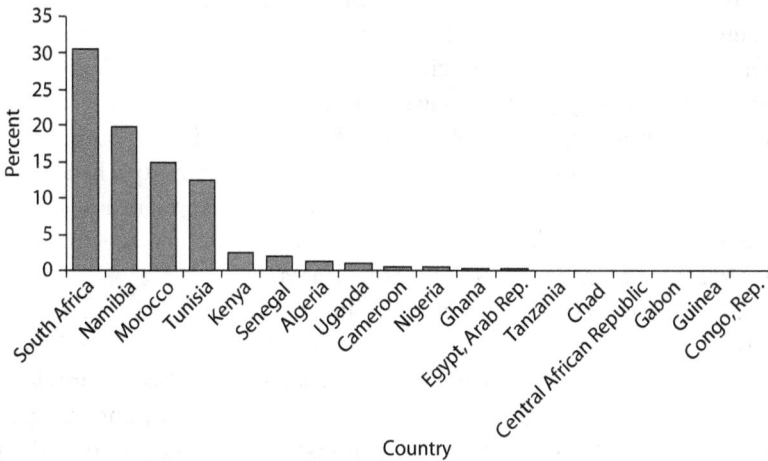

Source: World Bank mortgage debt database, 2010.
Note: Data are the latest available and vary between 2004 and 2009.

70 percent for the United States and 50 percent for Europe. If you take out South Africa, the rate falls to 2 percent of GDP. If you then take out North African countries, the rate for Sub-Saharan Africa falls to under 1 percent of GDP. In those countries where it does exist—such as Tanzania, Uganda, Ghana, and Nigeria—the number of loans is rarely more than a few thousand. These loans are also often limited to the wealthiest segment of the population, who pose the lowest credit risk. This means that the existing loans are far from subprime and are typically issued only after extensive documentation requirements, large down payments, and often additional guarantees from an employer or other forms of collateral besides the property.

An alternative to mortgage lending that has proved popular in developing the housing finance system in South America is housing microfinance. This medium-term financing can allow for much more rapid incremental construction and some bulk buying of materials. There is extremely limited information on this form of financing, but other than some initiatives in South Africa it has yet to develop to any significant scale in Africa. In part, this reflects the slower development of microfinance more generally in Africa than in other regions, as well as the continent's much lower urban densities. The density of urban areas may have helped accelerate the development of housing microfinance in the South American context where lenders are able to benefit from reduced distribution costs.

An alternative yet significant means of accessing housing is through the rental market. Finance is still required, however. The landlord must acquire the property initially, and a system is also needed for rental payments to be effected. African cities in Sub-Saharan Africa are predominantly populated by people living in rental housing. Much of the housing in cities such as Lagos, Nairobi, Accra, Kinshasa, and Khartoum is substandard and without sanitation, running water, or electricity. The absence of a functioning rental framework often means that there are limited incentives for landlords to improve housing stock. Tenants face insecurity, high rents, and higher deposits for their leases.

It is often remarked that "cities are built the way they are financed." This is especially true for Africa, where the absence of long-term financing means that long-term planning becomes difficult. This, in turn, leads to a lack of urban design, poor utility connections, and poor transport links. Residential, commercial, and industrial areas can also end up being mixed together through lack of proper planned zoning. The outcome is an urban sprawl with largely informal, low-quality housing. As urbanization accelerates, the situation is likely to worsen as more pressure is brought to bear on the limited existing resources and services, and as the limited housing production becomes ever-more inadequate.

Table 4.1 provides testament to government's inability to fully tackle the growth of urban slums. The table shows some of the worst-affected

Table 4.1   Urban Population and Slums, Selected African Countries

Country	Total population (millions, 2009)	Urban population (millions, 2008)	Urbanization rate (percent, 2008)	Slum population (millions, 2005)	Urban population living in slums (percent, 2005)
Somalia	8.9	3.3	37.3	2.8	96.5
Central African Republic	4.3	1.8	39.3	1.5	92.5
Niger	14.7	2.4	17.2	1.9	90.7
Sudan	41.3	18.0	44.4	13.9	88.1
Nigeria	151.2	73.1	49.5	41.7	64.0
South Africa	48.74	29.6	61.8	8.1	29.0
Egypt, Arab Rep.	81.5	34.8	43.5	5.4	16.4
Morocco	31.6	17.7	56.7	2.4	14.4
Tunisia	10.3	6.9	67.2	0.2	3.6
Africa	984.3	385.8	40.1	175.0	50.2

Sources: Millennium Development Goals Database 2010; *World Bank's World Development Indicators* 2010; author's calculations.

countries, down to those with the lowest levels of slums. The overall total for Africa shows that in 2005, there were some 175 million city dwellers living in slum conditions equivalent to over 50 percent of the urban population. While some progress has been made in reducing this ratio as part of the Millennium Development Goals program, the absolute level of slum dwellers remains high.

Housing Finance as a Driver of Growth

A central theme of global policy is currently how to stimulate job creation and find the road back to growth. The benefits of promoting housing as a policy objective include both the tangible improvement in people's living conditions and the potential impact of constructing housing as a way to create jobs. Many of the jobs will be low skilled and are therefore very accessible and can come on-stream rapidly. For countries such as Nigeria, which currently have unemployment reaching as high as 50 percent of the population, the types of jobs that housing development would create would have broad benefits for all strata of the population. This section of the chapter considers a theoretical framework of benefits arising from housing finance.

Economic Benefits of Housing Finance

The section below provides some theoretical background on the importance of housing finance as a driver of growth, as well as some of the other externalities that result from investing in housing. Much of this background is directly applicable to the current situation in Africa:

- *Deepening financial access.* There is a broad literature on the impact of deepening financial access on poverty levels (Beck, Demirgüç-Kunt, and Levine 2007; Honohan 2008). Gaining access to finance can be a way out of the perpetual cycle of poverty that is prevalent at the bottom of the income pyramid. This poverty trap is well illustrated in the book *Portfolios of the Poor: How the World's Poor Live on $2 a Day* (Collins et al. 2009), which chronicled in detail the financial lives of households in India, Bangladesh, and South Africa. It describes how, without credit, it can be extremely difficult to climb out of poverty for the poorest among us. Credit allows unexpected events to be confronted without causing a slide back down to the bottom of the income distribution.

- *Improving property rights.* Property rights that are reliable provide the means to expand access to finance using secured lending. This reduces the risk for lenders and improves repayment discipline. Providing collateral against a loan can be especially important in environments where credit history, formal payment records, and credit bureaus are nonexistent. Enhanced access to finance allows households to smooth consumption patterns and manage unexpected costs, and also to invest in education, health, or directly into a business. In addition to benefits accruing directly to the household, there are also broader benefits for the economy as a whole. A recent IMF paper (Singh and Huang 2011), looking specifically at the issue of financial deepening in Sub-Saharan Africa, found that there was causality between financial deepening and poverty reduction as well as income inequality reduction. Singh and Huang also concluded that stronger property rights reinforce the effects of private credit expansion on poverty reduction.

- *Unlocking "dead" capital.* The classic exposition of the power of property in enhancing access to finance is de Soto's book *The Mystery of Capital* (2000). De Soto sets out convincing arguments about the vast sum that is locked in property. Improving property rights and allowing this property to be used as collateral for loans could unlock a wave of investment at the bottom of the pyramid. In practice, some of de Soto's arguments may have been exaggerated, in the same way that the subprime crisis has demonstrated that lending purely on the basis of collateral is not a good approach. De Soto also implied that poor households were all budding entrepreneurs capable of making informed business and investment decisions. As with those in the rest of the income distribution, this is not always the case. Many households will be risk averse and prefer not to risk losing what little property they do own by putting it up as collateral.

- *Housing as a driver of construction.* Duebel (2007) postulates that housing finance is a direct driver of construction output. However, he also suggests that this relationship holds only where the construction sector is able to freely expand, a circumstance that is dependent on access to serviced urban land and also to developer financing. Mexico and Malaysia are both good examples of countries that have seen their housing production rise as a result of expanding the housing finance system.

- *The housing multiplier effect.* This is a central argument in favor of housing investment. The premise is that every unit spent on housing will generate a multiple benefit for the economy, as it creates jobs through both horizontal and vertical supply chains. This includes jobs in areas such as raw material production, mining, cement production, timber, and aggregates. In addition, there are also impacts on local economies where the construction jobs are created, and in the service industries linked to housing—such as mortgage lending, real estate agents, and retailers of home goods such as furniture or white goods. Although this argument is used regularly, there is no clear methodology or agreement on how to calculate the multiplier effect. There are several country studies that look at this effect, some of which are listed below. However, unfortunately, very few have looked at the multiplier effect in emerging markets.

  ○ *United States.* The multiplier effect accounts for the fact that income earned in other sectors of the economy as a result of a home sale is then recirculated into the economy. The National Association of Realtors' macroeconomic modeling suggests that the multiplier is between 1.34 and 1.62 in the first year or two after an autonomous increase in spending. This means that each dollar increase in direct housing activity will increase the overall GDP by $1.34 to $1.62.

  ○ *Argentina.* A 2006 study found that just on the production side of raw materials and direct inputs for housing there was a 1.6 multiplier effect. Further indirect employment effects are also present in related industries (see Duebel 2007).

  ○ *Australia.* The total multiplier for output and employment in the construction industry is estimated by the Australian Bureau of Statistics to be 2.866. So, for every $A 1 million increase in construction output, there is an increase in output elsewhere in the economy of $A 2.9 million (Duebel 2007).

  ○ *Scotland.* Some of the most detailed work has been done looking at multiplier effects for Scotland (Whitehead and Monk 2010). Whitehead and Monk's results show that the gross value added to the economy through different multiplier effects and channels in housing is higher than all other industries. Housing exhibits roughly a twofold multiplier effect in Scotland, so for every British pound (GBP) spent on housing, GBP 2 are generated for the economy.

o *Philippines*. The National Economic and Development Authority of the government of the Philippines found that for every peso spent on housing activities, an additional 16.61 pesos contributed to the GDP. One commentator concluded: "More housing investments and construction mean increases in job generation and sales for allied industries of the shelter sector" (Uy 2006). This result appears to be an outlier relative to the other measures shown above.

Social Benefits of Housing Finance

Numerous benefits can be ascribed to improving access to housing finance and thereby housing. Homeownership has long been promoted as a way of giving individuals a stake in society and a stake in the economy. By having a stake that can increase in value, it provides an incentive for the homeowner to look after the property and also to maintain the neighborhood in which the house is situated. This theoretically results in lower crime levels and improved quality of life. Another social benefit that has been observed arising from homeownership is lower fertility rates. This is a less intuitive benefit, but if the house is fully owned, parents in emerging markets where there is no pension system no longer have to rely on their children in their old age for somewhere to live. Further benefits include improved health, which comes about because of better and safer construction and improved sanitation.

The above provides some compelling arguments in favor of housing, but this list is not exhaustive and the exact magnitude of the economic benefits will depend on the environment in which policy reform is made. A financial system that benefits from a developed capital market and an efficient land allocation system will clearly be in a much better position to serve housing demand and expand housing output, reaping the benefits throughout its economy of housing expansion.

Housing Needs

There is a vast black hole in available data relating to housing needs, housing construction levels, and housing quality in Africa. Few countries are able to accurately determine how many houses/apartments are built on an annual basis in either the formal or informal sectors. Despite this, housing policy is formulated within this knowledge vacuum. Grandiose plans are announced to build 1 million, 2 million, 5 million houses "over the next *x* years." These plans rarely come to fruition. The reality is that, for the majority of African countries, new housing production is often limited to a few thousand units, often targeted at the very highest income groups: the expatriate market and the diaspora who like to invest in a house in their home country to which they can retire.

Some calculations can be made for the future housing needs. Two principal determinants dictate the housing need in African countries over the long term. These are, first, the net population growth rate and, second, the level of internal migration. The latter factor is essentially the urbanization process that occurs when villagers leave their homes in rural areas and go to live in the cities. This is a simplified model that also needs to take into account the average household size in rural and urban areas. The household size is used where available; where not available, the African average is used. This average is 4.79 people per household in urban areas and 5.28 in rural areas. Household size does change depending on cultures and relative levels of wealth. It is also likely to change over the analysis period, but changing household size is not allowed for in the model. This methodology can be put to use with UN population data to predict housing needs over the next 50 years. Figure 4.2 shows the housing needs for Africa as a whole.

Figure 4.2 shows the magnitude of the housing gap looming ahead. It shows that the current need across the continent stands at 4.4 million houses. This can be broken down into 1.9 million needed in rural areas

Figure 4.2   Annual Housing Needs for Africa

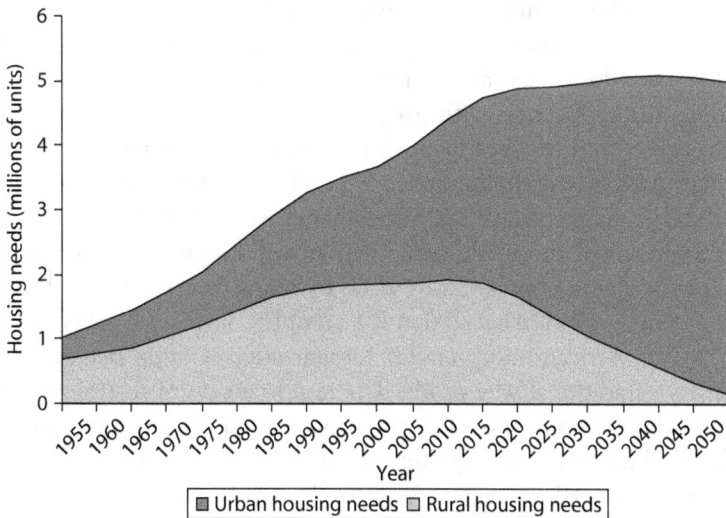

Sources: World Urbanization Prospects: The 2009 Revision Population Database; STATcompiler; author's calculations.

and 2.5 million in cities. The balance of urban to rural need varies from country to country, with many less-urbanized countries seeing the primary need in rural areas. The proportion of urban to rural need has important policy implications of how to finance the housing gap. For example, in Nigeria, which is fast urbanizing, 550,000 houses are needed in cities and just 144,000 in villages. Contrast this with the situation in Kenya, which requires just 65,000 urban dwellings but 136,000 rural dwellings on an annual basis. As the figure shows, this balance for Africa as a whole is gradually shifting, so that by 2050 almost the entire housing need will be in urban areas.

Alongside this analysis, it should also be remembered that most African countries are not starting in a position where all housing needs are met. Housing shortages already exist, and meeting only the forecast housing needs would preserve the status quo. Housing production needs to go beyond this if the pre-existing housing gaps are to be closed. These existing gaps are very difficult to quantify, however. Estimates often vary by several million within the same country, depending on the source of the data. The gaps also tend to reflect a qualitative shortage in housing rather than an absolute lack of shelter. The number of truly homeless households will be small, but those living in overcrowded or unsanitary conditions will be much higher.

The forecasts in the housing need analysis are from the United Nations and do presuppose a growing level of urbanization. The world as a whole now lives predominantly in cities, with the 50 percent urbanization mark passed in 2009. However, Africa remains largely rural. The extent of urbanization does vary across the continent by country. Nigeria, for example, has eight cities with over 1 million inhabitants and one of the largest urban metropolises in the world, Lagos. In contrast, some countries with large populations, such as Ethiopia, have four out of five inhabitants still living in rural areas. Sub-Saharan Africa, which now accounts for 12 percent of the world's population, will account for more than a third of the global population by 2100 by many projections.

The debate about urbanization is a complex one, and it meets a lot of resistance in African policy circles. Urbanization is often perceived as a threat to a traditional way of life. The important point to realize is that setting deliberate policy to slow the urbanization process has rarely succeeded and ignoring it completely is likely to result in unplanned cities. Once informal settlements appear, it is difficult to then reorganize a city in line with a central urban plan. The data in this report give a clear indication of what is likely to happen in the coming years. Planning the housing and infrastructure for an urban area, along with planning for its financing, needs to be done at an early stage.

Housing Affordability

This section links the availability of finance, the demand for housing, and how much it costs—specifically how much housing costs relative to incomes in each country.

Household Income

The previous section described an annual housing need of 4.4 million houses across the continent (see figure 4.2). This section will attempt to look at the capacity to pay for this housing based on the current situation. By looking at household incomes, house prices, and the availability of finance, some conclusions can be reached on the best way to finance future housing needs.

Starting at the household level, an analysis can be done to help construct income pyramids on a country-by-country basis. There are data constraints for many countries, and not all of the data are up to date, but even allowing for these lacunae a stark picture emerges. The vast majority of the population subsists on very low levels of income; only a very small proportion of the population sits at the top of the pyramid with high incomes. This is a pattern repeated throughout Africa to different degrees.

Figure 4.3 shows the income pyramid for Africa as a whole. The figure was constructed using income data derived from World Development Indicators income distribution data combined with the latest GDP estimates. These data suggest that—even when including South Africa and the North African countries—just 5 percent of African households have an income of US$6,646 or above. The people represented by the bottom half of the pyramid subsist on incomes of less than US$966 annually, which is barely more than US$2.50 a day. Clearly the scope for creating a mortgage market to finance the housing needs is going to be very limited, and alternative solutions are required for the lower-income majority. Nevertheless, some African countries do have a relatively large higher-income segment. For instance, the top decile of the income distribution in Namibia has an average income of US$32,328; South Africa's top decile average is US$22,050; in Mauritius the top decile average is US$26,901; in Libya, it is US$25,916; in Botswana, US$27,681; and in Angola, US$19,393. There are some limits to the reliability of these statistics, and these figures may represent a handful of hugely wealthy

Figure 4.3   Household Income Distribution in Africa (US$)

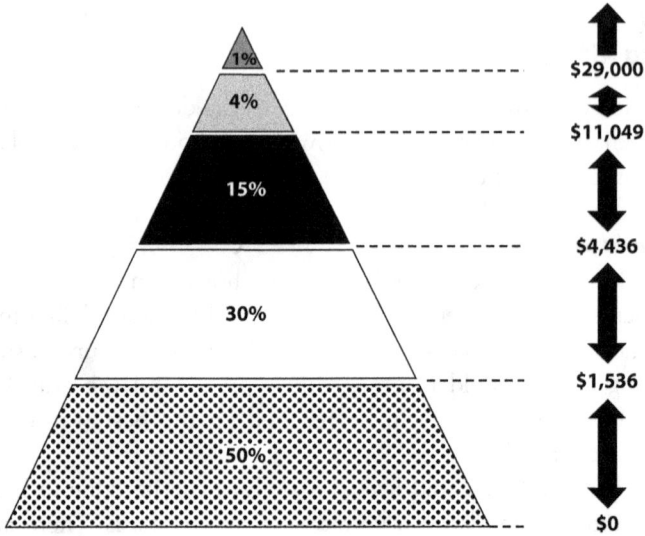

Pyramid segments (top to bottom): 1%, 4%, 15%, 30%, 50%

Income markers (top to bottom): $29,000; $11,049; $4,436; $1,536; $0

Sources: World Development Indicators; Economist Intelligence Unit database; author's calculations.

individuals that skews the overall distribution, but it is also clear that some wealth and income are present. Given economic growth rates in Africa, this is likely to be an expanding segment.

Cost of a Mortgage

The next step in the affordability analysis is to estimate what the potential cost of a mortgage would be to the borrower. Representative interest rates have been obtained from the IMF's International Financial Statistics (IFS) data set, which seem to correspond relatively well with actually observed mortgage rates in those countries where they are offered. Interest rates show a wide variance, from lows of 6 percent in Morocco and Libya to a high of 352 percent in hyperinflated Zimbabwe. The typical rate across Africa (median, mode, and average) was 15 percent in 2010. Because mortgage lending is done on a longer-term basis than the definition used by the IFS for determining lending rates, the addition of a margin could be used to reflect this; however, for consistency the original data from the IFS have been used in this analysis.

Given the relatively high rates of interest, there is little point in extending maturity over long periods. The additional principal that could be borrowed by extending the maturity is very small. Figure 4.4 illustrates this quite clearly. Assuming a constant mortgage payment of US$1,000, there is very little benefit to be had from extending a mortgage loan past 12 years if the interest rate is 20 percent. The figure shows the line flattening out at that point. Conversely, a 5 percent loan can be extended for as much as 40 years, allowing a borrower to assume a loan of four times the size with the same repayment amount as for a 20 percent loan over the same period. Thus, for the affordability analysis, a range of loan maturities will be used based on the level of interest rates in each country.

The last input needed for the affordability calculation is the price of a typical affordable property. As with property markets anywhere, this will be highly dependent on location, local demand, supply of new properties, and all the other factors that go into determining the price of a property. One striking fact that is relatively constant across Africa is the high cost of a new build. This reflects many elements, among them the lack of scale of many housing developers; the cost of raw materials; the cost of importing many raw materials and transporting them; the difficulty encountered in

Figure 4.4   Size of Mortgage Loan Relative to Loan Maturity, Assuming a Constant Monthly Repayment of US$1,000

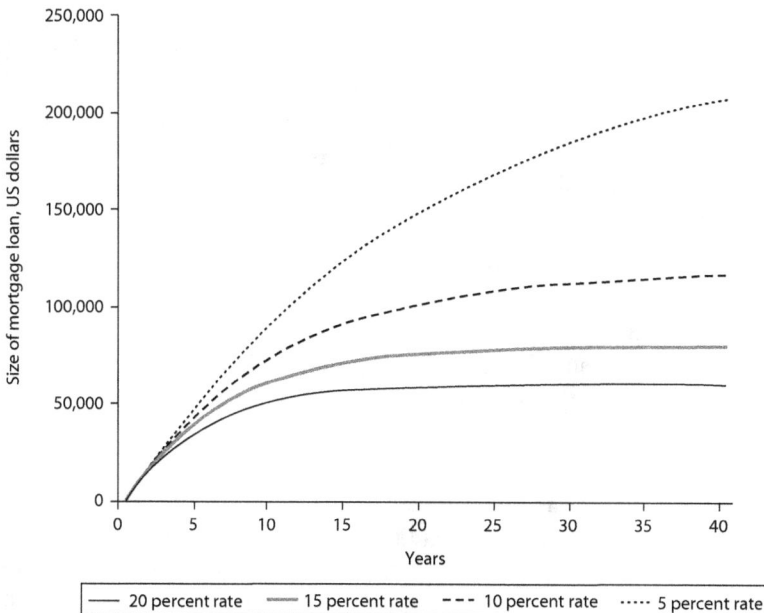

Source: Author's calculations.

obtaining developer financing; the cost of land, which can be high; and the cost of providing utility connections, access roads, and other services that typically end up being provided by the developer. This means that the cheapest property available in the formal sector, with access to electricity and water, is rarely lower than US$30,000 and in many cases will be much higher. In some urban centers it is virtually impossible to find a property that has full title and can be mortgaged for less than US$50,000. Again, lack of data is a big constraint here, so for the purposes of the calculation, an assumption will be made of a typical property of US$30,000.

It is worth noting that this does not compare well to other markets, such as India, where properties are available for prices as low as US$8,000 (see box 4.1).

Based on the parameters set out above and also based on safe lending standards, which would require a 20 percent deposit and a maximum payment-to-income ratio of 40 percent, a minimum income level can be calculated that shows at what point in the income distribution a mortgage loan becomes affordable. The mortgage payment would be US$468 per month, which means a minimum annual income of US$14,034. Using the income distribution pyramid in figure 4.3, this shows that the cut-off point for mortgage affordability is at the 2.9 percent population level.

Potential Size of Mortgage Market

The findings of this analysis have important implications for the formulation of housing policy. There is often a belief that, first, a bustling middle class has a vast pent-up demand that is not fulfilled because of a lack of housing supply; and, second, that developing a mortgage market alone represents a crucial missing link to unleash private capital into the housing market. From the analysis above, it is clear that mortgages alone cannot hope to meet even a fraction of the required housing investment.

However, a final step in the calculation shows that developing a mortgage market is a worthwhile and necessary activity to pursue from the perspective of financial sector development. Based on the 2.9 percent of the income distribution pyramid where mortgages are affordable and prudent, and ignoring the fact that those at the very top of the pyramid are unlikely to need mortgage loans, the potential market size for mortgage loans in Africa can be estimated at around 6 million loans. Assuming an average loan size of US$50,000, this represents US$300 billion of mortgage loans, or 18 percent of Africa's total GDP. Excluding South Africa, this would mean a debt-to-GDP ratio of around 12 percent for the continent.

Box 4.1

Affordable Housing in India

Rapid urbanization has led to an increase in the number of low-income house-holds in India's cities. Despite a vibrant housing market in India, decent housing in the formal sector is beyond the reach of the vast majority of these lower-income households. Monitor Inclusive Markets conducted a study in 2006–07 for India's National Housing Bank (funded by FIRST Initiative and with active sup-port by the World Bank), which found that even the cheapest houses in the market were at best affordable for the top 15 percent of the urban population. Customers in the next 30 percent income segment generally rented rooms in slums and low-income neighborhoods. They lived in poorly constructed houses with deplorable sanitary conditions (shared toilets, bad drainage, and water-logging) and lacking basic neighborhood amenities (few common spaces or gardens, unsafe alleys, open gutters). Many families had tiny quarters, for which they paid high rent and yet remained at the mercy of their landlords. Moreover, these customers aspired to live in and could afford to buy houses between 250 and 400 square feet in suburban areas at current market prices, but there was virtually no supply of houses and almost no access to mortgages from traditional financial institutions (this situation was even more severe for informal sector customers).

However, in the last three years, the low-income housing market has seen a series of encouraging developments. The macroeconomic recession has led to some traditionally upmarket developers switching their target customer seg-ments and beginning to seriously consider providing low-income housing. Furthermore, the efforts of dedicated "market-makers" and "field-builders" (includ-ing the National Housing Bank, the World Bank, the International Finance Corporation (IFC), the Michael and Susan Dell Foundation, and Monitor Inclusive Markets) are committed to market-based, alternative models of building com-mercially viable housing for the lower-income segments. These efforts have dem-onstrated the value of and the opportunity in the urban low-income housing market, which has resulted in the beginnings of a robust supply curve in low-income urban housing.

Source: http://www.mim.monitor.com.

Housing Finance Systems

The supply of long-term finance for housing purposes is extremely limited at present in most African countries. This section looks at the providers of the housing finance products and also at the possible funding sources for longer-term housing finance.

Housing Finance Lenders

Lenders come in many forms and sizes across the continent. The **traditional banking sector** has grown remarkably over recent years, particularly in countries such as Nigeria that, even allowing for the recent crisis, have seen a rapid expansion of banking. Despite this, levels of access to formal financial services remain limited. Even within the subset of those with access to formal services, those who have access to long-term housing finance are even more limited. Commercial banks in much of Africa have focused their efforts on deposit collection, which is then invested into government securities or, in the best-case scenario, lent out to companies at relatively short maturities. Pure retail banking has yet to really take off in many countries in Sub-Saharan Africa, excluding South Africa. Even in South Africa, access to housing finance among the poorer black majority remains extremely limited (see box 4.2 for information about one program in South Africa).

Where commercial banks have feared to go in the past, **state housing banks** have often sought to bridge the gap. Many African countries have experienced state housing banks: these have occurred in Gabon (Compte de Refinancement de l'Habitat du Gabon), Mali (Banque de l'Habitat), Tanzania (Tanzania Housing Bank), Cameroon (Crédit Foncier du Cameroun), and Rwanda (Caisse Hypothécaire du Rwanda). Almost without exception these institutions have failed in their mission to expand access to housing finance. Many have also required large bailouts from the state when they became insolvent. The reasons for the failures are repeated across the institutions and include poor management, political interference, and a perception by borrowers that they are receiving a grant rather than a loan with little consequence if they do not repay. The demand for loans by state housing banks, which are typically given at a below-market rate, by far outstrips their capacity to deliver loans. This leads to some rationing of loans, which creates an opportunity for corruption or political patronage. The other systemic failure of state housing banks is the displacement effect they have on the private sector. By offering loans at below-market rates, it makes it difficult for private lenders

Box 4.2

South Africa: National Urban and Reconstruction Agency (NURCHA)

The National Urban and Reconstruction Agency (NURCHA) was established in 1995 in South Africa. It is funded by the South African government in partnership with the Soros Foundation, various overseas donors, and other commercial lenders. It provides bridging finance to contractors and developers involved in the construction of subsidy and affordable housing, community facilities, and infrastructure.

NURCHA is specially geared to provide construction finance for contractors or developers who cannot easily access finance from the conventional financial institutions. It can either provide finance directly for those who do not have access to conventional bank lines of credit, or assist in securing bank lines of credit for those more experienced developers.

It sets itself the following developmental goals in providing its financing:

• Extend the housing market.
• Maximize options for the construction and financing of housing and related facilities and infrastructure.
• Promote synergy and cooperation between public and private sectors.
• Use NURCHA loans to contribute to the emergence of a new generation of successful, black-owned construction companies.

Another feature of the initiative can provide assistance from start to finish of a project by assisting developers with project appraisal, cost assessments, getting guarantees, sourcing of building materials, project management, and so on.

Source: Author.

to compete. So although it may seem a politically attractive way to expand housing finance, the experience has been quite the opposite, with large, inefficient organizations that rapidly accumulate portfolios of non-performing loans. This situation is by no means unique to Africa, but in the absence of other providers it makes the failures all the more stark.

The supply of **housing microfinance** loans to the informal sector remains limited and typically confined to nongovernmental organizations (NGOs), pilot exercises, and donor-funded institutions. Lenders can be classed into general microfinance lenders offering a housing product and those more focused on loans for housing purposes. The term *housing microfinance* may be relatively new, but the concept has been around for a long time. These institutions make small loans that are typically used for incremental building or home improvement. The loan may come after a savings period or be the result of earlier successful loan repayments. This is the way a borrower is qualified for a larger, longer-term loan in the absence of any formal credit history. One of the more successful providers in Africa has been the Kuyassa Fund in South Africa, which may provide a possible model for other markets. Given the relative wealth of borrowers and the level of informality in terms of both income and property ownership, housing microfinance has enormous potential, but it needs to gain scale for it to become viable as a commercial activity.

Some African countries have gone down the route of specialized single purpose nonbank mortgage lenders, or **monoline lenders**. Most notable among these countries are Nigeria, which has primary mortgage institutions; the Arab Republic of Egypt, which has mortgage finance companies; Kenya, which has housing finance companies; and South Africa, which has financial services providers specializing in mortgage lending. Typically these institutions have a narrow banking license that limits their activities; in particular, they are restricted on deposit collection. This means that they typically rely on wholesale funding on the liabilities side of their balance sheet. This type of institution has proved to be particularly vulnerable during the crisis, when its cost of funds has risen to a much greater extent than those lenders who have a deposit base. One response has consolidation in the financial sector, with banks acquiring specialist mortgage businesses or starting up their own. This is the case in Kenya (S&L acquired by KCB); in Egypt, where a number of mortgage finance companies have been acquired by banks; and in Nigeria, where banks have been setting up primary mortgage institution subsidiaries to carry out their mortgage lending business. This bank/subsidiary model allows a specialization in mortgage lending, and it may attract some regulatory benefits, but it avoids the funding downside because the bank can fall back on a large deposit base.

The final category of lenders in Africa comprise those that operate in the semi-formal area. They are often collectively referred to as *savings and credit cooperatives* (SACCOs), but can include community banks or credit unions. They operate in the space between the formal banking sector and the much more informal microfinance lenders or the "susu" savings schemes. How well established these semi-formal lenders are and the degree to which they are regulated vary from country to country, but they are present across most of the continent. Very few offer any form of loans with a term beyond one or two years, but their loans are commonly used for housing materials in the incremental building process.

It is also worth highlighting that, in the absence of any widespread provision of housing finance by banks, some countries have seen the growth of lending through other channels such as **social security funds or employer-funded loans**. Housing and real estate represents a major investment for many social security funds, so providing loans to buy these assets is part of a broader investment strategy, as well as providing additional services to members. Staff loans are also common, especially within banks themselves who see such loans as presenting a low credit risk and a way of testing products before a wider launch.

Funding of Housing Finance

A range of funding options—from traditional deposits to, in some countries, secondary mortgage markets—is available to housing finance lenders. A major common difficulty faced across Africa is in matching the maturity of the loan assets with an equally long-term funding base.

The traditional and most abundant form of funding for banks is **deposits**. These may be retail deposits from consumers or deposits from corporations or government bodies. Those lenders operating in the informal space are also largely reliant on deposits and savings from their customers. A major issue preventing the development of longer-term housing loans is the reluctance of banks to engage in any form of maturity transformation. This may be driven in part by conservative regulators wary of creating any mismatch positions. The reality is that a large proportion of deposits are "sticky," and although they may be contractually short-term or demand deposits, behaviorally they are the same as long-term funds. This is especially true for deposits from government departments. This is a fundamental precept for mortgage banking, on which building societies in Europe were founded. Even taking 5 or 10 percent of deposits as "behaviorally" long term can create a sufficient funding base to initiate a large lending operation with terms extended out beyond 10 years. This needs to be done with prudence, regular contractual and behavioral analysis, and monitoring and reporting of deposits to the regulator, but it does provide a core foundation for mortgage lending that can then be complemented by other "wholesale" sources of funds.

Aside from deposits, the funding options in Africa remain limited—so much so that often the only other source of long-term funds can be the institution's own **capital**. This is a source of funds that is both expensive and limited, given that it cannot easily be increased.

Secondary mortgage markets have developed to different extents in Africa, but the only true secondary mortgage market of any scale is in South Africa. Although it is worth noting that Morocco and Tunisia have developed securitization legal frameworks (in 1999 and 2001, respectively), the actual usage of the instrument has been limited: three transactions occurred in Morocco (US$150 million total) and two in Tunisia (US$80 million), by a single institution in both cases. Morocco is currently working to establish a mortgage-covered bond system, similar to the European system, which would be the first of its kind on the African continent.

Three key factors have enabled South Africa to develop the secondary mortgage market where others have not been able to (see box 4.3). First, there is a deep, active, and liquid government debt market. With some exceptions this is a necessary precursor to private debt markets. It allows "risk free" pricing points or benchmarks to be set, which allow the pricing of private issuances. Second, an active and developed institutional investor community is necessary. The life blood of secondary mortgage

---

Box 4.3

Pension-Backed Housing Loans in South Africa

Pension-secured housing loans are increasingly forming a critical part of the financial sector's housing finance armory in South Africa. Some 257,000 loans, valued at R 4.8 billion, have been extended in the five-year period since inception of the Financial Sector Charter in January 2004. In this case, the loans provided by financiers to individuals are for housing purposes, and the collateral for the loan is some percentage of the borrower's accumulated retirement savings.

Proponents of the product see pension-secured housing loans as an integral part of the private sector's housing finance solution, which offers an opportunity for low-income earners to release equity "trapped" in pension/provident funds to satisfy immediate housing needs. They also see these loans as a means to ultimately create wealth over the long term. Others view these loans as the first step on the road to penury, putting people's retirement savings at risk and, in the long term, compounding the state's burden of having to provide adequate social support for an aging population.

Source: Sing, 2009.

markets is the long-term funds provided by pension funds, insurance companies, and other investors. These institutions are seeking assets to provide long-term returns for their long-term liabilities in the form of pensions or insurance contracts. Residential mortgage-backed securities are able to provide this with a rate pickup over government securities. As will be discussed later, the financial crisis has highlighted some of the issues around transfers of risk in this market, but in theory a well-structured secondary mortgage market will be an important component in an efficient financial system. The third prerequisite is a robust institutional, legal, and regulatory environment. There needs to be an efficient and cheap way of accessing the capital markets, investor rights need to be protected, and the markets should be easily traded and liquid. Ideally a legal framework should give clarity over the ability of an issuer to engage in a "true sale" of assets, which is the full separation of the issuer from the assets that are being packaged as securities for investors.

A simpler alternative to securitization can be a **mortgage liquidity facility,** which helps lenders to obtain long-term funds but does not carry the same level of complexity or risk transfer as residential mortgage-backed securities do. This is a popular model that many of the French-speaking African countries have adopted in the form of Caisse de Refinancement Hypothécaire, which is based on the French institution Caisse de Refinancement de l'Habitat (CRH). Such institutions exist, have existed, or are planned in Gabon, Rwanda, Tanzania, South Africa, Nigeria, Egypt, and the West Africa Economic and Monetary Union countries (WAEMU) (see box 4.4 for an example in Egypt). The basic concept is a simple one: mortgage lenders are allowed to use their mortgage assets as collateral for loans from a centralized bond issuer. The bond issuer or liquidity facility is typically owned by the banks, which use it for refinance purposes. The facility is therefore a sort of mutual organization providing a service to its members. Unlike with securitization, the bonds it issues are plain corporate bonds without any direct risk transfer from the mortgage loans. They are simple obligations against the balance sheet of the liquidity facility. The institution gains its strength from a strong capital base and careful lending that is secured by mortgage assets as collateral.

Lenders can use a mortgage liquidity facility in two ways. It can be used as a direct source of long-term funds to help overcome the maturity mismatch, or it can just be used as a backup option in the case of liquidity problems. Because the facility provides a safety net, a lender is able to make better use of its short-term deposits: the lender is safe in the knowledge that any liquidity imbalances can quickly be overcome by presenting

Box 4.4

The Egyptian Mortgage Refinance Company (EMRC)

The Egyptian Mortgage Refinance Company (EMRC) is a private liquidity facility operating on commercial principles with a profit-making goal. It is majority privately owned by its users, predominantly mortgage finance companies and active banks. Many public and private lenders have participated in the capitalization of the EMRC, which indicates their interest in expanding their mortgage lending. The central bank of Egypt is a strategic investor, with around a 20 percent ownership share; the Mortgage Finance Fund (a government housing subsidy agency) has a small, 2 percent ownership share; and 19 banks and 6 mortgage finance companies have the remaining shares. The initial debt financing for the EMRC was provided through a US$37 million loan from the World Bank.

The EMRC neither takes deposits nor lends directly to households. It simply provides loans to mortgage lenders secured by a charge over some of their eligible mortgage assets. Its presence helps to promote prudent lending standards while enhancing competition in the mortgage market by creating a funding source also accessible to nondepository institutions. Its business is the refinancing of long-term residential mortgage loans originated by primary lenders for which it will raise term funding by issuing bonds in the capital markets.

This narrow mandate will strengthen the credit quality of the bonds and thereby help to keep the EMRC's cost of funds relatively close to rates on government bonds. By borrowing from the EMRC, or at least by having the EMRC available when needed to serve as a first-resort source of finance, mortgage lenders will be better enabled to offer longer-term financing for residential housing development at market terms and conditions that are favorable for many potential homebuyers. Lenders also view the EMRC as a source of liquidity they can tap at short notice.

Source: Walley 2008.

mortgage assets to the liquidity facility in exchange for long-term funds. Essentially this arrangement allows banks to repo their mortgage loans. During the crisis, this function was undertaken by a number of central banks to support their mortgage markets in the absence of a mortgage liquidity facility.

Saving for housing schemes is not widely developed in Africa. This represents a significant opportunity, especially in markets where lenders are unable to obtain the credit histories of borrowers. Requiring borrowers to save for a period allows lenders to verify the potential borrower's capacity for regular saving and ability to meet a mortgage payment, as well as building up a deposit and some equity in the purchase of a property. There are, nonetheless, some countries, such as Nigeria, where the national housing fund mechanism requires a six-month savings period before a borrower is eligible to access a loan. This is a closed saving scheme that relies on the amount saved to disburse the loans to borrowers. A six-month savings period qualifies many more potential borrowers than can be serviced by the fund, which is therefore fundamentally unsustainable. The other better example is in Kenya, where housing bonds can be invested in and allow borrowers to build up the necessary equity for the purchase of a house. The government actively encourages this scheme by providing tax concessions to savers. A similar scheme also exists in Uganda, although without the tax break.

Impact of the Financial Crisis

Given the low level of development of many housing finance markets in Africa, the direct impact of the crisis has been limited. This, in part, reflects Africa's lack of connection to the global capital markets, which to some extent insulated it from the contagion effects of the global crisis. There have certainly been some secondary effects resulting from the rise in food prices, for instance, or the lower levels of growth that have impacted incomes. However, the conservative nature of much of the lending has meant that the feed-through to nonperforming loans has been minimal, with no appreciable rise in levels of delinquencies. The lower level of world growth will also have had an impact on remittances and investments into property by the diaspora.

Another secondary impact has been felt in the longer-term development prospects of housing finance. Many banks had ambitious expansion plans across Africa and capital/debt raising plans. Banks with a strong presence across the continent—such as Stanbic, Barclays, Ecobank, and Societe Generale—have all scaled back their expansion plans, although they still have a positive long-term outlook on Africa (*The Economist* 2010). This is particularly the case for many Nigerian banks—such as the Union Bank of Africa, which had very ambitious continent-wide plans that have had to be scaled back dramatically in the wake of the banking crisis in Nigeria. Alongside expansion plans there had been tentative signs that some banks would look to international capital markets such as the

Eurobond market to fund some of their balance sheet growth. These plans have been put on hold in the wake of the crisis.

The bigger impact coming out of the crisis, and the one on which this section will focus, is seen in the lessons that have been learned for future development. The collapse in the U.S. subprime mortgage market led to a fundamental reexamination of housing finance systems and their regulation. This process remains ongoing, but some lessons are already apparent:

- *Asset-based loan underwriting should be avoided.* Mortgage lending should be done with the focus on the borrower's ability and willingness to repay the loan, not merely on the basis of collateral. Asset-based lending creates distorted incentives to keep on lending as long as asset prices are rising. To some extent this is the genesis of the "asset bubbles" seen in many developed markets. The core banking principles of underwriting a loan based on a borrower's capacity to repay should prevail. Collateral is posted as a safety net that can help lower the levels of loss in case of a default, improve a borrower's willingness to repay, and thereby reduce the loan rate.

- *There is a need for balanced funding models.* Over-reliance on a single source of funding can lead to exposure, to funds drying up, or to changes in the cost of funds. This has been shown to be true for lenders relying on mortgage-backed securities as a principal source of funding; examples include Northern Rock in the United Kingdom and Countrywide in the United States. This is also true of lenders relying on other capital market instruments, such as short-term debt in the Eurobond market. When this source of funds dried up, it created severe funding difficulties for many European and central Asian economies, most notably Kazakhstan.

- *Monoline lenders are vulnerable.* The dangers of over-reliance on a single source of funding is nowhere clearer than in the case of specialized mortgage lenders, which have been especially vulnerable during the crisis. The risk is twofold and comes both from the single source of funding and from the concentration risk of having such a focused line of business. In many cases, real estate lending was subject to overinflated property markets and stretched affordability. This model has run into difficulties in the United States, Mexico, and the United Kingdom. The crisis does not necessarily spell the end for this model, but it is likely to reemerge in a slightly different form. For instance, specialist lenders in Kenya, Egypt, and Nigeria are all being bought by banks or created as greenfield ventures by banking "parents." This allows for the necessary degree of focus, specialization, and branding of a monoline provider but with the diversified funding base that comes from a banking parent.

- *Responsible lending standards should be set by regulators.* The crisis has highlighted numerous cases of inappropriate products being sold to consumers. This could include products that are potentially unaffordable over their lifetime, products with hidden or unclear interest rate resets, or products that lead to overindebtedness. Many of these products have been sold to unsuspecting consumers with low levels of financial literacy. Although blaming lenders may seem easy, the issue can be more complex. Lenders may start competing in a market by offering loans with reasonable loan-to-value and payment-to-income ratios, but as competition grows there is pressure to relax standards. Those lenders who resist end up with no market share in booming markets. What develops is a "race to the bottom" because lenders are forced to lower standards to stay in the market. At some point, it is now clear, regulators need to step in and set minimum standards. How and at what level those standards are set is still being debated. There is a strong movement away from just regulating institutions to also regulating products.

- *There are dangers in foreign currency mortgage loans.* A specific case related to the point above is that of foreign currency–denominated mortgages. These proved popular in much of Eastern Europe during the boom period in the 2000s. Lending in euros, U.S. dollars, Swiss francs, or Japanese yen allowed banks to fund the loans more easily and also provided an attractive nominal interest rate differential for the borrower. It also increased the quantum of risk for the borrower, who not only faced the risk of interest rate movements, falling house prices, and unemployment but also movements in currency prices. The crisis brought about all of these risks at once to countries such as Hungary. At present this is not a major concern in Africa, but it is an issue that has the potential to grow rapidly. Especially in markets where the property market is already dollarized and where local currency funding is limited, these products can take hold rapidly with negative long-term consequences for market development.

- *Effective consumer protection is needed.* Again, this point is a variant of the two preceding issues, but consumer protection is less about prudential regulatory standards and more aimed at disclosure standards and financial literacy. A clear lesson from the crisis is the need for an effective consumer protection framework. The creation of consumer protection agencies with direct responsibility for financial services in both the United Kingdom and the United States is a clear sign of intent by the authorities. The need for such regulation is especially important in housing finance because of the size of the financial commitment relative to income, as well as the length of the commitment. In Africa, consumer protection is often seen as a luxury part of market development that only "developed" markets can afford. Quite the contrary: given that much of the maturity transformation that is at the heart of housing finance is based on confidence in the banking system, creating mechanisms to underpin that confidence is crucial. This is all the more necessary in markets where mortgages are not well understood and levels of financial literacy are very low. A recent good example is the new mortgage law passed in Tanzania, which explicitly requires lenders to disclose pricing and terms and conditions of the mortgage loans in a standard way that is comparable across lenders. As well as having laws and regulations, having the systems to enforce them is also important. Thus, having a clear complaint-handling procedure, and having dispute resolution mechanisms or an ombudsman system are all important parts of a working consumer protection framework.

In summary, the direct impact of the crisis on housing finance markets in Africa has been relatively muted. This is in large part due to the overall lower level of development of the mortgage sector and the lack of contagion effect to Africa's capital markets, which are not yet well integrated into the global system. There are undoubtedly also some indirect impacts resulting from the slower world growth that has had an effect on incomes and prices. The expansion plans of large banking groups may also be subject to some retrenchment. This reduction may slow the expansion of financial access and development of new products. Equally, however, many of the lessons learned and a more considered approach to opening new housing finance markets could create better foundations for future market development.

Obstacles to Financing the Housing Gap

Many constraints currently limit the growth of the housing finance market. Figure 4.5 attempts to categorize some of the most prevalent obstacles hampering the growth of housing finance across Africa. Each country

Figure 4.5   Obstacles to Housing and Housing Finance in Africa

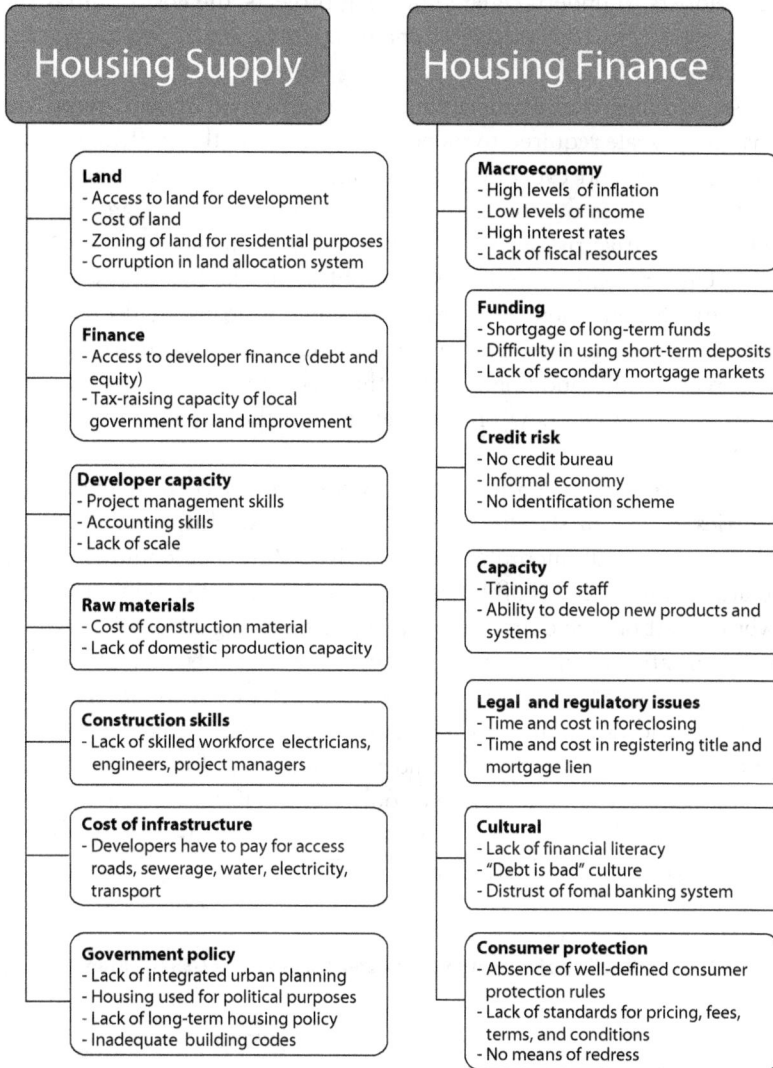

Housing Supply

Land
- Access to land for development
- Cost of land
- Zoning of land for residential purposes
- Corruption in land allocation system

Finance
- Access to developer finance (debt and equity)
- Tax-raising capacity of local government for land improvement

Developer capacity
- Project management skills
- Accounting skills
- Lack of scale

Raw materials
- Cost of construction material
- Lack of domestic production capacity

Construction skills
- Lack of skilled workforce electricians, engineers, project managers

Cost of infrastructure
- Developers have to pay for access roads, sewerage, water, electricity, transport

Government policy
- Lack of integrated urban planning
- Housing used for political purposes
- Lack of long-term housing policy
- Inadequate building codes

Housing Finance

Macroeconomy
- High levels of inflation
- Low levels of income
- High interest rates
- Lack of fiscal resources

Funding
- Shortage of long-term funds
- Difficulty in using short-term deposits
- Lack of secondary mortgage markets

Credit risk
- No credit bureau
- Informal economy
- No identification scheme

Capacity
- Training of staff
- Ability to develop new products and systems

Legal and regulatory issues
- Time and cost in foreclosing
- Time and cost in registering title and mortgage lien

Cultural
- Lack of financial literacy
- "Debt is bad" culture
- Distrust of fomal banking system

Consumer protection
- Absence of well-defined consumer protection rules
- Lack of standards for pricing, fees, terms, and conditions
- No means of redress

Source: Author.

will face a different set of challenges and consequently no single solution can be offered.

Chief among these obstacles is the shortage of affordable housing available for purchase. Africa is characterized by a severe shortage of housing at a price within reach of most households. A range of issues lie behind this barrier, including access and availability of land, the capacity of developers to undertake large housing projects, the cost of infrastructure (sewerage, road access, water, and electricity), and access to construction finance.

A second major set of constraints is the capacity of lenders to provide loans on the scale required to meet needs. This is partly a reflection of the skills shortages and capacity issues at financial institutions, the lack of long-term funds to overcome the maturity mismatch issue, and the relatively conservative risk-averse attitude shown by financial institutions in Africa. Until recently, one of the big problems in the financial sector was not so much delinquent loans as the absence of loans. Banks tended to prefer the easier alternative of investing in high-yielding, low-risk government treasury bills and bonds rather than facing the administrative difficulties of developing new product ranges and the attendant operational systems.

A third constraint is the macro environment faced in many African countries. A lack of stability in inflation, uncertain future interest rates, and concerns about unemployment are all inhibitors of lending for banks and also put households off borrowing. Yet a period of stability leading to lower interest rates and, importantly, longer financing can have a dramatic impact on affordability. Table 4.2 shows the amounts that can be borrowed for a fixed US$200 monthly payment but with different loan maturities and different rates. The table clearly shows that for the same monthly payment a borrower could receive a loan of either US$34,212 over 25 years at a 5 percent rate or only US$7,549 over 5 years at a rate of 20 percent. The potential market size and the cut-off point on the income pyramid could alter dramatically with even relatively small

Table 4.2   Affordability of a Mortgage Loan with a Constant US$200 Monthly Payment

Interest rate charged (%)	Length of mortgage loan					
	5 years	10 years	15 years	20 years	25 years	30 years
5.0	$10,598	$18,856	$25,291	$30,305	$34,212	$37,256
7.5	$9,981	$16,849	$21,575	$24,826	$27,064	$28,604
10.0	$9,413	$15,134	$18,611	$20,725	$22,009	$22,790
12.5	$8,890	$13,663	$16,227	$17,603	$18,343	$18,740
15.0	$8,407	$12,397	$14,290	$15,188	$15,615	$15,817
20.0	$7,549	$10,349	$11,388	$11,773	$11,916	$11,969

Source: Author.

changes in the macroeconomic outlook. Governments can do more to develop mortgage lending by sound economic stewardship of the economy than any number of fiscal resources or subsidies put into affordable housing.

A final constraint worth highlighting is access to titled land. In his seminal book *The Mystery of Capital*, Hernando de Soto set out the vast potential of unlocking land and property as a source of collateral for the huge disenfranchised poor population (de Soto 2000). Although the book may have overstated the potential benefits, improving property rights can clearly help to expand secured lending and the residential mortgage market. Not only are strong and secure property rights necessary, but an efficient institutional framework for recording land rights and an enforcement mechanism are needed. A framework for registering is another requirement. Whereas there is often a presumption that Africa is a special case because of the complicated land rights arising from postcolonial changes and customary land rights, this need not be an insurmountable obstacle.

It can rightly be argued that the traditional African way of life is also moving from rural—in some cases nomadic—occupations toward urban living. For this transition to happen, land tenure also needs to change. The traditional land rights and customary rights need modernizing. As deSoto describes, this is a process that has occurred in almost all countries. The United Kingdom moved from a feudal system; the United States moved from multiple land ownership systems following its Civil War; other countries all have their own peculiarities and histories. The key issue, though, is that an equitable transition is needed. This should involve compensation where appropriate and a clear and transparent dispute resolution mechanism. Combining strong property rights with an expansion in financial access can be a powerful mix for generating economic expansion among lower-income groups and unlocking "dead" capital.

Recommendations

Making recommendations applicable to a whole continent is a difficult task, especially given the diversity that exists on the African continent in terms of both economic development and financial sector development. The following broad recommendations represent the key development pillars for growing housing finance systems and tackling access to housing finance for lower-income groups.

Box 4.5

Rwanda Land Reform Program

Rwanda has achieved what few other countries in Africa have been able to achieve: it has a working one-stop shop for land transactions and titling. Its success is in part the result of its small size, but also in part the result of a singular approach that has effectively moved away from customary land rights. Property rights are clear, and past claims respected. The country has created a modernized system for administering these rights and claims. Importantly, there is also a functioning dispute resolution mechanism that covers boundary or claim issues. It is estimated that there are 9 million plots of land in Rwanda; all of these have now been mapped and a systematic registration program is under way. This clarity can open up the possibility of land being used as collateral for small rural loans and to expand financial access.

Source: Sagashya and English 2009.

Land Reform for Modern Efficient Property Rights

Land issues have loomed large during much of Sub-Saharan Africa's post-colonial period. Many of the difficulties are inherited from the colonial systems that were imposed. Many countries now have a blend of colonial laws, customary laws, and sometimes even laws from other countries such as India mixed in with other forms of tenure and legislation. Even where legal certainty does exist, the multiplicity of forms of land ownership and tenure can itself cause operational problems, as each type of land is recorded in a different register and it becomes a complex exercise to check for encumbrances on a property when registering a lien.

Land is often seen as an untouchable political subject, but without reform and a move toward a modern system, collateralized lending not only for households but also businesses will be difficult, if not impossible. However, some countries such as Rwanda (see box 4.5) have managed remarkable progress and created efficient functioning systems.

The recommendations therefore are to:

- Adopt a clear policy framework for land reform and regularization of existing land rights.
- Introduce an adequate and fair compensation methodology for cases where property claims and tenure claims may compete.

- Introduce a clear, efficient, and transparent dispute resolution mechanism that is accessible at minimal cost, but is also one that does not allow prolonged and repeated appeals to be used as a delaying tactic.
- Introduce a modern computerized title system, which to the extent possible minimizes opportunities for fraud.
- In creating a cadastral system, opt for an operational system on general boundary principles rather than the perfect mapping system with new plans drawn for all properties and lots. This ensures rapid processing and mapping of regions. It is important to have a boundary dispute resolution mechanism through which any contested boundaries can be quickly resolved and clarified.
- Where possible, unify the land registry, the immovable property registry, and the mortgage register. Creating a one-stop shop is more efficient and eliminates the possibilities for fraud and operational problems.

Affordable Housing

The preceding discussion has focused largely on mortgage lending and the role it can play in fomenting financial sector development. As has also been shown, mortgage lending will not resolve the housing gap for the vast majority of the population. Other targeted, innovative solutions are needed. A number of alternatives are considered below, including rental market, housing microfinance, public housing, and construction finance solutions.

Affordable housing encompasses a wide range of possible solutions that can be found on either the housing supply side or the housing finance (demand) side. On the supply side, it is clear that any efforts to reduce the cost of construction, facilitate access to land, and lower the cost of infrastructure will have a beneficial impact on the price of housing. The first sections of this chapter clearly lay out the size of the coming housing needs; these needs can be met only by leveraging private sector funds. Thus, any steps taken on the housing supply side need to help build the right environment for private developers to come in and deliver affordable housing. The following represent some of the main considerations in addressing housing affordability.

- *The effective demand for housing must be understood.* This can be accomplished by understanding the income distribution in the country and what households in different deciles of the population are able to afford versus what the market can provide in terms of both housing and housing finance. Homeownership may not be the most appropriate option in all cases.

• *Rental housing can offer more affordable and flexible options for low-income urban living.* In urban areas such as Lagos or Nairobi, rental is the main form of housing tenure, often accounting for over 85 percent of all housing. This is often informal housing, with few rights for the tenant but equally little legal recourse for landlords in the case of disputes. The reality is that formal rental frameworks rarely exist. The result is poor-quality housing with little incentive for the landlord to improve or invest further in developing the rental stock. Rents are high and often require two or three years of rent in advance. Enforcement of disputes occurs outside the court system, with brutality as a final arbiter of disputes. Creating a rental framework that is investor friendly while also balancing the rights and needs of tenants is important to attract private sector resources into developing rental housing units.

• *Housing microfinance can be an option for incremental construction.* The majority of workers in many African countries work in the informal sector, with irregular income that can be difficult to verify. Although advances can be made in including these workers in formal housing finance systems, a good alternative—especially for lower-income households—is to provide nonsecured, shorter-duration loans akin to microfinance. These can be based on the group lending model; there can also be models where the lender is actively engaged in the construction process. The loan can be disbursed against bills of sale for construction materials, for example. There are many models of such shorter-duration loans, but their main feature is that they run for a longer term than traditional microfinance but a shorter term than a mortgage. Even though interest rates may be high, the availability of financing allows for a much more efficient construction process, with big economies of scale. This can speed up the delivery of a final unit down to 2 or 3 years, rather than the current process, which can take up to 10 years. This is a major benefit and one that can be achieved with relatively small loans. Equity Bank in Kenya, for example, launched a rural housing finance product at the end of 2011 with loans for as little as US$250 to buy materials for different types of housing modules. Developing housing microfinance does require support from the government and the central bank to ensure that standards are set and lending occurs in a safe way (see box 4.6).

Box 4.6

Progressive Housing Case: KixiCredito in Angola

The case of KixiCredito, in Angola, serves as a great example of microfinance help-ing the poor address their incremental housing needs.

The conflict in Angola accelerated the urbanization process. Now, 60 percent of Angola's population resides in cities, and 75 percent of those urban residents live on informal/semi-formal land called *musseques*. Angolan urban migrants commonly aspire to own their own homes in the city. Urban residents consider themselves to be established in the city when they are living in their own houses, and renting is perceived as being unstable. However, clear title is rare in Angolan *musseques*, with a mere 9 percent of land transfers involving the regis-tered transfer of a legal title. Households lead the home-building process on their own—sometimes starting with rudimentary cardboard and plastic shelters—and moving to more durable materials as they save up, or when financing is obtained.

KixiCredito recognized this need in their clients, with evidence suggesting that as much as 30 percent of their enterprise loans were going to shelter. In response, KixiCredito developed a product—KixiCasa—intended for housing, and developed a management process around it. KixiCredito adapted its group-lending methodology to fit a housing product by forming subgroups of three to five people for the KixiCasa product. Loan amounts for housing started with a limit of US$800 over the initial 10-month tenure, but have increased to up to US$2,500 per year. The KixiCasa product gives households a financial tool that complements their progressive building approach. Families accelerate or slow down their shelter timeline based on whether household income increases, stag-nates, or decreases. Arguably, this can be better than a mortgaged house pur-chase that could trap families into a long-term payment commitment that does not account for the cyclical variability, and vulnerability, of informal sector incomes.

Source: Based on Kelly and Bauman 2011.

- *Housing finance subsidies can be a partial solution.* Although there may be limited scope for direct government transfers in many African coun-tries, others may want to consider introducing some limited incentives to help move housing finance downmarket. South Africa and Egypt have both introduced subsidies linked to the mortgage product in an effort to leverage private sector resources. Any scheme needs to be extremely well designed to ensure delivery of "smart" subsidies that target the right population and provide the right incentive structure.

- *Guarantee or insurance mechanisms also have a role to play.* Another way to incentivize lenders to move downmarket is to create a guarantee or insurance mechanism. Morocco has a particularly successful scheme, described in box 4.7. As with subsidies, the schemes have to be carefully designed to have the right impact and target the right population. Guarantees should also be properly accounted for and represent a contingent liability on the balance sheet of government. Private insurance schemes are unlikely to be successful currently given the lack of data, which is essential in managing the risk and pricing private mortgage insurance.

Sound Macroeconomic Management

This recommendation may seem obvious, but the actual impact of stable inflation is often underestimated. This chapter presents several examples

---

Box 4.7

The Moroccan FOGARIM Guarantee Scheme for Low-Income Housing Finance

Created in 2004, FOGARIM (**Guarantee Fund for Irregular and Modest Earners**) targets primarily low-income households with irregular earnings. It provides guarantees covering 70 percent of losses on mortgage loans. Because of the type of income of the borrowers, the main selection criteria are prices (limited to US$25,000) and the level of monthly installments, capped at about the equivalent of US$200 (at the upper-income threshold) and 40 percent of the households' income (at the lower threshold). Guarantee can be enforced after nine months in arrears, once the foreclosure process has been initiated. After an initial phase where guarantees were granted for free, FOGARIM switched to a risk-linked premium system, where the amount of premiums is inversely linked to the size of the down payment.

In 2009, FOGARIM was merged with another guarantee fund that targeted the moderate-income civil servants, middle-class independent workers, and nonresident Moroccans buying or building houses worth to US$100,000. The consolidated fund, Damane Assakane, was guaranteeing DH 9.3 billion at the end of 2010 (US$1.2 billion), while its own funds amounted to DH 0.95 billion.

Source: Author.

of the impact of extending the terms of mortgage loans and the impact on affordability. By reducing inflation expectations, the implied discount rate falls. This drop has the double benefit of reducing the rate of interest and making it economically viable to discount a loan over a longer period.

Across much of Africa, interest rates are often in the range of 10 to 15 percent; at these levels, there is little benefit in extending mortgage terms beyond 10 years. This automatically puts a severe constraint on affordability.

It is no coincidence that the two most successful housing finance markets in Africa are Morocco and South Africa, both of which have benefited from strong macroeconomic indicators that make long-term finance favorable.

Another key macro variable that should be subject to much greater scrutiny in the countries of Africa is the price of real estate. Real estate price bubbles can destroy mortgage markets and set back efforts to develop housing finance. The bubbles may be caused by speculation on land or real estate and may be fueled by a credit expansion. Whatever the causes, the monetary authorities need access to the data and information as early as possible so they can take corrective action. In African countries where the supply of housing may be limited, together with limited price elasticity of supply, any increase in credit can rapidly result in house price inflation.

Key macroeconomic management recommendations (to the extent that they directly impact housing finance) are as follows:

- *Manage inflation and inflation expectations.* Inflation increases the cost of long-term money and does more to constrain affordability than almost any other single factor.

- *Develop fixed income markets.* Consider the role of government in fostering the development of fixed income markets through its debt management policy. A yield curve can be constructed through the strategic issuance of benchmark bonds at different maturities. A regular debt issuance program is needed to maintain liquidity and secondary trading. The yield curve allows for improved pricing and transparency in long-term financing.

- *Actively monitor real estate prices for residential and commercial property.* Together with bank exposures to real estate, such monitoring can provide an early warning mechanism. Ideally this should be designed to indicate that overheating in the property sector may be taking place and policy action may be needed.

Create Long-Term Funding Mechanisms

The funding mismatch between short-term deposits and long-term mortgage loans is one of the biggest constraints to scaling up the mortgage market. It is worth noting that there are no shortcuts to resolving this. For a secondary market to develop, the primary market must be working efficiently and there has to be a strong institutional investor base. The following represent some key recommendations toward extending the funding profile for mortgage lending.

- *Consider a mortgage liquidity.* As the first step to linking capital markets with a primary mortgage market, a mortgage liquidity can be considered. This is a simple institution that allows lenders to effectively mutualize their access to the capital markets. Thus, in a situation where it is uneconomic for individual lenders to issues bonds, even small lenders can have access to capital markets on the same terms as larger lenders.

- *Standardize underwriting processes and procedures.* Having such standard procedures in place will prepare for a secondary mortgage market where standardization is key in managing risks.

- *Take a long-term view by considering requirements for securitization.* Some markets may want to start thinking about what the necessary steps are for securitization with a 5- to 10-year lead time. The legal process for introducing this can be lengthy. A working group could be set up to identify the main obstacles and create a long-term action plan and milestones for getting there. This step would be appropriate only for a number of the more developed markets such as Kenya, Nigeria, and Botswana, as well as the North African countries where securitization is not yet present.

- *Make better use of deposit funding.* Regulators and lenders can be overly cautious in enforcing term mismatch regulations. There is often a stark difference between contractual maturities for deposits and behavioral maturities. A large portion of deposits are often sticky, are not very responsive to interest rate movements, and behave like long-term funds. Within safe bounds and based on analysis of the funding term structure, a percentage of demand deposits could be allocated toward long-term asset origination.

- *Introduce covered bonds.* This European instrument can be seen as an intermediary step between a mortgage liquidity facility and securitization. It provides a capital market instrument with less complication and lower risk transfer than securitization. It does, however, require a reasonably large mortgage market to ensure regular issuance. It is currently being rolled out in Morocco.

Create Necessary Primary Mortgage Market Infrastructure

As stated in the opening of this chapter, a housing finance system is a series of connected links forming a chain. The strength of all the links is important for the overall efficiency and health of the system. Thus, when wanting to develop housing finance, the following primary market links—where improvements may be required—should be considered:

- *Credit bureau.* A key risk mitigant, the more data—positive and negative—that the credit bureau can provide, the easier it becomes to manage credit risk. This should result in lower interest rates.

- *Property valuation.* Having a professional body of property surveyors and valuers is critical for banks in assessing the value of their collateral. If the valuers are not reliable, banks will typically be more conservative and the value of housing as a collateral is diminished along with affordability.

- *Payment systems.* Having a good payment infrastructure where monthly mortgage payments can be made automatically helps both customers and lenders. Relying on checks creates delays, inefficiencies, and possible fraud.

- *Sound legal framework.* Property rights and the ability to enforce collateral underpin the principles of secured lending. Having a fair process with limited delays and costs in enforcing collateral in the case of default strengthens the value of collateral.

- *Efficient titling and property transfer mechanism.* Alongside the enforcement action, there is also a need for an efficient mechanism to record property rights and register liens on property. This system should be cheap, efficient, and reliable. In addition, taxes related to property transactions should carefully balance fiscal revenue-raising needs with the efficient working of the property market.

The recommendations laid out here are just a beginning. Africa's housing needs are vast and especially difficult to manage because they are so diverse. But, as these recommendations show, there is much that can be done to begin to address the issues and look for solutions. Each country will need to find its own way forward, but many lessons have already been learned, and there are many ways to improve the situation. Some of them have been presented here.

References

Beck, T., A. Demirgüç-Kunt, and R. Levine. 2007. "Finance, Inequality and the Poor." *Journal of Economic Growth* 12: 27–49.

Chiquier, L., O. Hassler, and M. Lea. 2004. "Mortgage Securities in Emerging Markets." Policy Research Working Paper 3370, World Bank, Washington, DC.

Chiquier, L., and M. Lea, eds. 2009. *Housing Finance Policy in Emerging Markets.* Washington, DC: World Bank.

Collins, D., J. Morduch, S. Rutherford, and O. Ruthven. 2009. *Portfolios of the Poor: How the World's Poor Live on $2 a Day.* Princeton, NJ: Princeton University Press.

de Soto, H. 2000. *The Mystery of Capital: Why Capitalism Triumphs in the West and Fails Everywhere Else.* New York: Basic Books.

Deb, A., A. Karamchandani, and R. Singh. 2010. *Building Houses, Financing Homes.* Monitor Group. http://www.mim.monitor.com/downloads/whitepaper-BuildingHousesFinancingHomes-final-screen.pdf.

Duebel, A. 2007. "Does Housing Finance Promote Economic and Social Development in Emerging Markets?" IFC. http://www.finpolconsult.de/mediapool/16/169624/data/IFC_Duebel_HF_Impact_Study_Final_SV_07.pdf.

The Economist. 2010. "Africa's Banking Boom: Scrambled in Africa." *The Economist,* September 16. http://www.economist.com/node/17043662.

FSD Kenya (Financial Sector Deepening Kenya). 2009. *Costs of Collateral in Kenya: Opportunities for Reform.* Nairobi: FSD Kenya. http://www.fsdkenya.org/pdf_documents/09-11-24_Costs_of_Collateral_Study.pdf.

Hassler, O. 2011. *Housing and Real Estate Finance in Middle East and North Africa.* Washington, DC: World Bank. http://siteresources.worldbank.org/INTMNAREGTOPPOVRED/Resources/MENAFlagshipHousingFinance.pdf.

Hassler, O., and S. Walley. 2007. "Mortgage Liquidity Facilities." *Housing Finance International* 22 (December): 16–22.

Honohan, P. 2008. "Cross-Country Variation in Household Access to Financial Services." *Journal of Banking and Finance* 32: 2493–500.

Kelley, P., and T. Baumann. 2011. *How Can Microfinance for Housing, Land, and Infrastructure Catalyze Slum Improvements and New Settlements?* Habitat for Humanity International. Global Microcredit Summit, commissioned workshop paper, November 14–17, Valladolid, Spain. http://www.habitat.org/gov/suppdoc/Microfinance_Improving_Slums.pdf.

Safavian, M. 2008. *Financing Homes: Comparing Regulation in 42 Countries.* Washington, DC: World Bank.

Sagashya, D., and C. English. 2009. *Designing and Establishing a Land Administration System for Rwanda: Technical and Economic Analysis.* http://www.fig.net/pub/fig_wb_2009/papers/sys/sys_2_english_sagashya.pdf.

Sing, L. 2009. *Pension-Secured Loans: Facilitating Access to Housing in South Africa?* FinMark Trust, June. http://www.housingfinanceafrica.org/wp-content/uploads/2009/06/Pension_secured_loans.pdf.

Singh, R., and Y. Huang. 2011. "Financial Deepening, Property Rights and Poverty: Evidence from Sub-Saharan Africa." Working Paper WP/11/196, IMF, Washington, DC.

UN-HABITAT. 2010. *The State of African Cities 2010: Governance, Inequalities and Urban Land Markets.* Nairobi: UNEP.

Uy, W. J. 2006. "Medium Rise Housing: The Philippines Experience." Presentation Paper for the 5th Asian Forum, Subdivision and Housing Developers Association, 2006.

Walley, S. 2008. "Case Study: Egypt Mortgage Refinance Company. Johannesburg, November 4." Wharton Housing Finance Workshop, World Bank, Washington, DC.

———. 2011. "Developing Kenya's Mortgage Market." Report No. 63391-KE, World Bank, Washington, DC.

Whitehead, C., and S. Monk. 2010. *What Does the Literature Tell Us about the Social and Economic Impact of Housing?* Report to the Scottish Government: Communities Analytical Services, Cambridge University Centre for Housing and Planning Research.

World Bank. 2011. *Doing Business 2011.* Washington, DC: World Bank. www.doingbusiness.org.

World Bank, Financial Sector Assessment Program. Technical Notes on Housing Finance for numerous Africa countries, unpublished.

PART III

Safeguarding Finance

CHAPTER 5

The Reform Agenda for Financial Regulation and Supervision in Africa

Michael Fuchs, Thomas Losse-Mueller, and Makaio Witte

The financial crisis has refocused government authorities around the world on the financial stability agenda. It has exposed a number of weaknesses in the way international financial markets have been regulated and supervised, and the international community has responded with a concerted effort to strengthen international supervisory and regulatory standards.

In Africa, where financial sector deepening and financial inclusion remain the most important challenges for financial sector policy, policy makers are paying renewed attention to safeguarding the sustainability of financial sector growth. The crisis and new international reform proposals offer a valuable opportunity to revisit the regulatory and supervisory landscape in Africa and to look at the priorities for the continent. There is a broad recognition that African priorities in financial regulation and supervision differ substantially from the issues discussed internationally

The authors would like to thank Carmencita Cequena Santos, David Scott, Pierre-Laurent Chatain, Constantinos Stephanou, Martin Vazquez Suarez, Haocong Ren, Thouraya Triki, Pietro Calice, Achim Deuchert, Ed Al-Hussainy, and Thomas Jaeggi for valuable inputs and comments on earlier drafts of this paper. This paper is part of a continuous World Bank work program on regulation and supervision in Africa in cooperation with the Deutsche Gesellschaft für Internationale Zusammenarbeit (GIZ).

by the G20, the Financial Stability Board (FSB), or the Basel Committee on Banking Supervision (BCBS). Given the nature of African financial markets and taking into account the financial, technical, and human resource constraints under which African supervisors operate, there is a need to identify priorities for financial and supervisory reform.

Reform Is on the Agenda

When defining the regulatory and supervisory reform agenda in Africa, policy makers need to carefully assess the costs and benefits of implementing international standards. Rather than applying these standards wholesale, appropriate sequencing and prioritization of different building blocks of reforms that correspond to the regional implementation environment and risks might offer a more successful alternative.

This discussion about the supervisory and regulatory agenda in Africa focuses on banking, which dominates African financial sectors. With a few exceptions (for example, Botswana, Namibia, South Africa, Swaziland), the banking sector accounts for more than 75 percent of total financial system assets; in a number of African countries, the share is above 90 percent (Lukonga 2010).

The purpose of this chapter is to stimulate discussion about African reform priorities and to outline some of the questions facing African regulators when looking at the regulatory and supervisory reform agenda. The chapter compares and contrasts key elements of the international reform discussion with the priorities for reform in Africa and advocates a "building block" approach to defining reform roadmaps for regulatory and supervisory reform. Considering that the capacity to implement regulatory standards in Western markets also turned out to be insufficient at a very fundamental level, African supervisors may find merit in reviewing their own capacity needs and possibly adopting a more selective, realistic, and effective strategy with regard to the implementation of international standards.

Crisis Experience and Future Risks

Africa largely evaded direct impacts from the global financial crisis. Low levels of integration with international financial markets limited the exposure to "toxic" assets and the volatility of international markets. With a number of important exceptions, nonperforming loans remained stable despite the slowdown in economic growth. African financial sectors went into the crisis with a cushion of high levels of capitalization and liquidity.

This reflects a broader trend of enhanced financial stability in African banking over the past decade. The 1980s and 1990s still saw a series of costly systemic and nonsystemic banking crises in Africa. As discussed by Honohan and Beck (2007), these banking crises of the late 20th century had a different face than non-African banking crises. They were caused mostly by governance problems, either on a bank or a regulatory level, or simply by bad banking practices. This did not hold only for countries whose banking systems were dominated by government-owned banks, but also for countries with predominantly private banking systems—both local and foreign banks.

Important steps have been taken in most countries to improve the governance of banks (and regulatory entities), but these issues continue to be a challenge in some countries. Privatization has helped in some instances by reducing the conflict of interest that public authorities face as both owner and supervisor of the same institution; in others, however, the process was not smooth and at first exacerbated governance challenges and fragility. Improved asset quality and increased capitalization are the two dimensions where African banking systems have made the most progress over the past two decades. Both have helped Africa weather the financial crisis. As a result, Laeven and Valencia (2008) report no single systemic crisis on the African continent between 2000 and 2007 (see figure 5.1).

However, underneath this rather benign picture lie a number of more worrisome developments. The limited impact of the international financial crisis should not blind one to the potential future risks in African financial markets, which are largely homemade and not related to global market developments. Africa experienced an unprecedented period of credit growth when the international crisis hit. Throughout 2008 and 2009, the volume of credit to the private sector grew by over 30 percent year-on-year in more than two-thirds of African countries. Once the crisis hit, average credit growth cooled down, but remained positive, and many banks continue to expand rapidly. Given the fast pace of growth, a buildup of risks is not unlikely. Most prominently, a couple of African banking systems—such as those of Nigeria and Ghana—have come under considerable pressure in the past years. These domestic crisis episodes occurred because of domestic structural and governance weaknesses, which varied from country to country and highlight the need to reinforce the regulatory and supervisory reform agenda across the region.

Figure 5.1   Systemic Banking Crises in Africa

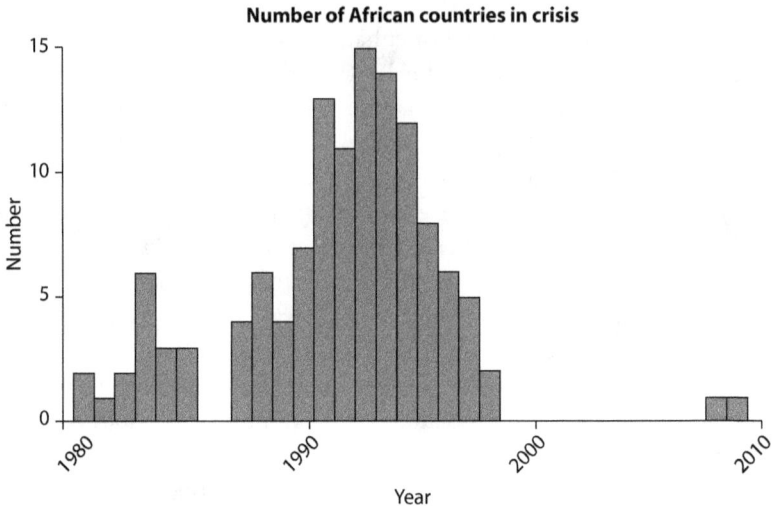

Source: Laeven and Valencia 2008.

Two Pillars of Financial Stability: Capital and Supervisory Capacity

In Africa, as in other regions, bank capital and the capacity of banking supervisors to identify and correct risks are at the heart of the financial sector stability agenda. The relationship between the strength of the supervisory process and the strength of the capital base provides a useful framework for a discussion about the priorities for banking supervision and regulation in Africa going forward.

In most African countries, supervisory capacity remains low. Supervisory resources, including qualified staff and the availability of analytical tools, are limited. Many regulators are not independent in their decision making, and legal frameworks often limit the corrective and remedial powers of supervisors. Supervisory processes focus on compliance with regulatory standards, but they are not set up to identify and manage the changing risks in the banking system. The ability to monitor risks on the institutional and systemic levels is hampered by insufficient data quality and poor reporting processes.

Traditionally, African regulators and supervisors have used capital as the main stability anchor for the banking system, aiming to balance limited regulatory capacity with high capital requirements across the region. Regulatory capital ratios are significantly higher than the minimum required by international standards and even increased slightly during the crisis. Leverage as measured by capital to nominal assets is much lower than in most developed markets (see figure 5.2). Though accounting weaknesses and a lack of transparency concerning the composition of capital may put the quality of capital into question in some cases, capital structures in Africa are generally simple and, even with the necessary caveats about the quality of capital, overall levels of capital are still high.

Against this backdrop, the weight that international reform discussions put on increasing capital requirements to safeguard financial stability is less relevant to Africa. African supervisors are confronted with a more delicate balancing act with respect to capital levels: on the one hand, historically high macroeconomic volatility makes increased levels of capital and liquidity a necessity, and without investments in supervisory capacity, capital provides the only stability anchor. On the other hand, further capital increases are likely to have little impact on stability, especially compared with the much higher expected benefits of investing in supervisory capacity. Capital cannot compensate for a lack of supervisory capacity in the long run and has very high opportunity costs. High capital

Figure 5.2 Bank Capitalization in Sub-Saharan Africa

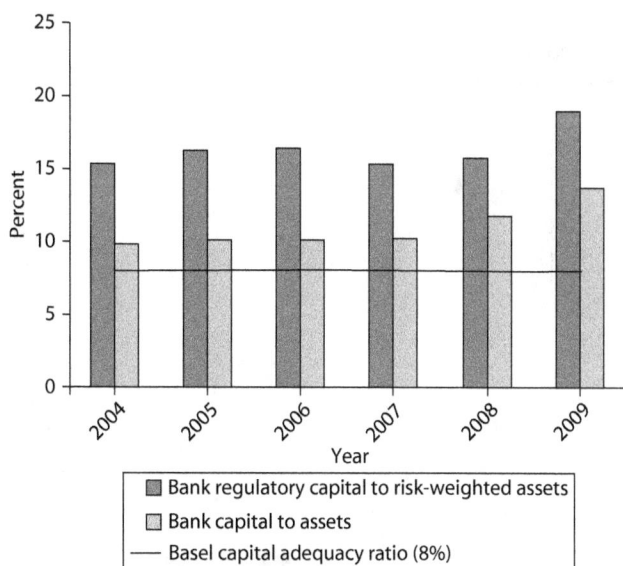

Source: IMF's International Financial Statistics database 2010.

levels make banking more expensive, reduce the volume of credit, and hamper the mobilization of domestic resources for productive investment.

Strengthening Banking Supervision

Strengthening supervisory capacity needs to be at the core of the reform agenda going forward. A survey by Gottschalk and Griffith-Jones (2010) carried out in Botswana, Ethiopia, Ghana, Kenya, Lesotho, Tanzania, Uganda, and Zambia points out that the lack of skills, technical capacities, and staff constitutes the major challenge in moving toward more complex capital regimes in Sub-Saharan Africa.

An assessment of compliance with the Basel Core Principles by Fuchs, Hands, and Jaeggi (2010) substantiates that view. The Basel Core Principles for Effective Banking Supervision (BCPs) define minimum standards for the way that banking supervision is organized and implemented by regulatory authorities. On average, the 16 African jurisdictions where BCPs have been assessed were largely or fully compliant with only 20 out of 30 principles.[1] Among the principles that pose challenges in compliance are important ones such as BCP 1.2 (Independence, accountability, and transparency); BCP 7 (Risk management process); BCP 18 (Abuse of financial services); and BCP 23 (Corrective and remedial powers of supervisors) with median ratings being materially noncompliant (see figure 5.3).

Figure 5.3   Compliance with Basel Core Principles (BCPs): Median Assessment Results, 16 African Low-Income Countries

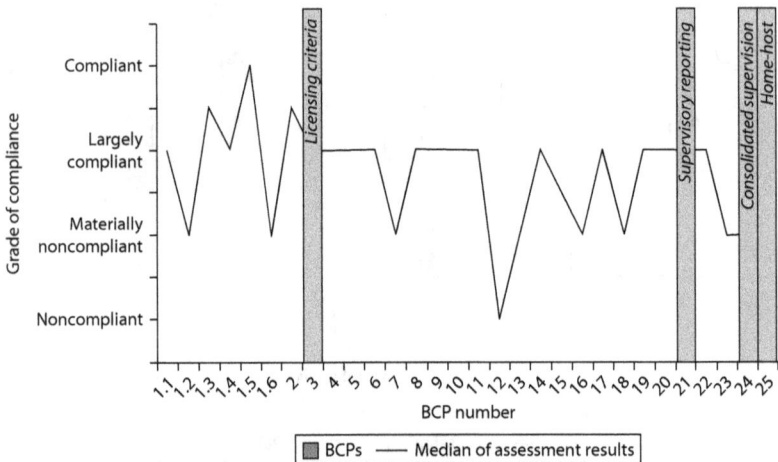

Source: Fuchs, Hands, and Jaeggi 2010.

Compliance with the BCPs is an important stepping stone toward effective supervision. Clearly an assessment of compliance with particular standards is not synonymous with the effectiveness of supervision in practice. Good supervisory practice also relies on the skills, capacity, and values that the supervisors bring to the task; the empowerment of people and organizations to be proactive risk managers; and the broader governance and transparency framework of social and economic interaction. As a result, the empirical correlation between BCP compliance and the effectiveness of supervisory practices in minimizing a financial crisis has proven to be weak. Be that as it may, the fundamental ground rules embodied in the BCPs provide useful goalposts for strengthening supervisory capacity.

Fuchs, Hands, and Jaeggi (2010) suggest that reform efforts focus on selected BCPs for African regulators rather than the whole set. From an international regulatory perspective, it is desirable to converge around an internationally harmonized set of standards to safeguard financial stability as a "global public good." In the absence of any resource constraints, all principles should certainly receive the same and immediate attention. However, the dramatic reality of limited budgets and supervisory capacity in Africa forces regulators to make difficult choices and focus scarce resources on those building blocks of financial supervision that offer the largest immediate benefits to their financial systems. Although this strategy represents a temporary deviation from the ideal of assigning equal importance to all the BCPs, it may yield a higher payoff in terms of financial stability both nationally and internationally. In the long run, African regulators should, of course, strive to achieve full compliance with all the BCPs.

The authors propose a focus on compliance with international minimum requirements. This includes the four principles singled out in the FSB Framework (BCP 3: Licensing criteria, BCP 21: Supervisory reporting, BCP 24: Consolidated supervision, and BCP 25: Home-host relationships), which are discussed below and highlighted in figure 5.3. A focus should also be on establishing the independence of the supervisor (BCP 1.2: Independence, accountability, and transparency); enhancing risk management practices in banks and building up the capacity of supervisors to assess these risk management practices as a fundamental step in establishing risk-based supervision (BCP 7: Risk management process); effective implementation and documentation of supervisory policies and procedures (BCPs 19 and 20: Supervisory approach and supervisory techniques); strengthening and applying in practice the powers of supervisors to take action (BCP 23: Corrective and remedial powers of supervisors);

and strengthening the capacity of the authorities to implement anti-money laundering practices (BCP 18: Abuse of financial services).

The fact that many African countries are materially noncompliant with some of these fundamental requirements—in particular concerning the independence of the supervisor and its capacity to enforce regulation and take corrective measures—gives further weight to this choice.

FSB Framework for Strengthening Adherence to International Standards

The *FSB Framework for Strengthening Adherence to International Standards,* published by the FSB in 2010, sets out minimum requirements for non-FSB member jurisdictions (FSB 2010b). These requirements include a subset of four of the BCPs (3, 21, 24, 25). The framework explicitly establishes a *global* standard and includes provisions to enforce the standard also in non-FSB member countries. Initially, the FSB will focus on consultations with countries that are deemed systemically relevant, but it has announced that the number of countries subject to the FSB Framework process will be expanded in the future. While it is rather unlikely that African low-income countries will be blacklisted or excluded from international capital markets in case of noncompliance, the FSB Framework constitutes a pronounced shift in the governance of international financial markets to push more strongly for adherence to international standards beyond the members of the G20, the FSB, and the BCBS.[2] In addition, by requesting countries to ensure compliance with some minimal standards essential for financial stability, the FSB has at least implicitly endorsed a building block approach to the implementation of the BCPs.

Compliance with the FSB Framework will advance fundamental aspects of supervisory capacity by strengthening licensing procedures and establishing transparency as a first-line defense against the participation of unsatisfactory entities and individuals in the market (BCP 3: Licensing criteria); ensuring adequate information flow to the supervisor (BCP 21: Supervisory reporting); conducting supervision on a consolidated basis by including all foreign and nonbank subsidiaries in the supervisory assessment (BCP 24: Consolidated supervision); and establishing effective mechanisms to exchange information with supervisors in other jurisdictions where parent companies or subsidiaries of African banks are operating (BCP 25: Home-host relationships).

Some of the relevant BCPs included in the FSB Framework are easier to implement than others. Empirically, of the four selected BCPs, the implementation of consolidated supervision (BCP 24) has posed the biggest challenge. For example, lack of consolidated supervision is one factor that allowed the buildup of risks in subsidiaries of Nigerian banks that caused the recent banking crisis and was not addressed as part of the supervisory process.

Implementation of International Capital Standards

In the past, discussion of the regulatory framework for banks has largely been driven by the evolution of international standards developed by the BCBS and, recently, the principles and policies put forth by the FSB. However, in developing a roadmap for Africa, it will be important to look at the specific requirements in the region. International standards offer orientation, but because they were designed for developed economies, they need to be translated into the largely low-income economy context of the region.

In September 2010, the BCBS published a revised capital adequacy framework ("Basel III"), which follows the initial Basel I capital adequacy framework and major revisions under Basel II and was publicly endorsed by the G20 at the Seoul Summit in November 2010. These capital frameworks define minimum standards for the calculation, composition, and size of regulatory capital that banks need to hold in relation to the assets on their balance sheet. The implementation of the capital adequacy frameworks is mandatory only for members of the BCBS; South Africa is the only Sub-Saharan Africa member country from the continent. Basel II and Basel III include additional demands on the supervisory process, but the BCPs remain at the core.

The three Basel regimes put different weights on regulatory capacity and capital requirements. Given the low regulatory capacity in the region, authorities in Africa need to consider the relationship between regulatory capacity and capital requirements that each of the different frameworks implies when choosing a regulatory framework and defining the African reform agenda.

Moving from Basel I to Basel II?

Basel I, which was adopted by most African countries following its introduction in 1988, defines a relatively simple approach to regulatory capital that concentrates on the capture of credit risk in broad risk categories. Risk categories are highly standardized, static, and independent of asset risk ratings. Basel I confirmed the international norm of a minimum capital adequacy ratio of 8 percent, but supervisors were encouraged to set higher ratios, as was the case in most African jurisdictions.

In 2004, the Basel II reforms introduced additional risk-sensitive options in the calculation of capital requirements based on the greater use of risk assessments provided by banks' internal credit and market risk systems. Most important, the intention of the reforms under Basel II—to allow banks to use capital more efficiently and broaden the framework's scope by including operational risks—resulted in lower capital requirements for most credit risk classes, which are the predominant form of risk for African banks. Against the background of the strategic development dilemma of the need to maintain high capital as a stability anchor versus the need to leverage capital to mobilize funding resources, it is important to note that Basel II did not lower capital requirements per se, but instead increased the risk sensitivity of capital requirements. This provided for a more efficient use of capital, assuming, of course, that banks have the necessary capacity to manage risk according to the more sophisticated approaches of Basel II and also that supervisors are able to monitor banks' risk management capacity.

According to the *Results of the Fifth Quantitative Impact Study* (BCBS 2006), banks that used the new option of the advanced internal ratings-based approach (IRB) reduced their minimum required capital by up to 30 percent more than banks using Basel I. IRB-based capital reductions were especially strong for retail mortgages (82 percent), small and medium retail loans (72 percent), and corporate loans (27 percent). Basel II predicates these reduced capital requirements on a significant increase in supervisory requirements—and therefore demands on supervisory capacity—including the need for supervisors to assess individual bank risk management systems. It requires supervisors to exercise considerable judgment in reviewing and evaluating a bank's internal risk management practices, its exposure to risks, its funding structure, and its overall risk profile.

Figure 5.4 illustrates the relation between overall regulatory capacity and capital adequacy under the three different frameworks. Today most African countries operate under Basel I, which—in comparison with the more recent revisions—is characterized by higher capital and less-defined demands on supervisory capacity. Most African frameworks are characterized by an even higher reliance on capital and lower levels of supervisory capacity than implied by the full observance of the BCPs, which complemented Basel I. A potential move to Basel II is a formidable challenge for any regulator. It requires a significant step-change in supervisory capacity,

Figure 5.4   Relation between Capital Requirements and Supervisory Capacity

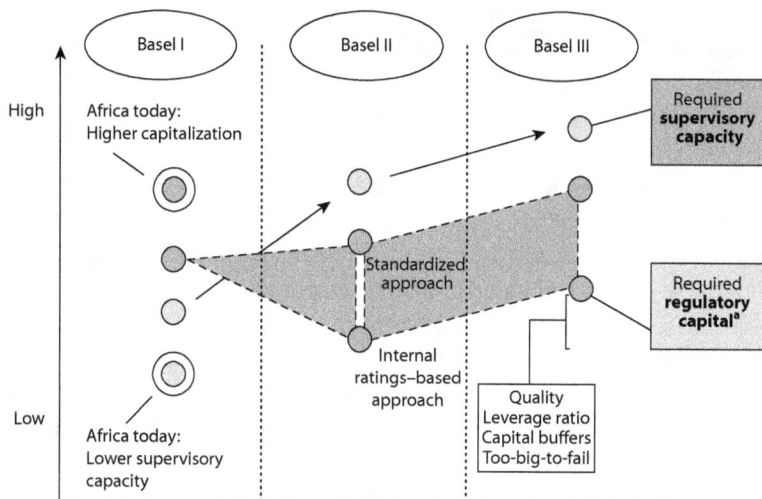

Source: Authors.
[a]Required regulatory capital for the same amount of corporate credit risk under Basel I, Basel II, and Basel III. The gray dots connected by the dotted line indicate the level under all three frameworks.

which is even more daunting when starting from a low base. At the same time, Basel II allows banks, especially those adopting the advanced IRB approaches, to considerably reduce regulatory capital. There is a fundamental difference, though, between a move from Basel I to Basel II and the adoption of the 2010 Basel III reforms: Basel III does not include a trade-off between the two stability anchors—capital and capacity—but it does contain elements that increase demands on capital and supervisory capacity at the same time. The potential value of these latest proposals for the reform agenda will be discussed below.

In essence, the introduction of Basel II into African jurisdictions requires a significant buildup of supervisory capacity to allow banks to leverage capital more efficiently. Conversely, Basel II does not provide an adequate framework to enhance financial stability in African countries if supervisory capacity remains low. African supervisors often view high capital requirements as a way of compensating weak supervisory practices to safeguard financial stability. But capital cannot replace adequate supervision—rather, it creates a false sense of security and can impose a significant burden on banks' ability to intermediate the depositor funds at their disposal. The goals of ensuring the maintenance of financial stability and enhancing intermediation efficiency can be achieved jointly only if supervisory capacity is considered a precondition for lowering capital requirements. Without a significant strengthening of supervisory capacity in Africa, the implementation of Basel II is built on shaky ground.

Implementing Basel II will carry significant costs for banks and regulators alike. Building up supervisory capacity—including staff training, new processes, and substantial investments in information technology (IT) infrastructure—is beyond the budget scope of many regulators in African low-income countries. For the European banking sector, Europe Economics (2009) estimated that the introduction of new capital rules would cause average one-off expenses of 1.57 percent of annual operating costs for large banks and 0.92 percent for small banks. These figures apply to the adoption of the equivalent European Union directives for European banks. Costs for African banks are likely to be higher since the initial IT and staff capacity is relatively low.

Yet many African supervisors look toward implementing Basel II with a view to enhancing financial stability. In 2010, 15 out of 20 African respondents to a survey of the Financial Stability Institute stated their intention to implement Basel II, including four countries that indicated their objective was to go beyond the Standardized Approach. These findings are in line with other surveys in the region and the general thrust of regulatory reform objectives underlying the policy dialogue in Africa.

African regulators state a variety of reasons why Basel II is so high on the agenda, despite it not being mandatory outside the BCBS member states. They are concerned that Basel I is coming to be perceived as an inferior standard by international investors and that African markets may be penalized by international market participants (Tran 2005) or that African banks will be denied access to foreign markets in the future if they do not comply with the latest Basel standards (Ward 2002). According to a Financial Stability Institute (2004) study, the main driver for non-BCBS countries to move toward Basel II is that foreign-controlled banks or local branches of foreign banks operating under Basel II expect low-income country regulators to adopt the framework as well. Whether or not these concerns are justified, they have accelerated the dispersal of the Basel accords in Africa and elsewhere.

Low regulatory capacity and the costs of implementation warrant caution not rush in moving to implement the Basel II capital framework in Africa. The BCBS itself encourages worldwide adoption, but recognizes that Basel II "may not be a first priority for all non-G10 supervisory authorities" and recommends carefully considering the benefits of such a framework in the context of domestic banking systems when "developing a timetable and approach to implementation" (BCBS 2006). The BCBS also stresses that before moving to Basel II, countries need a "good base-line supervisory system," characterized by successful BCP implementation, including its preconditions for effective banking supervision (BCBS 2004, 2).

In the medium term, the adoption of the more complex approaches under Pillar 1 of the Basel II framework (Minimum Capital Requirements) should not be a priority in most African countries. Countries have the option to limit the calculation of risk weights to the "Standardized Approach," which is based on external ratings, or the "Simplified Standardized Approach," which is very similar to the risk categories under Basel I. Given the lack of external ratings in most African countries, the adoption of both approaches would in effect result in capitalization requirements very similar to those under the current Basel I regime.

Nevertheless, Basel II does provide valuable elements for strengthening the regulatory infrastructure. For instance, introducing a capital charge for operational risk is equally as important in low-income countries as in the developed world. Under Basel II's Pillar 2, the Supervisory Review Process, the supervisor is expected to evaluate banks' own risk management techniques and internal control processes, as well as to develop bank-specific capital requirements. These are important elements needed to empower supervisors by enhancing their ability to ensure that capital more accurately reflects risk and to move toward a risk-based supervisory approach. This would facilitate more efficient use of capital and give supervisors greater comfort in reducing currently high capital requirements in appropriate individual institutions. However, compliance assessments and transactional checks will still play an important role as long as data are not sufficiently available and reliable to support the move to risk-based supervisory approaches. A combined approach will be more appropriate for the transition phase.

The provisions under Pillar 3, Market Discipline, are of particular relevance in Africa, given the generally underdeveloped frameworks for transparency, reporting, accounting, audit, and corporate governance. Supervisors are asked to develop disclosure requirements for banks that are sufficient to allow market participants to assess key pieces of information on the scope of application, capital, risk exposure, and risk assessment processes, and hence to enforce additional public oversight over the performance and stability of the banking sector. However, disclosure requirements will lead to increased market discipline only if market participants are able and willing to exercise appropriate control and it requires a renewed focus on strengthening both data quality and accounting and external auditing practices, as well as increasing financial literacy and creating a culture of an active and critical financial community. Last but not least, disclosure should be targeted and selective because a flood of irrelevant information may only contribute to a lack of transparency.

Basel III: Applying Lessons Learned from the International Crisis to Africa

The concerns about supervisory readiness apply to a much lesser extent to the latest revisions under the new Basel III framework, which is scheduled to be adopted in BCBS member states by 2019. Basel III focuses on increasing capital requirements rather than leveraging existing capital and broadens the supervisory scope at the same time. Applying specific elements of Basel III might be beneficial in safeguarding African financial systems, without demanding huge additional supervisory capacity. Key elements of the reforms include:

- Raising the quality, consistency, and transparency of the capital base
- Strengthening the risk coverage of the capital framework
- Introducing a leverage ratio as a supplementary measure to the Basel II risk-based framework
- Introducing a series of measures to promote the buildup of capital buffers in good times that can be drawn upon in periods of stress
- Introducing a global minimum liquidity standard for internationally active banks.

However, most of the measures proposed under Basel III are of limited immediate relevance to African banking sectors, since the weaknesses they address are largely a result of regulatory philosophies and market practice in developed markets. This is not to say that they are irrelevant for enhancing regulatory frameworks in the future, but that they are of limited practical application today:

- Basel III outlines various measures to raise the quality, consistency, and transparency of the regulatory capital base, focusing largely on the definition of Tier 1 capital. In most African states, bank capital structures are a relatively straightforward composition of common shares and retained earnings and thus already fulfill Basel III quality requirements.

- Measures to improve the risk coverage of the capital framework for counterparty credit risk will have little immediate impact since African bank activity in derivatives, repos, and securities financing is limited. But these measures should be included in the regulatory approach of African jurisdictions going forward.

- Given the high levels of liquidity in most African markets, global minimum liquidity standards would imply little change for banks. However, given data quality and systems constraints, more basic approaches— such as the simple customer loans–to-deposit ratio seen in some low-income countries—appear more appropriate and easier to implement. Care would need to be exercised to balance prudent liquidity controls with the risk of excessively constraining loan growth and consequent economic development.

- A leverage ratio may offer an important safeguard for all low-income country jurisdictions, especially those that may consider the introduction of Basel II because of its limitations on the risks that insufficient historical data and spotty risk assessment and modeling capacity introduce into risk capital calculations. However, in practice, African banks' leverage is significantly better than the suggested standards.

Countercyclical Capital Buffer Regime

The proposed measures to promote the buildup of capital buffers in good times that can be drawn upon in periods of stress warrant closer attention. The fast pace of credit growth in Africa in recent years poses significant risks. Median year-on-year credit growth reached 30 percent across the region in 2008, with some markets growing significantly above 50 percent (see figure 5.5). This credit growth started from low absolute levels of credit provision and is supported by relatively high levels of capitalization in most African economies. However, the potential buildup of risks is significant and African regulators need to be prepared to respond with adequate guidance in a potential downturn.

The application of the specific Basel recommendations for countercyclical rules has some significant limitations with respect to Africa, and low-income countries more generally, though. From a technical point of view, the focus of the proposed measure on trend deviations of private sector credit as a percentage of GDP and not on absolute private sector credit growth is problematic. It limits its applicability to the dynamics of African markets, where sudden economic booms (driven by resource

Figure 5.5   Year-on-Year Growth Rates of Credit to the Private Sector in Sub-Saharan Africa

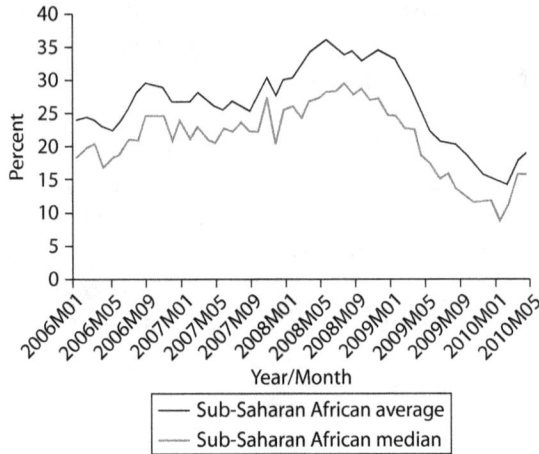

Source: IMF's International Financial Statistics database 2010.

windfalls, peace dividends in postconflict situations, or donor bubbles) followed by busts induced by internal or external shocks are not uncommon.

The experience of various African jurisdictions prior to the financial crisis highlights the limitation of focusing primarily on the ratio of credit to GDP. The more volatile macroeconomic environments put additional demands on decision makers.

For example, in Ghana, Nigeria, and Zambia, high growth in private sector credit (above 30 percent) prior to the crisis was offset by commodity-driven GDP growth inflating the denominator. Additionally, economic development from a low base is likely to have a disproportionately high initial trend trajectory. In Ghana, for example, credit to GDP has more than tripled in a decade, with nominal credit growth frequently rising above 30 percent, but the ratio of credit to GDP remained below the trend level in the years before the crisis. The high trend momentum was caused by fast growth from a low base of credit to GDP, and would make it more challenging for authorities to determine appropriate buffers (see figure 5.6). In low-income countries in general, buffers would need to be triggered by also looking at nominal private sector growth.

The implementation of such a countercyclical buffer regime poses significant challenges in building supervisory capacity and establishing

Figure 5.6   Private Sector Credit in Ghana and Nigeria

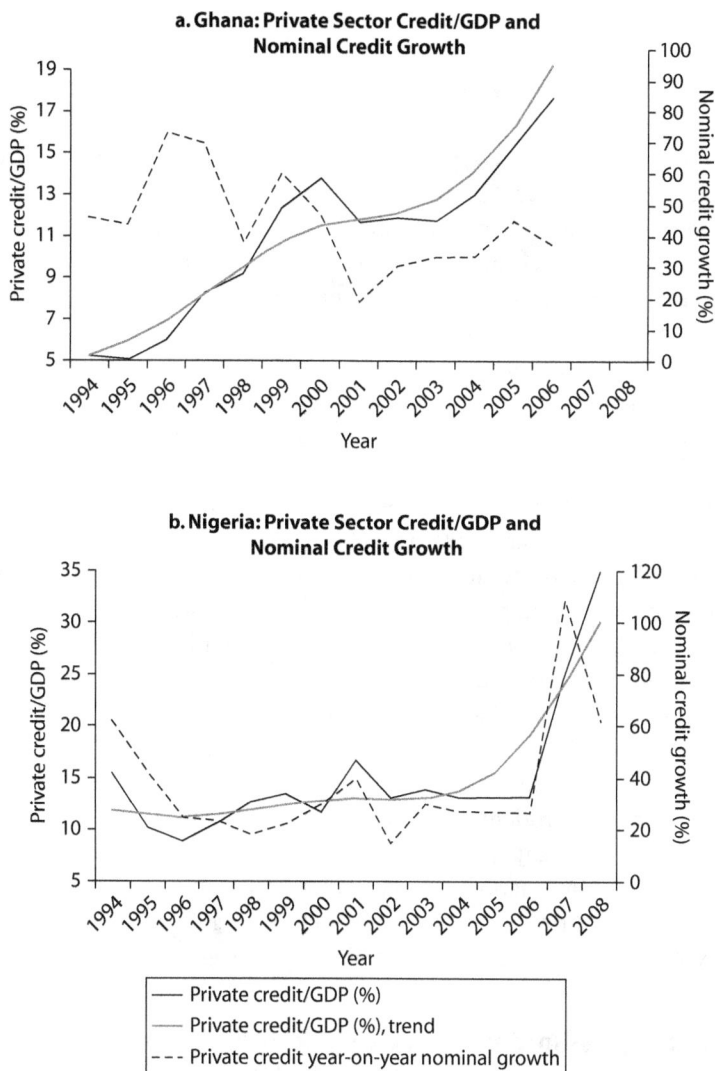

a. Ghana: Private Sector Credit/GDP and Nominal Credit Growth

b. Nigeria: Private Sector Credit/GDP and Nominal Credit Growth

——— Private credit/GDP (%)
——— Private credit/GDP (%), trend
- - - Private credit year-on-year nominal growth

Source: IMF's International Financial Statistics database 2010.

the authority of the regulator to implement triggers. With most African jurisdictions not yet set up to properly conduct risk-based supervision, it is unclear how they would institute a regime that goes even further than this in terms of exerting judgment, as well as how they would communicate and enforce decisions.

Macro-Prudential Oversight

Most regulators in Africa view macro-prudential regulation as a key challenge, and the development of macro-prudential supervisory capacity—with the exception of a very few countries—is in its infancy. Independent of the adherence to new international standards, the development of macro-prudential supervisory capacity is of crucial importance to most African supervisors. The economic structure of many African economies often results in high direct and indirect risk concentrations in a few sectors, often natural resources, and macroeconomic risks are often more significant for financial stability than the risks of individual institutions.

Still, most central banks lack dedicated surveillance units, and the buildup of macro-prudential supervisory capacity imposes a range of new demands that many regulators are unable to meet at this point. It requires new cross-cutting skills combining macroeconomic analysis and regulation, new modeling techniques, data collection and analysis, and practical criteria for triggers and intervention. The additional resource demands are considerable, particularly with regard to skills, training, modeling, technology, and data. In addition, macro-prudential supervision requires a cultural change from a passive rules-based supervisory approach to active risk management. Regulators may lack the legal authority for intervening on the basis of macro-prudential factors (rather than institution-specific factors). Regulators need to work with governments to determine how far they are prepared to intervene in the event of a buildup of systemic risk.

As a stepping-stone, African regulators might focus first on establishing dedicated macro-prudential surveillance units before moving to full-fledged macro-prudential supervision (including intervention powers). The development of international standards for tools and measures to monitor macro-prudential risks could inform similar exercises that are adjusted to the existing resource and data constraints by African regulators.

Regional Cross-Border Supervisory Coordination and the New International Supervisory Architecture

Cross-border supervisory issues are increasingly important for African regulators. The continent has long had an international banking presence. Recent inward investment by international banking groups and the emergence of Africa-based regional banking groups have significantly increased cross-border banking activity. Although international banks continue to play a vital role on the continent, African markets are in fact dominated by the cross-border operations of African financial groups.

Figure 5.7 shows that the total assets of African banks in Sub-Saharan African operations by far exceed the engagements of large international banking groups in the region, such as Barclays, Citibank, and Standard Chartered.

Effective supervision of cross-border financial institutions requires closer cooperation between the supervisors in the respective institution's home country and in the host country where the institution's subsidiary is operating. This is also a key issue in advancing consolidated supervision.

Figure 5.7   Cross-Border Operations of African and International Banking Groups

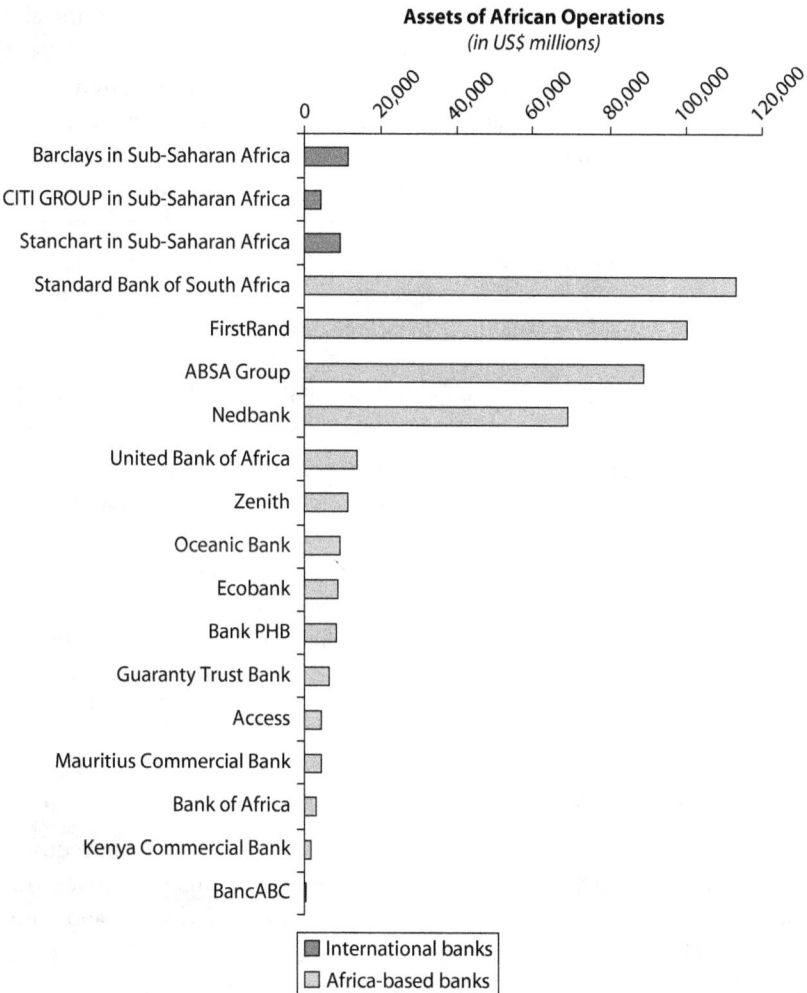

Assets of African Operations
(in US$ millions)

Source: Lukonga 2010.

Recent reforms of the international supervisory architecture have focused on the constitution of colleges of supervisors for all internationally operating banks. The representation of African supervisors in these supervisory colleges remains a weak point, given the current asymmetry of the size of operations of large international banks between developed markets and most African markets. Although the activities of an international banking group in Africa may make up a very small part of its total balance sheet, that bank may be of disproportionate importance for certain African countries. The South African ABSA Group is a case in point: though the group makes up only 2 percent of Barclay's balance sheet, it is the largest consumer bank in South Africa and systemically important for the host country. This asymmetry introduces an inherent complication in the design of college arrangements—namely, that African supervisors have a large interest in being included in the supervisory college, but may be overlooked by the home supervisors because of a biased view of their significance for the efficiency and effectiveness of the supervisory process. To these issues may be added the relative cost to low-income country regulators of attending colleges in distant locations: not only in terms of transport costs, but also in terms of time that relatively scarce senior qualified personnel must spend away from the home bank.

Closer to home, the emergence of regional banks headquartered in African jurisdictions requires significant investments in regional cooperation platforms and information exchange regimes across the region. African home supervisors need to champion the establishment and effective implementation of regional college agreements for the large regional banks. Legal mechanisms, including bilateral memorandums of understanding, to facilitate cooperation and information exchange need to be put in place. Further, restrictions to information sharing relating to the confidentiality of banking information need to be addressed to enable regulators to pass on information to other regulators.

Crisis Response Mechanisms and Bank Resolution

Effective banking supervision and robust bank capitalization requirements are important to minimize the likelihood of financial crises, but these will not completely prevent episodes of banking distress and bank failures. The difficulties experienced by governments in managing bank failures during the financial crisis have demonstrated that effective bank resolution is a weakness in developing and developed countries alike. Prompt and effective responses to potential financial distress are important to avoid poor ad hoc decisions and to minimize the costs of banking failures to the financial system and ultimately the taxpayer.

Though the number of systemic banking crises has declined sharply in Africa, the recent Nigerian experiences in responding to bank failures and several self-assessments by other African countries have highlighted the need for establishing and rehearsing effective crisis response mechanisms and bank resolution procedures before the actual events occur. Bank depositors in Africa have, to a large extent, relied on the implicit guarantee of the authorities that, as recently seen in Western markets, bank depositors would not be exposed to the failings of bank risk management. What is more, given the comparatively small size of the financial sectors in Sub-Saharan Africa, many banks are of systemic importance on a national scale and the too-big-to-fail problem is ubiquitous.

The continent's overall record of resolving failing banks in the form of ad hoc interventions is mixed. If it was successful, it often depended on the de facto power and capacity of the executive branch to impose bank resolutions on shareholders, as well as the limited practical ability of shareholders to challenge government interventions.

Since only a few countries on the continent have established formal crisis response mechanisms, authorities tend to be inadequately prepared to deal with potential crises. Proper procedures need to be established to define efficient information sharing, analysis, decision making, and internal and external communications, as well as appropriate contingency plans for funding the resolution of banks where necessary. Without an appropriate legal framework in place, supervisors lack the required legal powers and independence in their decision making to intervene in a timely and forceful way. As banking systems grow, it will be increasingly important for supervisors to be able to take prompt corrective actions, and, as the need arises, resolve insolvent banks in an orderly way.

Developing Country-Specific Roadmaps for the Regulatory and Supervisory Reform Agenda

Focus group discussions with African supervisors have found that they are pursuing a vast reform agenda that goes far beyond the implementation of the BCPs and the Basel capital frameworks.[3] Besides introducing risk-based supervision and effective consolidated supervision, issues such as introducing deposit insurance, promoting financial inclusion and consumer protection, regulating electronic money, adopting International

Financial Reporting Standards, adopting contingency planning and bank resolution frameworks, and supervising microfinance institutions ranked high on supervisors' list of priorities. Although some of these efforts may follow a political rather than an economic rationale or may even be donor-driven, it is striking that African supervisors often deal with a much broader reform agenda than their counterparts in developed countries. The breadth of the reform agenda documented in the focus groups is a challenge for the already constrained capacity of supervisors; many supervisors felt overwhelmed with the demands on them.

The focus group discussions also indicated that some African supervisors already take a very pragmatic, building block–like approach to the implementation of international standards. Some regulators have decided to introduce risk-based supervision without implementing the entire Basel II framework, while others focus on macro-prudential supervision as their priority. There is a strong consensus among African supervisors that a more systematic approach to identifying regulatory priorities was required to focus the reform agenda. In identifying reform agendas, international standards should not be viewed as a blueprint for sequencing reforms.

Based on the discussion in this chapter, it is suggested that African regulators adopt a "risk-based approach" to identifying building blocks and developing country-specific roadmaps for regulatory and supervisory reforms. In doing so, policy makers and their partners need to move beyond the classic assessment framework for financial stability and develop a roadmap diagnostic framework that aids decision makers in prioritizing certain building blocks of the reform agenda over others.

Any roadmap needs to be grounded in a set of basic supervisory conditions and requirements (for example, the availability of data, sound accounting practices, minimum staffing and resources, independence and authority of the supervisor) that will need to be in place before it makes sense to concentrate on other supervisory aspects or variations of the capital adequacy regime. These preconditions form a necessary foundation for implementing country roadmaps.

The choice of focus areas for reform should be based on an assessment of (the gaps in) existing regulations and supervisory capacity and the specific risk drivers in each country, for example, prevalent risk concentrations, or risks inherent in the financial structure and the structure of the economy. National authorities should choose those building blocks that will have the greatest immediate impact on strengthening the effectiveness of financial supervision and safeguarding financial stability.

Conclusion

The agenda for regulatory and supervisory reform in Africa is substantial, but progress in recent years is a source for optimism and should motivate a continued and focused process. Regulatory capacity remains at the heart of the reform process, and efforts for developing capacity are the biggest priority. African supervisors across the region understand existing risks well and have a clear sense of priorities, but they are often limited in their scope of action by a lack of resources and empowerment.

Notes

1. In fact, there are only 25 BCPs, but for the purpose of analysis BCP 1 has been divided into six subcomponents.

2. The FSB's work on the intensity and effectiveness of supervising systemically important financial institutions provides another example for this shift in international financial governance (FSB 2010a). Pointing to weaknesses in compliance with basic and essential principles of banking regulation and supervision, such as the operational independence of the supervisor, the FSB notes, "Such failures should be considered unacceptable and more pressure should be placed on jurisdictions who do not comply" (FSB 2010a, 4).

3. The focus group discussions were conducted in the context of a regional policy workshop on "The African Approach to the Implementation of International Standards for Banking Supervision and the Basel Capital Framework" on April 29, 2011. The workshop was convened by the African Association of Central Banks, the Partnership for Making Finance Work for Africa, and the Bank of Uganda and brought together supervisors from 25 African central banks.

References

BCBS (Basel Committee on Banking Supervision). 2004. "Implementation of Basel II: Practical Considerations." Basel: BIS. http://www.bis.org/publ/bcbs109.pdf?noframes=1.

———. 2006. *Results of the Fifth Quantitative Impact Study.* Basel: BIS. http://www.bis.org/bcbs/qis/qis5results.pdf.

Europe Economics. 2009. *Study on the Cost of Compliance with Selected FSAP Measures: Final Report.* London: Europe Economics. http://ec.europa.eu/internal_market/finances/docs/actionplan/index/090707_cost_of_compliance _en.pdf.

FSB (Financial Stability Board). 2010a. "Intensity and Effectiveness of SIFI Supervision Recommendations for Enhanced Supervision." Financial Stability Board, November. http://www.financialstabilityboard.org/publications/r_101101.pdf.

———. 2010b. "FSB Framework for Strengthening Adherence to International Standards." Financial Stability Board, January. http://www.financialstability board.org/publications/r_100109a.pdf.

FSI (Financial Stability Institute). 2004. "Implementation of the New Capital Adequacy Framework in Non-Basel Committee Member Countries: Summary of Responses to the Basel II Implementation Assistance Questionnaire." FSI Occasional Paper No. 4, Bank for International Settlements, June. http://www.bis.org/fsi/fsipapers04.pdf.

———. 2010. "2010 FSI Survey on the Implementation of the New Capital Adequacy Framework: Summary of Responses to the Basel II Implementation Survey." FSI Occasional Paper No. 9, Bank for International Settlements, August. http://www.bis.org/fsi/fsipapers09.pdf.

Fuchs, Michael, Richard Hands, and Thomas Jaeggi. 2010. "Recent International Reform Initiatives to Strengthen Post-Crisis Banking Supervision and the International Regulatory Architecture: Priorities and Potential Pitfalls for LICs." April 2010, World Bank, Washington, DC.

Gottschalk, Ricardo, and Stephany Griffith-Jones. 2010. "Basel II Implementation in Low-Income Countries: Challenges and Effects on SME Development." In *The Basel Capital Accords in Developing Countries: Challenges for Development Finance*, ed. Ricardo Gottschalk, 75–96. Hampshire and New York: Palgrave Macmillan.

Honohan, Patrick, and Thorsten Beck. 2007. *Making Finance Work for Africa.* Washington, DC: World Bank.

Laeven, Luc, and Fabian Valencia. 2008. "Systemic Banking Crises: A New Database." IMF Working Paper 08/224, World Bank, Washington, DC.

Lukonga, Inutu. 2010. "Regulatory Frameworks in Sub-Saharan Africa: Ensuring Efficiency and Soundness." http://www.palgrave.com/PDFs/9780230580503 .Pdf.

Lukonga, Inutu, and Kay Chung. 2010. "The Cross-Border Expansion of African LCFIs: Implications for Regional Financial Stability and Regulatory Reform." IMF Research Paper, World Bank, Washington, DC.

Tran, Hung Q. 2005. "Basel II and Emerging Markets." Presentation at the Conference on the Future of Banking Regulation, London School of Economics, April 7–8, 2005. http://fmg.lse.ac.uk/upload_file/400_Hung%20Tran.ppt.

Ward, Jonathan. 2002. "The New Basel Accord and Developing Countries: Problems and Alternatives." Working Paper No. 4, Cambridge Endowment of Research Finance, Cambridge, UK.

PART IV

Financial Sector Reform: Activism and Local Political Conditions

CHAPTER 6

The Potential of Pro-Market Activism for Finance in Africa: A Political Economy Perspective

Florence Dafe

How can governments in the political and economic environments typical of Sub-Saharan Africa intervene to increase the financial resources available for productive investment? This is the question that drives this chapter. The policy relevance of research on this question is widely acknowledged: there is strong empirical evidence that an efficient and inclusive financial system is essential for private investment, and ultimately for economic growth.[1] However, the majority of African financial systems are highly exclusive: in Africa,[2] more enterprises than in any other part of the world report that access to finance is a major constraint to their operations. Particularly small and medium enterprises (SMEs)

This chapter draws on a paper written within a wider research project on the political economy of financial reforms in Africa, commissioned and funded by the Deutsche Gesellschaft für Internationale Zusammenarbeit (GIZ). The views expressed in this chapter are those of the author alone and do not necessarily represent the views of GIZ. This paper has gone through a major rewrite in response to helpful comments from Kathrin Berensmann, Christian von Haldenwang, Matthias Krause, and Mick Moore. Special thanks are due to Karen Losse, Thomas Losse-Müller, Christian von Drachenfels, and Peter Wolff for valuable comments on earlier drafts.

179

lack access to external investment resources (Honohan and Beck 2007, 166). Moreover, even relative to other developing countries, financial systems in Africa have remained poorly developed in terms of size and efficiency (Allen et al. 2010; Honohan and Beck 2007).

The lack of financial intermediation into higher levels of domestic investment results, to a substantial extent, from market failures that make providing financial services to SMEs prohibitively costly or, because of an uncompetitive market environment, unattractive.[3] The need for banks to downscale operations and find less expensive ways of serving SMEs is limited, as banks operate very profitably: subsidiaries of foreign banks in Sub-Saharan Africa have higher returns on assets than subsidiaries of the same banks in other world regions (Honohan and Beck 2007, 36). In light of the alarming situation in the financial sectors of many African countries, policy makers are taking a renewed interest in the question of how governments could govern the financial sector so that it better serves the needs of the real economy.

African policy makers asking this question received different advice in different eras of economic thinking. In the 1960s and 1970s there was a consensus that developing-country governments should assume an activist role and intervene directly in the financial sector to increase outreach; in the 1980s and 1990s, the dominant view of the Washington Consensus was that governments should take their hands off the financial markets. Today the appropriate role of the state in the financial sector is still a controversial issue. Acknowledging that the private financial sector has often not been very successful in providing finance for productive private investment, the debate now focuses less on whether governments should intervene and more on the degree and the best way to intervene (Beck, Fuchs, and Uy 2009). The key proposition of the current consensus on the role of government is that governments should concentrate on creating an enabling environment and on supporting activist actors outside the government, thus promoting access to finance. Moreover, based on more recent experiences, it is increasingly accepted in some parts of the debate that governments could themselves assume an activist role if they have appropriate governance (Beck, Fuchs, and Uy 2009; De la Torre, Gozzi, and Schmukler 2007). So far, however, there is only a dearth of research exploring the circumstances under which activist government interventions could be a successful tool for increasing the financial resources available for productive investment in developing countries.

This chapter makes three main arguments.

- First, it argues that although the current view on the role of government in the promotion of access to finance offers a realistic way forward toward making finance work for Africa, the associated policy implications remain unclear. This is because of the lack of a fully developed positive approach to government activism that provides a framework helping to evaluate ex ante whether a government has the political will and capacity for efficiently playing an activist role. This chapter seeks to contribute toward developing such a framework, because it would help development practitioners assess whether activist government interventions have a chance to succeed in a particular country.

- The second argument is that political economy could provide the theoretical foundation for such a framework, because political economy allows for the modeling of policy choices as the outcome of a bargaining process between interest groups that cut across state and society.

- The third argument is that a political economy framework would not only help in evaluating the chances of efficient government interventions but could also inform policy making in countries that currently lack the conditions to govern finance through activist policies.

These arguments build upon two strands of literature: the welfare economics argument in favor of government interventions to address market failures and an interest group model of political economy focusing on the role of state–private sector relationships. Empirically the arguments are based on experiences with activism in the developing world both within and outside of Africa. Thus, the chapter focuses on the role of government in banking and not in the securities market, because banks still account for the vast majority of financial sector assets in poor countries (excluding central bank assets) (Demirgüç-Kunt, Beck, and Honohan 2008, 10).

The chapter is organized as follows: the next section examines in more detail the current consensus on the potential of activist government interventions to increase access to finance for private productive investment. It begins by presenting the welfare economics argument in favor of activism and proceeds with an overview of developing-countries' experience with activism and of the new, more political perspective on government activism. The following section discusses the problems that development practitioners currently face when it comes to prioritizing reforms without having a positive theory of activism. The next section sketches some start-ing points for thinking about the determinants of efficient government interventions in the financial sector and explores how such a framework could inform policy making, and the final section draws conclusions from the arguments presented in the whole chapter.

Activism in Financial Markets: Theoretical Perspectives and Practical Experiences

This section discusses the current consensus on the potential of govern-ment activism to promote greater outreach of financial systems to the private sector. It begins by exploring the rationale for activist government interventions and compares this welfare economics point of view to the actual experiences with government activism over the past five decades. Most examples are drawn from Africa, but some also refer to Asia or Latin America, where the debate on the potential of activism has been similar. The remainder of this section discusses the role attributed to poli-tics in the current view on activism.

Before delving into the arguments, it is necessary to offer a definition of *activism*, a popular term in the current debate on access to finance.[4] Since the question behind this chapter is how African government offi-cials can intervene to increase finance for productive private investment, the definition proposed here is very broad: a government is referred to as *activist* when it deliberately intervenes in the financial sector to promote the outreach of financial services to segments of the private sector that have been underserved. The discussion focuses on SMEs in agriculture and industry as examples for underserved segments. Although it is not only governments that can play such an activist role but also elements of the private sector—in particular nongovernmental organizations (NGOs) and foreign donors—if not stated otherwise, the term *activism* in this chapter refers to government activism.

The Welfare Economics Argument in Favor of Activism

From a welfare economics point of view, government intervention might be called for when market failures need to be corrected. The financial sector relies heavily on gathering and processing information, as well as on the enforcement of contracts. This makes finance prone to a variety of market failures that, if not corrected, limit the outreach of financial ser-vices (Besley 1994; Stiglitz and Weiss 1981). The following examples from the market for corporate lending in developing countries shed some light on how market failures can make providing credit to SMEs prohibitively costly and less profitable than the alternative options of commercial banks, such as those serving large corporations or governments.

Asymmetric information (especially adverse selection and moral hazard) and enforcement problems add substantially to the transaction costs for lenders. Because of such market failures, lenders need to spend resources to screen and assess the creditworthiness of borrowers and monitor them. In poor countries, these costs are particularly high because SMEs often lack a credit history or formal and stable sources of revenue or assets that can be used as collateral.

Moreover, private banks may not find it worthwhile to incur the high costs of screening and monitoring SMEs because once these borrowers have a good credit history, they can obtain credit from other lenders who will not have to bear the initial costs for screening. This suggests that information on creditworthiness is basically a public good, in the sense that once it has been generated, it is very costly to exclude anyone from using it. When the market fails to let banks appropriate the returns of information about their costumers, banks will underinvest in the acquisition of such information.[5]

Besides asymmetric information, enforcement problems, and the public good character of borrower information, high minimum efficient scales in the provision of financial services may impede the functioning of credit markets. Credit, like the provision of other financial services, involves fixed costs and, to a certain extent, increasing returns to scale. If financial markets are small, as in most African countries, the lack of economies of scale substantially adds to the unit costs of transactions. Low population densities exacerbate this problem. Moreover, high minimum efficient scales increase market concentration, which eventually—although not necessarily—reduces competition and increases prices.[6]

High costs for providing credit that have a negative effect on profits should be an incentive to innovate and find less expensive ways of providing credit. Yet market failures reduce investments in credit market innovations to a point below what is socially optimal: innovations are a public good and therefore innovators bear all the costs in case of failure, but they find it difficult to prevent other investors from adopting the new technology once it has proven to be successful. Without the chance to internalize more of the positive externalities they create, the incentive for private banks to invest in socially profitable but financially relatively unattractive innovations will remain low. This holds in particular where markets are uncompetitive and easy outside options are available.

In sum, high transaction costs reduce the profitability of dealing with SMEs, especially in light of the small amounts of money involved in transactions with these clients. More attractive alternatives—such as serving large enterprises with tangible assets that can be used as collateral and that fit with the existing business model—tend to lower the banks' incentives to reduce prices, compete for market shares in underserved segments, or innovate and find more inexpensive ways of serving SMEs. Moreover, the failures of the credit market in developing countries tend to reduce not only the supply but also the demand for credit. If the unit costs of provision are high, credit becomes less affordable for some smaller firms, such as SMEs, and this, in turn, reduces the demand for credit from the formal banking sector.

These examples demonstrate how market failures can impede the development of inclusive financial systems. They provide an argument, based on welfare economic theory and information economics, that some form of government intervention going beyond financial regulation and supervision to remove market failures might increase social welfare.[7] Thus, governments should choose their policy to mitigate a particular market failure depending on the nature of this market failure, in order to achieve the best possible economic outcome.[8] For instance, if the major constraint on the operation of a payment system is a problem of scale and small market size, policies that spur regional financial integration might be appropriate. In cases where several ways of addressing a specific market failure are possible, welfare economic theory suggests that governments should seek to implement those policies that address the market failure most directly and provide the highest benefits at the lowest costs.

Thus, normative economic theory does not only provide a basis for considering activism as a way to enhance social welfare, but it also offers some guiding principles for choosing and designing government interventions. However, contrasting these theoretical insights with actual experiences suggests that governments often lack the capacity or willingness to design activist policies in a way that achieves the positive outcome predicted by the theory.

The Experience with Activism

Assessing the actual experience with activist policies is not straightforward. First, it is difficult to provide empirical evidence of whether economic growth or productive investment would have been higher or lower in the absence of interventions—the counterfactual. Second, convincing evidence on whether the government-supported expansion of financial services increases private investment remains limited because of the non-random nature of interventions: although private banks favor serving governments and large companies, activist policies tend to target less-developed sectors and companies. The associated selection bias complicates the identification of the causal impact of activist policies on the private sector. Third, the returns of activist policies may be long term, which makes it difficult to assess the success of more recent—and in the short term, sometimes even distorting—activist policies.

For these reasons, the following historical overview of experience with activism adopts a broad definition of what constitutes a successful activist policy. While a narrow definition would consider activist policies to be successful only when they increase investment and economic, sectoral, or enterprise development, policies are also categorized as successful in this section if they increase the outreach of financial services to the target group.

Decades of market-replacing activism. In the 1960s and 1970s governments in developing countries were expected to play a prominent role in the financial sector. In line with welfare economic theory, the consensus was that the lack of bank finance for private investment was a result of market failures (Gerschenkron 1962). Mainstream economic thinking held that an active public sector involvement in mobilizing and allocating financial resources was called for to overcome market failures in order to broaden access to finance for groups and sectors that were shut out of the formal financial market. These excluded groups included poor households, agriculture, and sectors depending on long-term finance. This activist approach toward financial sector development was part of a broader interventionist agenda that regarded governments as drivers of the development process and sought to replace markets that failed to generate growth and substantially reduce poverty.

The main instrument for broadening access to finance in developing countries during the period of market-replacing activism was directly providing funds through public or development banks. By the 1970s, the state in developing countries owned, on average, 65 percent of the assets of the largest banks, compared with about 40 percent in developed countries (De la Torre, Gozzi, and Schmukler 2007, 13). In those countries that had adopted central planning and had nationalized the banking system—such as Guinea, Tanzania, and Benin—government-owned banks constituted the entire banking system. Governments used public or development banks to support the pursuit of their developmental agenda through the selective allocation of credit. Consistent with the market failure rationale, government-owned banks sought to focus on areas where private markets failed, such as agricultural lending (Brownbridge, Harvey, and Gockel 1998).

In theory, government-owned banks might have an advantage over private banks in increasing outreach through, for instance, better access to information, exploiting economies of scale, being less risk averse, or solving the problems of externalities. However, the overall experience with public banks has been negative: strong empirical evidence shows that greater government participation in bank ownership is associated with lower levels of financial development, less credit to the private sector, wider intermediation spreads, slower economic growth, and recurrent fiscal drains (La Porta, Lopez-De-Silanes, and Shleifer 2002). However, there are case studies at the country level that find that some public banks—such as the village bank system of Bank Rakyat in Indonesia (Yaron, Benjamin, and Charitonenko 1998), the Bank for Agriculture and Agricultural Cooperatives in Thailand (Townsend and Yaron 2001), or, to some extent, the Botswana Development Corporation (Harvey 1998, 20)—were quite successful in reaching out to their targeted clientele while still operating in a financially viable manner.

Another major tool used to broaden access in developing countries in the decades of market-replacing activism was the imposition of lending requirements that obliged private banks to allocate a certain share of their loans (often at preferential interest rates) to priority sectors or regions. In East Asia, all countries directed credit to varying degrees (Stiglitz and Uy 1996). In India, only about 20 percent of bank deposits were allocated freely; the rest had to be invested in government bonds or were directed to priority sectors such as agriculture and SMEs. In Brazil, commercial banks were required to allocate between 20 and 60 percent of their sight deposits to agriculture (De la Torre, Gozzi, and Schmukler 2007, 15–16). In Africa, this form of activism was most extensive in planned economies such as Tanzania, where nationalized banks provided direct credit allocations to public enterprises and priority sectors on the basis of their annual plans. Yet, even in countries where banks were relatively independent of the government, private banks were pressed to extend loans to public sector enterprises and government projects (Daumont, Le Galle, and Leroux 2004, 40).

The experience with directed credit programs has been negative in most developing countries. On average, these programs failed to reach their intended beneficiaries and more influential borrowers were favored

(World Bank 2005, 165). In some countries, such as Ghana or Nigeria, sectoral lending requirements were on the books, but not applied effectively (Daumont, Le Galle, and Leroux 2004, 25). However, there are examples of successful directed credit programs, although most of them are from East Asia (Stiglitz and Uy 1996; Vittas and Cho 1996).

Another common tool used to broaden access to finance in rural areas was to compel banks wishing to expand their networks of urban branches to also set up branches in rural areas. A prominent example is the Indian experiment of the late 1970s and 1980s, where the government imposed the so-called 1:4 license rule. This rule stated that banks could open one branch in an already-banked location only if they opened four in unbanked locations (Burgess and Pande, 2005). Other countries where rural branching legislations were in place include Botswana, Nigeria, and Zambia (Brownbridge, Harvey, and Gockel 1998).

The effectiveness of such legislation has been mixed at best. In Botswana and many other countries where rural branching legislation was tried, it was not enforced effectively (Brownbridge, Harvey, and Gockel 1998; Daumont, Le Galle, and Leroux 2004). While the prominent rural branch expansion program in India terminated because of high bank loan default rates, it is also regarded as one of the success stories: the rule not only caused banks to open relatively more rural branches in Indian states with lower initial financial development and broadened access to finance, but also significantly reduced rural poverty (Burgess and Pande 2005).

The "modernist" period. Although some examples of market-replacing activism were successful, in most cases it was not and might even have impeded development. From the 1970s onward, it was increasingly accepted that two major assumptions of the market-replacing approach— that governments know how to replace markets and that they always seek to maximize social welfare—were flawed. A growing body of work found that public authorities in developing countries often had limited technical capacities for running financial institutions and that their willingness and capacity to govern financial institutions in a way that increases private investment depended on the interests of the political leadership (Brownbridge, Harvey, and Gockel 1998).

In response to these insights, a consensus emerged in the 1980s that governments should withdraw from markets, including the financial sector. The costs of government failures were regarded as exceeding those of market failures, and direct government interventions were therefore seen as counterproductive. The new benchmark became the best-practice institutions of the industrialized economies. Policies of this "modernist" approach sought to transplant these institutions to the developing world (Honohan and Beck 2007, 7–12).[9] As a result, developing countries around the world started liberalizing and privatizing their financial systems in the 1980s and 1990s.

The evidence for the effectiveness of modernism has been mixed. By the end of the 1990s, countries in Sub-Saharan Africa, as in other regions, had made significant progress in macroeconomic stability and bank restructuring, usually including the reentry of foreign capital and the privatization of banks (Beck, Fuchs, and Uy 2009, 14–15). Yet in many African countries the institutional mechanisms needed to supervise and regulate banking in the modernist system were absent when reforms started. Thus, the first decade of financial liberalization was accompanied by macroeconomic instability, and liberalization often had devastating effects on the real economy, as evident in the growing disintermediation in the 1980s and early 1990s.[10]

The success of the modernist approach in building inclusive financial systems has fallen short of expectations. By the end of the 1990s, access to finance in Sub-Saharan Africa was still limited for those groups that had been traditionally shut out of the market, such as lower-income households or SMEs. The operations of the newly licensed domestic and foreign commercial banks have concentrated on government lending and international assets, avoiding lending to the domestic private sector and in particular to agriculture (Chang 2009, 494–97; Honohan and Beck 2007, 29–34). The experience has been similar in other world regions (Hanson 2003). In response to the overall disappointing record of both market-replacing activist and modernist approaches, the debate has shifted again, back toward more government involvement but this time emphasizing the need for pro-market orientation (De la Torre, Gozzi, and Schmukler 2007; World Bank 2007, 145–46).

Pro-market activism. Over the past decade a consensus has emerged that the role of government needs to go beyond ensuring macroeconomic stability, toward building the necessary institutions for an inclusive, efficient, and stable financial system, in a form of activity termed *pro-market activism.*[11] This view is informed by a more recent body of literature that provides strong empirical evidence for the key role of institutions for economic development and the removal of market failures (Acemoglu, Johnson, and Robinson 2001; Rodrik, Subramanian, and Trebbi 2004).

A major focus of public action has been on developing contractual and informational institutions. At the top of the agenda are collateral and bankruptcy law reforms that aim to protect the rights of both borrowers and lenders in order to facilitate lending. Other major reforms aim at improving the court system or building alternative dispute resolution mechanisms and establishing asset and collateral registries. Public action also focuses on strengthening independent bank regulation and supervision, including the formulation and implementation of accounting and disclosure standards. Such measures intend to increase not only the stability of the financial system but also its capacity for competition and innovation, two key determinants of outreach.

It has become part of mainstream economic thinking that there is room for pro-market activism in the form of carefully designed, market-friendly government interventions in the financial sector to address specific market failures "while the fruits of ongoing institutional reform are still unripe" (De la Torre, Gozzi, and Schmukler 2007). In contrast to the earlier market-replacing approach, pro-market activism is based on the assumption that markets can broaden access to finance, and therefore the goal of government interventions is to develop or enable markets, not to replace them (Beck, Fuchs, and Uy 2009; De la Torre, Gozzi, and Schmukler 2007). To improve the intermediation of financial resources into higher levels of investment, proponents of pro-market activism recommend that governments use a combination of sticks (disincentives), such as moral suasion, and carrots (rewards), such as tax incentives. Considerations of financial sustainability have become central to the design of pro-market interventions (De la Torre, Gozzi, and Schmukler 2007). Although government interventions are acknowledged to possibly create inefficiencies in the short-term allocation of resources, the key underlying assumption is that time-bound pro-market activist policies may increase long-term productivity.

Pro-market activism can take the form of affirmative regulatory policy. One of the most prominent examples of such policy is the establishment of credit registries. Credit registries give access to clients' credit history and increase the transparency of borrower quality, which makes it safer for financial institutions to lend to new customers. Credit registries also allow borrowers to build reputational collateral that increases their bargaining power for the terms of credit. Banks are not always supportive of building credit registries, if doing so will entail the compulsory sharing of their information with other lenders, thereby increasing competition. In some countries the authorities have therefore started to push beyond the boundaries of information sharing with which bankers are comfortable. In Kenya, for instance, a private operator struggled for several years to initiate a credit registry because of the lack of interest among banks. The Central Bank of Kenya (CBK) finally took the initiative and issued a regulation mandating financial institutions to share information with credit bureaus. Similar approaches were taken in Ghana and Uganda (Mylenko 2007). Although these examples show that activism can be successful in addressing coordination failures and first-mover disincentives, the fact that reforming or establishing credit registries stagnates in the majority of African countries (Beck, Fuchs, and Uy 2009) indicates that both technical capacity and political will are important intervening variables in the success of pro-market activism.

It is also increasingly acknowledged that activism might have to go beyond competition policy and first-best institution building. A case in point is the moral suasion exercised by South African authorities that caused banks in that country to introduce the Mzansi (basic transaction) account in 2004. The Mzansi account is an entry-level deposit account, developed by the South African banking industry, offering lower charges and no overdraft facilities. To mitigate the financial risks of offering a low-cost account, participating banks shared the costs of product development and marketing. Although the expectations of participating banks in terms of revenue (where breakeven was the expectation) were not met, they were exceeded with respect to take-up: by December 2008, more than 6 million Mzansi accounts had been opened, about two-thirds of them by people who had never had a bank account before (Bankable Frontier Associates 2009).

Yet there are many examples where moral suasion has not worked. For instance, frustrated by the results of earlier attempts to induce the private sector to serve each district, in 2006 the government of Uganda mandated the establishment of savings and credit cooperatives to be supported by services supplied by the poorly managed, government-owned Postal Savings Bank (Beck, Fuchs, and Uy 2009, 20). The difficulties many African governments face in persuading banks to ensure the interoperability of payment system infrastructure that spurs competition also indicate the limitations of moral suasion.

Another example of the promotion of market-friendly and activist financial governance is the key role that has recently been assigned to developing-country central banks in the design and implementation of consumer protection policies.[12] It is increasingly acknowledged that this role might go beyond regulation and supervision to protect customers from the potentially predatory behavior of financial institutions. The CBK, for instance, provides an overview of bank charges to the public to make it easier for customers to compare them (Candace and Angela 2008, 6); similarly, the Peruvian central bank requires banks to disclose the "Annual Effective Cost Rate," which is expressed like an interest rate but includes all costs associated with consumer credit, such as evaluation charges or credit insurance premiums (Alliance for Financial Inclusion 2010, 4). Moreover, cost information associated with financial services has to be published daily in newspapers. When this information was first published, interest rates dropped by as much as 15 percent in six months (Alliance for Financial Inclusion 2010, 3). However, since consumer protection has only recently been added to the list of priorities on the financial reform agenda, there is a lack of experience with activist consumer protection, and it is too early to more broadly evaluate the capacity and willingness of governments to intervene in this area.

Many governments continue using instruments that were common during market-replacing activism. Examples are credit guarantee schemes and direct public finance. Evidence of the effectiveness of these instruments in the past decade has—just like past experience— been mixed at best. In Chile, for instance, the government-owned Banco Estado has managed to broaden access to finance for micro-entrepreneurs by providing credit while operating profitably (Benavente 2006). Benavente, Galetovic, and Sanhueza (2006) show that the Fondo de Garantía para Pequeños Empresarios (FOGAPE) a credit guarantee scheme funded by the Chilean government, is also a success. African examples of successful government interventions might include the South African public business finance agency Khula Enterprise Finance, which promotes SME lending (Sapp Mancini, Yee, and Jain 2008, 7) and the Tanzanian SME credit guarantee scheme established by the Bank of Tanzania in 2005, which involves 50–50 risk sharing. However, in most African countries, public banks have not adjusted their business models, and government schemes fail to recover loans and impose heavy fiscal costs without reaching their target groups (Honohan and Beck 2007, 99–102). "Smart subsidies" have not yet had the expected take-up.[13]

The examples show that it is difficult to assess the effectiveness of pro-market activism, partly because the policies have been adopted quite recently, and partly because pro-market activism is a very broad and ill-defined category. Yet it is possible to draw a headline conclusion from existing experiences: there is, as with market-replacing activism, a broad range of examples of both successful and unsuccessful pro-market activist policies.

Remarkably, both in the past and today, developing-country governments around the world have been using similar activist policies. In most countries, these interventions have not achieved their goals. Yet the fact that some countries, primarily but not exclusively in East Asia, have had successful experiences and managed to design and use the instruments in an effective way suggests that under certain conditions, differing from country to country, activism might be a successful strategy to substantially increase the financial resources available for productive investment. Table 6.1 provides a stylized summary of the different approaches to financial governance in the developing world over the past seven decades.

Politics as a Key Determinant of the Effectiveness of Activism

Past experience suggests that activism is neither a generally harmful nor necessarily effective approach. Rather, the evidence indicates that, in line with the welfare economic argument, activism has the potential to promote finance for development if the country-specific environment is right. Although a number of arguments could be made to explain the failure of government interventions in markets—such as explanations based on ideas or ideology (Krueger 1993) or on the lack of expertise to identify binding constraints (Hausmann, Rodrik, and Velasco 2007)—the more recent literature examining interventions in financial markets has identified politics and a lack of good governance as key determinants (Demirgüç-Kunt, Beck, and Honohan 2008; Honohan and Beck, 2007; Stiglitz and Uy 1996, 273). There is a strong consensus that activist policies, which entail giving discretionary powers to governments, can easily be and have indeed been politically abused.

This section seeks to illustrate this perspective, which is more systematically developed in the next two sections. Contrasting African and East Asian experiences with market-replacing activism illustrates what effect politics and the resulting governance structures can have on the design and implementation of activist policies—negative and positive, respectively.

In many Sub-Saharan African countries, no attempt was made to set clear goals for government-owned banks, to measure their performance against these goals, or to undertake cost-benefit analyses (Honohan and Beck 2007, 99–107). A major reason for this lack of adequate governance structures seems to be that governments used the banking sector as a source of finance. In many cases, the practice of paying off political clients

Table 6.1 Summary of Approaches to Financial Reform in Developing Countries

Period	Approach to financial reform	Rationale/ideology	Dominant or main actors	Focus of policies	Efficiency of interventions
1940s–1980s	Market-replacing activism	Planning; states as drivers of the development process, replacing missing or failing markets	State agencies; donors	Support of sectors and industries excluded from formal financial system, such as agriculture, SMEs, and industries depending on long-term finance through directed lending, public credit, credit guarantees, and so on	Overall experience negative; the few examples of successful activism are primarily in East Asia
1980s–1990s	Modernism	Market-based adjustment; strong emphasis on states over markets	Private market participants; donors, especially international financial institutions (IFIs)	Transplantation of best-practice institutions such as central bank; independence from industrialized countries to the developing world; monetary stability; bank restructuring; market-based provision of financial services through privatization	Evidence has been mixed; often increase in macroeconomic stability but reduced or stagnant financial intermediation

(continued next page)

Table 6.1 *(continued)*

Period	Approach to financial reform	Rationale/ideology	Dominant or main actors	Focus of policies	Efficiency of interventions
Since the end of the 1990s	Pro-market activism	State and markets complementary; states as market enablers and market developers	Broad spectrum of actors: developing-country governments, IFIs, donors, private sector including civil society and social entrepreneurs	Role of government goes beyond ensuring macroeconomic stability and first-best institution-building; activism might take the form of affirmative regulatory policy: mandatory information sharing with credit bureaus for financial institutions, inducing banks to share interoperability of payments infrastructures, tax incentives, smart subsidies, and so on	Difficult to assess effectiveness of pro-market activism, partly because policies have been adopted quite recently; broad range of examples of both successful and unsuccessful pro-market activist policies

Source: Author.

distorted the lending decisions of government-owned banks so that many of them ended up lending to the wealthy and politically connected. Often public banks were used to make up for the losses of inefficient public enterprises; central banks also served to finance the state apparatus more generally (Brownbridge, Harvey, and Gockel 1998). For instance, the Uganda Commercial Bank (UCB), which used to be the country's largest public sector bank, failed to adequately appraise or monitor loans or to pursue their recovery because of the political nature of lending. The discipline of UCB's borrowers was low because they often regarded such loans as rewards for political support and, in some instances, politicians also told their constituents that loans from government banks need not be repaid (Nsereko 1995, 28–29). As a consequence, loan recovery rates for the lending schemes administered by Ugandan public banks were below 50 percent in the 1980s, and banks mostly failed to reach their targeted clientele (Brownbridge 1998a, 129–31).

Moreover, in many African countries, positions in development banks were used by public authorities to reward political clients. This may explain why the Nigeria Education Bank, a public institution intended to finance the higher education sector, had failed to make a single loan seven years after it was established, despite employing 261 staff in 21 offices (Alawode et al. 2000, 55). The political costs of laying off excess staff were a key obstacle to the privatization of government banks as part of the financial reform process.

Private banks in Africa also failed to serve the real economy in a way that increased broad-based private investment and instead provided financial resources mainly to the government and a small economic elite. Using political pressure, politicians and politically connected private investors in some countries appear to have been able to access loans from private banks at below-market rates, to fail to repay them, and to resist repayment successfully when banks took action to recover the loans. Moreover, African governments, chronically in fiscal crisis, used not only direct measures such as lending requirements to public enterprises but also indirect measures such as interest rate controls or high reserve requirements to govern private banks so as to finance the state apparatus (Brownbridge, Harvey, and Gockel 1998; Daumont, Le Galle, and Leroux 2004).

At the same time, private banks, in principle opposed to such government interference in the banking sector, often came to a profitable *modus vivendi* with the government. In many African countries, such as Botswana, Kenya, and Ghana, private banks did not have to compete with state-owned financial institutions. In these countries, private and public banks often served different market segments. Public banks focused on serving development priority sectors and public enterprises, and private banks served large enterprises. Where private banks were required to follow sectoral credit policies, cooperation was usually bought with profitable *quid pro quos* such as central bank discounting of loans, access to inexpensive funds from government placements, or controls on deposit rates that gave banks a profitable spread (Daumont, Le Galle, and Leroux 2004, 43; Haggard and Maxfield 1993, 301).

The lack of adequate financial governance also had devastating costs for the technical capacities of both public and private banks. Notable exceptions, such as the Ethiopian government banks, the government-owned Kenyan Commercial Bank (KCB), and private banks in Botswana (Brownbridge, Harvey, and Gockel 1998), did exist. Yet most African central banks lacked the necessary capacities for prudential regulation and supervision because the financial incentives of powerful political and economic agents determined financial policy making. Moreover, the politicization of lending decisions discouraged public banks, and to a lesser extent private ones as well, from building up capacities in liquidity, assets, and risk management.

In contrast, the literature on the East Asian Miracle emphasizes how the political leadership delegated authority to insulated economic bureaucracies (technocrats) so that they were able to develop efficient and growth-enhancing economic policies.[14] As in Africa, financial policy making was motivated by political objectives to secure power, finance the state apparatus, and ensure popular acceptance. To this end, governments intervened heavily in the banking system. Yet governance structures, incentive mechanisms, and the efficiency of interventions differed substantially between Africa and the newly industrialized East Asian countries.

Nissanke (2001) describes the financial governance structure as a performance-based system for the distribution of rents: policy makers sought to create rent opportunities ("contingent rents") through the same set of financial policies as in Africa, such as interest rate controls and entry regulations. The underlying assumption was in line with welfare economic theory that, in the absence of rent opportunities, banks would not have sufficient incentives to provide the socially efficient level of financial services to the private sector, given the prevalence of market failures. Yet in contrast to activist approaches in most African countries, the size of rents for banks was proportionate to their efforts in expanding their business. Rents were performance-indexed opportunities.

This governance structure appears to have created incentives for banks to expand their deposit base and improve their loan portfolio through more diligent monitoring. Unlike government-owned banks in many other developing economies, those in the Republic of Korea, Singapore, and Taiwan, China, and arguably Indonesia as well seem to have behaved prudently and were mostly successful in reaching their target groups (Stiglitz and Uy 1996). East Asian policy makers took several measures to minimize problems of political capture (although they were not able to eliminate them) by powerful economic interests. Taiwan, China, gave employees of public banks incentives to act prudently and penalized employees whose loans did not perform. Korea imposed strict performance criteria to guide banks' lending decisions. In order to insulate public banks from political pressure, public officials in Malaysia were not allowed to serve on the boards of public banks (Stiglitz and Uy 1996, 258–59). In contrast to most African countries, policy makers in Northeast Asia directed credit mainly to private enterprises and changed credit policies rapidly when policies were not functioning properly (Stiglitz and Uy 1996, 271–72). Thereby, banks were given incentives to develop close links with firms and relationship-based lending allowed banks to reduce the information costs related to financial intermediation and to adopt a long-term business perspective, which increased the provision of term loans. Through the close relationship between companies, banks, and a supervising and risk-taking government, the credit risks were socialized, as were the social benefits from higher private investment at a later stage of economic development (Kang 2003; Nissanke 2001).

The Northeast Asian experience highlights the importance of the governance structure activist states choose for the allocation of financial resources. Some examples show that activism can be a viable developmental strategy in Africa, as in the case of the Botswana Development Corporation and of the KCB: governments used these public banks to pursue their developmental agenda but made provisions to ensure that the banks were managed relatively efficiently, with governments deliberately abstaining from interference in day-to-day management and making sure that the majority of board members were private entrepreneurs (Brownbridge, Harvey, and Gockel 1998, 20–21, 84–86). Most African governments seem to have lacked the political will or capacity to design adequate governance structures that monitor and evaluate the financial sustainability of programs and the outreach to intended beneficiaries. However, within Sub-Saharan Africa, there is variation in the degree of success achieved by using activism as a tool to increase access to finance.

The degree of success, in turn, seems to depend on the political environment in which financial policy making takes place.

Based on these experiences, the current consensus on the role of the state in the financial sector takes it as a basic premise that the country's political realities have to be taken into account in the design of activist policies (Beck, Fuchs, and Uy 2009; Honohan and Beck 2007, 12). Although it is widely agreed that modernist approaches should be complemented through some form of activism to correct market failures and increase finance for private investment, it is not recommended that African policy makers put themselves in the lead in implementing the activist agenda by increasing their direct engagement in the provision of financial services (Honohan and Beck, 2007, 12). Rather, they are advised to smooth the way for private activists such as NGOs or social entrepreneurs. This view rests on the assumption that many African governments lack adequate governance structures (Demirgüç-Kunt, Beck, and Honohan 2008, 143; Honohan and Beck 2007, 6, 11, 12; World Bank 1997). As table 6.1's stylized comparison between African and East Asian experiences with activism highlights, appropriate governance structures seem to be the major precondition for successful market interventions. Where activism was successful, policies tended to be closely monitored and characterized by provisions that seek to hinder the political capture of policies by a powerful economic elite and the exploitation of the financial sector as a source of government finance (De la Torre, Gozzi, and Schmukler 2007; Stiglitz and Uy 1996).

Assessing the Current Approach toward Activism

The consensus on the role of government today is distinct from the predominant views of previous periods of market-replacing activism or modernism in that it sees governments' main role to be one of creating an enabling environment for financial markets. As noted earlier, it is increasingly acknowledged that sometimes this role might have to go beyond competition policies and first-best institution-building toward affirmative regulation and other more direct interventions, whereby good governance is regarded as a key determinant of the effectiveness of such policies (Honohan and Beck 2007, 12). For at least three reasons, this view on activism offers a realistic and promising way forward toward making finance work for Africa.

- First, the current consensus has the potential to spur on the development of inclusive financial systems because it has overcome the dualism of states versus markets of the Washington Consensus and sees a role for the state in improving the functioning of the market. This insight is important because it acknowledges that market failures could make providing financial services to some groups of society prohibitively costly and that a modernist approach alone is not likely to broaden access to finance in the medium term. It also acknowledges that—at a time of unprecedented concentration of capital in a small number of banks—uncoordinated, decentralized actions by civil society, business associations for underserved sectors, and social entrepreneurs are unlikely to result in substantially increased access to investment resources for SMEs or agriculture. Furthermore, the state might play an important role in negotiating and implementing large-scale, collective solutions involving public and private actors.

- Second, the current view on activism is promising because, informed by past experience, it recognizes that although globally acclaimed best-practice institutions might offer a first-best solution to market failures, transplanting these solutions to Africa without taking into account the region's local political conditions is unlikely to work. A consensus that "no size fits all" and that building best-practice institutions in Africa takes time has emerged; thus, in the meantime, public action could try to find alternative second-best solutions as transitional devices. This gives policy makers in countries at a lower stage of economic development more policy space.

- Third, the current view on activism offers a promising way forward because it has incorporated insights from research that identifies politics as a key explanatory variable for the success and failure of activism.[15] It is now widely accepted that the differences in the objectives and the functioning of institutions governing activist policies are the result of political factors. At the core of this "institutional turn" and the renewed interest in political economy are the propositions that states and markets are politically determined and that good governance is a precondition for the success of activist policies. The current approach to activism does not deny that other country-specific factors—such as ideology or the ability to identify the binding constraints in an economy—determine the effectiveness of interventions, but it is assumed that these concepts can explain only part of the cross-country variation in the effectiveness of activism and interact significantly with politics.

Although the current consensus on activism provides a positive perspective on the role of government in financial markets and offers a promising starting point for thinking about how to raise finance for investment in Africa, a major drawback remains: the associated policy implications are not quite clear. It is recognized that activism can work in principle, but it is not clear under what conditions governments are willing to pursue and capable of pursuing activist policies successfully. When do political leaders choose a governance structure that, on the one hand, resists political capture by private interests, and, on the other, avoids public authorities using their political power in a way that merely benefits the state apparatus, politicians, or their political supporters? It seems clear that without good governance conceived in this way, government interventions will rarely be successful. However, although it has become part of mainstream economic thinking that it is necessary to "get the political conditions right" before any type of government intervention, assessing ex ante whether a state will demonstrate adequate governance is less straightforward. This makes it difficult for donors to direct their resources for the support of activist policies only to those governments that are likely to implement them successfully.

A large body of literature on the welfare economics argues in favor of government interventions, but there is little research that tries to contribute to a positive theory of activism—that is, a concept that helps assess ex ante whether a state has the willingness and capacity to pursue activist policies successfully. The small body of research in political economy that explores the determinants of financial policy making has taken up this challenge, advancing us closer to such a concept of effective activism. Through its focus on endogenous policy choices, a political economy perspective would not only help to evaluate the chances for success of an activist approach, but could also inform policy making in those countries that currently lack adequate governance to pursue activist policies successfully. There is a high added value to country-level political economy research that explores the potential of activism, because it would allow prioritizing avenues for reform and, as a consequence, would offer more effective guidance for policy makers.

Activism as a Tool to Increase Finance for Private Investment: A Political Economy Perspective

Contrasting the positive experiences with activism in Northeast Asia with the failures in many African countries highlights the influence of politics on the effectiveness of activist policies and the need to study the political environment in which financial policy making takes place in order to be able to explain and predict the outcome of any government intervention.

This section sketches some starting points for thinking about a political economy framework of activism and demonstrates how such a framework could inform policy making. Based on the existing literature about the political determinants of financial policy making, the section begins by discussing the major factors that could be used to weigh the empirical support for using activism as a tool to increase finance for private investment in a particular country. Although the overall body of work on the politics of finance in developing countries is small and mainly focuses on middle-income countries in Latin America and East Asia, this literature provides a number of analytical cues on which future work on the political economy of financial reform in Africa could build. The rest of this section draws some policy implications from the political perspective on financial policy making by elaborating what reform strategies are possible in countries where the political environment is unfavorable to a successful implementation of government activism.

Policy Coalitions and the Politics of Finance in Developing Countries

The most substantial body of work that seeks to explain variation in financial policy making from a political perspective has emerged in the fields of historical institutionalism and the political economy subfield of fiscal economy.[16] This work suggests that *policy coalitions,* defined as coalitions of interest cutting across state and society, play an important role in shaping financial policy patterns: state and private sector actors form implicit or explicit alliances to lobby for desired policies. Other state actors and social groups may form alliances in opposition. The difference in strength of competing coalitions then shapes policy choices. This coalitional approach to explaining financial policy rests on three key underlying assumptions:

- State-business relations are based on interdependence (Maxfield 1990; Moore and Schmitz 2008).
- Financial interests shape behavior (Haber, North, and Weingast 2008; Haggard, Lee, and Maxfield 1993; Maxfield 1990; Rajan and Zingales 2003).
- The translation of interests into policy is mediated by the historically evolved organization of the private sector and the revenue base of the state (Boone 2005; Maxfield 1990; Winters 1994).

The interdependence of the state and the private sector. The proposition that state-business relations are based on interdependence is drawn from arguments about what has been termed the "structural power of capital." In most developing countries there are tendencies for state predation and political capture, but also incentives for cooperation: to take the risk of investing, the private sector needs the active support of the state to provide physical, social, and legal infrastructure. States, in turn, depend structurally on private investors for two main reasons, which form the basis of the "structural power of capital." First, the state apparatus depends on the inflow of financial resources to fulfill its functions, and private capital providing tax income, party donations, or—in the case of banks—credit, is often the primary source for government finance. Second, politicians need private capital to invest within their jurisdictions in order to maintain a minimum level of economic prosperity, which ensures the government popular acceptance and increases the chances of continuing in power (Bates and Lien 1985; Moore and Schmitz 2008; Winters 1996).

Private banks seem to have a privileged position among investors, not only because of their ability to withhold financial resources from government but also because they shape industrial and agricultural growth and hence macroeconomic performance more generally by channeling resources to the real economy (Thurow 1989; Zysman 1983). The structural dependence of governments on private actors, and in particular on private banks, is likely to increase their leverage over financial policy. Therefore, the assumption of interdependence between the state and the private sector should serve as a starting point for thinking about the actors involved and the influence of different policy coalitions to shape financial policy.

Financial interests as determinants of behavior. The second proposition, that financial interests shape behavior, is a key contention underlying all major political economy approaches to explain financial policy. Common interests between sections of the public and private sectors form the foundation of different policy coalitions. Related to the first assumption of state-business interdependence, this suggests that explaining reform trajectories requires an analysis of the financial interests of actors in the public and private spheres, such as private banks, business associations, central banks, and (bureaucrats within) ministries of finance.

Two issues deserve particular attention. First, the financial interests of private banks with respect to financial reforms seem to be particularly important, given that bankers tend to have leverage over policy because both the government and the productive sector rely on external bank financing.[17] Second, in analyzing the financial interests of "the state," states should not be conceived of as monoliths, because there might be intra-state variations in financial interests, and as a result in the demonstrated willingness to pursue particular reform strategies (Maxfield 1990). For instance, it seems likely that the interests of central banks in their role as monetary authorities with a focus on financial system stability differ from those of ministries of industry or ministries of economic development. As a result, central banks might seek to establish coalitions with partners in the private sector other than those the ministries would choose.

The translation of interests into policy. The existing literature with a coalitional approach to explaining financial policy highlights two factors that mediate the translation of financial interests into policy:

- First is the historically determined organization of the private sector (in particular of the banking sector) in relation to the government, as reflected in the private sector diversity and autonomy in relation to the state (Boone 2005; Haggard and Maxfield 1993; Maxfield 1994).
- Second is the revenue base of the state, as registered in the degree of reliance on the domestic private sector and on external sources of revenue (such as foreign capital markets, aid or exports of natural resources) for government income (Maxfield 1990; Rajan and Zingales 2003; Winters 1994, 1996).

These two factors influence financial policy making through their effect on the nature (who becomes part of a particular policy coalition) and the power (which of the competing policy coalitions are favored in a policy process) of particular policy coalitions.

Among the most significant works exploring how the organization of the private sector affects financial policy making is Boone's "State, Capital and the Politics of Banking Reform in Sub-Saharan Africa" (2005). Boone (2005, 401) argues that differences in banking reform patterns reflect "cross-national differences in the strength, diversity and autonomy of private capital *vis-à-vis* the state." She demonstrates that the process of banking reform is determined by historically produced state–private sector relationships, so that reform outcomes are, to a significant degree, path-dependent: government responses to pressures for financial reform in the 1980s and 1990s were conditioned by pre-existing patterns of state-society interaction, as registered in the concentration and ownership structure of the banking sector and in political alliances between the state and the banking sector. The stronger, more diverse, and more autonomous the private banking sector was in relation to the government, the further and deeper went the process of reform. Boone's findings are in line with other works on the determinants of economic policy making in the developing world. Bräutigam, Rakner, and Taylor (2002), for instance, examine the emergence of growth coalitions in Africa and find that, in countries where the private sector does not constitute a powerful partner in economic reform processes, government policies are less successful in economic restructuring. There is also evidence that in developing countries with highly concentrated, oligopolistic banking sectors, financial reforms are not as far-reaching and the privileges of banks are maintained, because governments try to preserve the political alliances established with these banks in pre-reform periods (Boone 2005; Haggard, Lee, and Maxfield 1993).

In light of these findings on the role of the organization of the private sector, it seems plausible that activist policies are more likely to succeed in African countries where the state is complemented by a diverse and autonomous private (banking) sector. There are at least two reasons for this. First, governments find it more difficult to exploit the private banking sector as a source of finance for government entities, patronage, or elections when it is stronger and more autonomous. Governments also have fewer incentives to do so if a developed private sector provides stable and substantial tax revenues. Second, the political capture of activist policies by powerful economic interests is less likely when the banking system is diverse and competitive. Thus, the structure of the banking sector might at least partly explain why activist policies in Kenya, which has a vibrant and competitive private banking sector, have been more successful than in Uganda, where the banking sector is still shallow, or Nigeria, where banking has only recently started to become more competitive.

However, while the analysis of historically determined state–private sector relationships carries substantial weight in explaining or predicting long-term policy patterns, it seems less suited to explain policy change. In a model where the power of different policy coalitions is entirely determined by internal, historically produced, and thus relatively static institutional structures, policy is path-dependent. This makes it difficult to account for genuine financial reform and institutional innovation.

Previous research on the politics of finance suggests that policy change is determined by external financial connections, pointing to the importance of the state's revenue base. Large and relatively stable inflows of financial resources from external sources (for instance, through international capital markets, exports of natural resources, or, arguably, foreign aid) make the government more independent from the domestic private sector and reduce the need to seek private sector support for particular policies (Haggard, Lee, and Maxfield 1993; Lukauskas and Minushkin 2000; Moore and Schmitz 2008, 36–41).[18] Activist, business-friendly policies seem, therefore, more likely to succeed when governments rely substantially on the domestic private sector as a source of government income and economic prosperity than when governments rely primarily on alternative sources of revenue (Brownbridge 1998b; Lewis and Stein 1997; Winters 1996).

However, this is not to suggest that access to external financial revenues has adverse effects in all circumstances. It seems plausible that, in the context of a concentrated and autonomous private sector, access to revenues from external sources (such as foreign credit, income from natural resources, or aid) reduces the vulnerability of governments to pressures from incumbent private firms. Such a reduction of vulnerability might increase the policy space for governments and diminish the likelihood of the political capture of activist policies (Maxfield 1994, 587; Moore and Schmitz 2008, 37; Rajan and Zingales 2003).

This discussion of the coalitional approach to explaining or predicting policy choices suggests that a framework to weigh the empirical support for using activism as a tool to increase access to finance for productive private investment could usefully take into account the role of the historically determined organizational structure of relevant private sector institutions and the revenue base of the state. Both factors have important impacts on the structural dependence of governments on domestic capital, and on where authority resides within the government (Winters 1994).[19] As a result, both factors influence government discretion over policy making and determine which particular public sector entities gain the upper hand in the process of policy making. Both factors also determine whether the domestic private sector (and which sections) constitutes a powerful ally in the design of activist policies. The added value of developing a coalitional approach to understanding financial policy choices is likely to be high, as few researchers have taken up this challenge (Boone 2005; Lukauskas and Minushkin 2000; Maxfield 1990).

Alternative Approaches to Explaining or Predicting Financial Policy Choices

The coalitional approach, which builds on historical institutionalist and fiscal economy literature to explain or predict financial policy making, differs significantly from state- or society-centered explanations as major alternative approaches in the literature on the political economy of finance.

Society-centered approaches. Society-centered approaches perceive policy as the outcome of struggles among societal interest groups such as sectors or classes (Frieden 1991; Pagano and Volpin 2001; Rajan and Zingales 2003). Policy is conceived as an exchange where politicians provide policies favorable to those interested constituencies on which their power depends. In this analysis, state interests and the state's capacity to implement policies are conceived as perfectly flexible in responding to societal preferences.

The major shortcoming of society-centered approaches is their vision of the state. In this view, the state is treated as a "black box" where the economic bureaucracy is essentially just reacting to private demands. This premise denies states an independent role as agenda setters proactively seeking to create alliances to gain support for their preferred policies. Successful examples of activism—such as the introduction of the Mzansi account in South Africa as a result of moral suasion, or the advent of mandatory information sharing with the credit bureau in Uganda—are difficult to explain with society-centered approaches. Moreover, society-centered analyses of activism neglect the role of state capacity as a precondition for effective government action. In particular, the translation of private sector preferences into policy choices is particularly problematic in poor countries not only because states might lack the political will, but also because they might not have the organizational, financial, or knowledge resources to implement the preferred policies of private sector groups effectively (Evans, Rueschemeyer, and Skocpol 1985; Skocpol 1985; Thomas and Grindle 1990; Winters 1996).

State-centered explanations: the political institutions view. In the realm of finance, state-centered explanations for financial policy choices predominantly focus on the role of political institutions such as electoral democracy for checks and balances (Girma and Shortland 2008; Haber, North, and Weingast 2008; Huang 2010). The key underlying assumption of this so-called political institutions view is that—in the absence of self-enforcing political institutions that limit government discretion—governments, relying on banks to provide them with a source of finance, have "strong incentives to govern the financial system so as to facilitate its own political survival at the expense of the development of a banking system that can finance the private economy" (Haber, North, and Weingast 2008, 2).

The major shortcoming of this approach is that it does not consider the possibility that the revenue imperative (the necessity of governments to generate income) might also provide incentives for governments to introduce universal business-friendly policies to increase tax income (Moore and Schmitz 2008; Tilly 1992; Winters 1996). Governing finance might consist of more than financing government, and the relationships between those controlling capital and those with political power are characterized by both conflict and cooperation.

The assumption of causality running from political institutions to financial policy choices also appears to be problematic. One reason for this is the endogeneity of institutions. An explanation of policy choices based on institutions automatically raises the question of why some states have democratic institutions and govern their financial sector well but others do not. Although it seems plausible that in the long run political institutions have the presumed positive effect, it is likely that, particularly in the short run, there are other factors at work that determine both financial reform processes and the transition to democracy.

The increasing empirical evidence that democracy has not always had the expected positive effect on economic development and reform in the developing world also suggests that a broader set of variables than those related to political institutions might be needed to explain or predict financial development and policy patterns (see, for instance, Bräutigam, Rakner, and Taylor 2002; Collier and Rohner 2008). As highlighted previously, historically those developing countries that were most successful in intervening in financial markets, such as Korea or Taiwan, China, were not electoral democracies (Kang 2003; Stiglitz and Uy 1996). Quantitative evidence also indicates that electoral competition alone does not cause financial development (Keefer 2007; Rajan and Zingales 2003).[20]

In light of the shortcomings of state-centered and society-centered explanations for financial policy choices, the added value of elaborating a framework to weigh the empirical support for activism using a coalitional approach to explain or predict financial policy is likely to be high.

Few researchers have taken up this challenge. Those who have, have mostly focused on Latin American and East Asian middle-income countries (Lukauskas and Minushkin 2000; Maxfield 1990).

Table 6.2 provides an overview of approaches in the existing literature that studies financial policy patterns. The review of society-centered,

Table 6.2 Approaches to Explain and Predict Financial Policy Patterns in Developing Countries

Approach to explain/ predict policies	Dominant or main actors	Main propositions	What should reformers do? Policy implications	Weakness of the approach	Exemplary works
Interdependence approaches	State actors, private sector	State and society are interdependent Financial interests of political coalitions cutting across state and society are major determinants of financial policy patterns	Engage in political economy analysis of policy coalitions to explore niches for engagement across public-private divide Broker coalitions	Narrow focus on historically determined organization of the private sector sees policy choice as path-dependent and neglects international factors Neglects the role of technical capacity	Boone 2005; Maxfield 1990
Society-centered approaches	Private sector	Policy is the outcome of competition among societal interest groups Policy is an exchange where politicians provide favorable policies to those interested constituencies on which their power depends	Strengthen those societal interest groups that have an interest in more inclusive financial systems	State interests and capacity to implement policies assumed perfectly flexible States as preference takers not preference makers Dismisses the role of state capacity	Pagano and Volpin 2001; Rajan and Zingales 2003

| State-centered approaches: The political institutions view | States | Politicians decide policy according to institutionally defined rules

Without political institutions that limit government authority, governments have strong incentives to use the financial system as a source of government finance at the expense of the private sector | Reform political institutions to limit the discretion of public officials | Link between democracy and economic development is not straightforward

Relationship between state and private sector is characterized by conflict and interdependence

Dismisses the role of state capacity | Girma and Shortland 2008; Haber, North, and Weingast 2008; Huang 2010 |

Source: Author.

state-centered, and interdependence approaches provides some guidance for building a framework to study the potential of activism as a tool to increase access to finance. The next section will further elaborate on the key elements and steps in a political economy analysis to weigh the empirical support for an activist approach.

Starting points for an analytical framework. Existing research on the political economy of finance highlights the need to systematically explore how the interests of different groups translate into financial policy outcomes in order to weigh the empirical support for activism as a tool to increase finance for private investment in a particular country. The review of the literature highlights two sets of factors as potential determinants of financial policy choices and of the nature of the policy coalitions that shape them: organizational factors and the state's revenue base. These are discussed below.

1. *Organizational factors.* Two main organizational factors in particular seem especially relevant:

- *The autonomy of the private sector (in particular of banks) relative to the government.* The more autonomous the private sector is relative to the government, the higher the state's structural dependence on it and the more likely it is that the private sector constitutes a powerful ally in the process of financial policy making (Boone 2005; Bräutigam, Rakner, and Taylor 2002). As a result, policy coalitions across the public-private divide that seek to reform the financial sector in a way that sustainably increases access to finance are more likely, which plausibly has a positive effect on the design and effectiveness of activist policies.

- *The degree of concentration in the private sector (in particular in the banking sector).* Concentration in the private sector—whether within the financial sector, among favored borrowers, or as reflected in financial-industrial conglomerates—increases the power of the concentrated segment in relation to the government (Haggard, Lee, and Maxfield 1993). Therefore, the political capture of activist policies by powerful economic interests seems more likely in countries where the private (banking) sector is concentrated. Correspondingly, it seems plausible that activist policies are more likely to succeed in countries where states are complemented by a diverse and competitive private (banking) sector. A prime example is seen in the case of Chile, where the banking sector has become more diverse and competitive in recent years and there is evidence that private commercial banks, forced to reach out to new customers, tend to support activist policies that help them to serve SMEs and that pro-market activism has become relatively effective (De la Torre, Gozzi, and Schmukler 2007; De la Torre, Martínez Pería, and Schmukler 2010). However, in the extreme case of a fragmented private sector, activist policies are less likely to work. Fragmentation constitutes an obstacle to collective action, so governments would have difficulties engaging with the private sector in policy making.

2. *The revenue base of the state.* When governments have access to sources of revenue other than domestic bank finance or taxes from domestic private sector activity through international links—such as credit from international capital markets or, as is more often the case in African countries, aid and exports of natural resources—governments are less structurally dependent on the domestic private sector (Boone 2005; Gordon and Li 2009; Maxfield 1990; Moore and Schmitz 2008; Winters 1996, 41). Thus, in a situation where the degree of reliance on the domestic private sector as a source of government income and economic prosperity is low, incentives to cooperate with the domestic private (banking) sector to promote business-friendly and activist financial policies are also likely to be low. However, the effects of government income from sources other than the domestic private sector are not adverse in all circumstances because these alternative revenue sources can give governments a degree of autonomy from the domestic private (banking) sector that can also be used wisely. This could particularly be the case if conditions are attached to the use of the external revenues, as in the case of aid or in the context of a strong private sector (Maxfield 1990, 1994; Winters 1994).

Future research on the potential of activism as a development strategy could also provide a high added value by considering the role of state capacity. Technical capacity (including adequate organizational and managerial resources) emerges as an important intervening variable in assessing the potential of pro-market activism as a tool to increase access to finance, especially because pro-market activist strategies often require a commitment to sustainable financial inclusion from multiple actors and effective coordination between them. Technical capacity seems to be a particularly important factor in the African context. Although private sector development has increased the political clout of the private sector in financial policy making in most African countries, the success of ongoing financial reform efforts across countries continues to vary. Some states reform relatively eagerly; others fail to respond to the pressures both from private bankers to improve the investment climate and from donors and financially excluded businesses to make the financial sector more development oriented. Such a variation suggests that technical capacity is a major mediating factor in explaining and predicting successful activism or policy choice more generally.

Table 6.3 summarizes the ideas presented in this chapter in an analytical framework, indicating key issues in the different arenas of the political economy analysis. Future research could analyze these arenas in the proposed sequence, and it might be useful to revisit, reassess, and reinterpret earlier information during the research process.

The framework also takes into account two more general issues: First, history plays an important role in policy choice through its effect on the organizational structure of the private economy as well as on the financial incentives of various private and public agents. Second, the state varies, and there are intra-state variations in state capacity.[21]

While it should not be seen as an inventory, this preliminary framework offers some starting points for thinking about which elements might be important to consider in an analysis of the potential of activism as a tool to increase finance for development in a particular country. The framework could also more generally inform research seeking to explore the political economy in developing countries faced with the task of governing finance in a way that supports national development and, at the same time, responds to pressures from international markets to limit the role of the state in financial markets.

Implications of the Approach

Supporting an activist strategy—a strategy of deliberate government interventions in the financial sector to promote the outreach of financial services to segments of the private sector that have been underserved— requires an understanding of the political environment, particularly of the financial interests and the political clout of key actors. If the political conditions suggest that government entities have governance that is good enough to pursue activist policies effectively, then, in line with welfare economic theory, there are convincing arguments for development

Table 6.3   Analytical Framework to Study the Potential of Activism as a Development Strategy

Stage 1: Defining the financial sector	
Key issues for the analysis	*Selected guiding questions*
Mapping key players in the sector (for example, ministries, central banks, bankers' associations)	What are the roles of the different actors in the financial sector?
	How much influence do different actors have in government and what is the historical basis for the differences?

Stage 2: Basic country analysis	
Key issues for the analysis	*Selected guiding questions*
Economic structure: Economic development, private sector development, revenue base of the state	What is the level of economic and private sector development (including technical skills base and autonomy from government)?
	What is the organizational structure of the private sector?
	What are the main sources of government income?
	To what extent is the government dependent on private sector taxation?
	How do these structural factors affect the composition and influence of key actors in the financial sector?
Financial sector development	What have been the main policy trajectories within the sector?
	How have sector roles changed over time, and why?
	What have been the consequences for policy making and implementation?
Government capacity	Does government exercise authority over bureaucracy, military, raising public revenue, and policy making?
Development of (political) institutions	How well institutionalized are the government apparatus, policy-making processes, and political parties?

Stage 3: Analysis of key organizational players in the financial sector	
Key issues for the analysis	*Selected guiding questions*
Roles and mandates	What are the official and unofficial roles and mandate of the organization?
Organizational structure	What is the structure of the organization?
	What form does the balance of power across the organization take?

(continued next page)

Table 6.3   *(continued)*

Management and leadership	Who are the key actors? What is the degree to which power is vested in individuals?
Financing	What is the financial balance of the organization? Is the budget sustainable? To what degree is the government self-financing? What is the effect of funding source on policy preferences?
Incentives and motivation	What opportunities for career advancement are present? What is the level and distribution of remuneration for different personnel? What would be the benefits and losses from changes in incentives?
Capacity	What are the skills and resources of the personnel? Is the information base of the organization adequate for what it needs to do? Does the organization have the authority to define and implement policy?
Historical legacies	How do historical legacies affect: • roles and mandates? • organizational structure? • management and leadership? • financing? • incentives and motivation? • capacity?
Relationship between key players	What is the historical foundation of these relationships? What is the power balance in these relationships? How and why have these relationships changed over time? What is the effect of alliances on policy preferences and policy processes? What impediments to and niches for collaboration across organizations and the public-private divide are present?

Sources: Adapted from Moncrieffe and Luttrell 2005; Moore 2001.

practitioners to support well-designed, time-bound activist policies to complement modernist approaches.

But what if the political economy analysis suggests that the preconditions are not in place and governments are not likely to pursue activist policies successfully? The political economy framework drawn up in the last section emphasizes that policy choices are, at least to some extent, outcomes of the historical development path of a country. These historical foundations do not lend themselves to simple policy proposals because they suggest that there is some element of path-dependency in policy making. However, by taking the political economy framework as a starting point, it is possible to propose strategies for economic change in the short and longer terms, and also to draw policy implications for those African countries with a political environment unfavorable to activism. The political economy perspective suggests that policy makers and advisors in these countries seeking to promote access to finance need to pursue alternative strategies. In countries where activism is unlikely to work effectively, there are two main strategies to align the interests and incentives of the political and economic elites with those of the wider society. The first is to change the power balance in society to expand the space for reform policies; the second is to work within this power balance.

Changing the power relationships within society. If the political economy analysis suggests that the political environment is not favorable to effective activist policy making, then one of the two main options is to implement policies that focus on changing the balance of power in society in a direction that is more favorable to inclusive financial systems. Such a strategy is clearly a complex, mid- to long-term, politically sensitive task. However, some donors, in concert with reform-oriented domestic constituencies and in some cases the diaspora, are already implementing strategies for strengthening the political power of those groups with an interest in a greater and more sustainable outreach of financial services.

There is a large body of work (Przeworski 2000; Wittman 1989) that argues that one potential way to change the power balance within society is to change the political institutions and to try to induce greater political competition because this would stimulate more socially efficient policies. This argument is in line with the political institutions view of financial sector development, which explains the cross-country variation in financial development by variation in the degree of access to political institutions (Haber, North, and Weingast 2008). However, as outlined in previous sections, democracy has been a poor predictor for successful activism in the developing world. Political power to influence financial policy making seems to derive not from the formal institution of electoral democracy, but rather from the control over economic resources and the ability of a group to organize itself into a political force.

The dependence of political influence on political organization suggests that public development strategies in countries where the political environment is not favorable to effective activist policy making should have two major goals: (1) To support those with an interest in inclusive and sustainable financial systems—such as small manufacturers, farmers, or even banks seeking to reach out to SMEs—to gain economic weight, and (2) to help them to organize themselves along interest lines. Middle- and lower-income groups as well as smaller entrepreneurs are often fragmented because they lack the resources to organize themselves into a viable political force. Therefore, policies to strengthen political organization should focus on encouraging what political economists call "political entrepreneurship."

A political entrepreneur—which could be an individual, such as a reform-oriented minister; an organization, such as a manufacturers' association; a political party; or, under certain conditions, even a venture capital fund—helps those who lack resources and have difficulties in forming a group to organize themselves into a political force. Political entrepreneurs do so through collecting and disseminating information, subsidizing the costs of organization and thereby facilitating collective action (Kosack 2009; Noll 1989). In many poor African countries, donors make up the single most important group of political entrepreneurs. Through financial and technical assistance, they seek to strengthen the political and technical capacity of business membership organizations and of financial institutions targeting the lower end of the spectrum, such as microfinance banks. This contributes to improving the enabling environment for government–private sector relations. In the long term, these efforts might strengthen the consumers of financial services, financial service providers interested in serving SMEs, and public entities that promote access to finance, thus making the financial system more diverse and inclusive. As long as the private sector does not constitute a partner and challenger to the state, governments are unlikely to be responsive to the needs of those affected by their policies (Bräutigam, Rakner, and Taylor 2002).

While many examples of political entrepreneurship have had positive effects, it is less clear how to encourage it on the ground. Further research is needed to shed more light on this issue. Although democracy is not a sufficient precondition for group formation, democracy may be helpful in encouraging political entrepreneurship because certain aspects of it—such as freedom of both speech and association—make political entrepreneurship easier.

Working within the existing power relationships of society. An alternative to shifting the political power relationships would be to try to work within them. The challenge here is to design policies that have the potential to increase access to finance for productive investment in weak institutional environments, but that are also incentive-compatible for those with economic and political power.

In some parts of the financial development debate today, modernist policies are regarded as the preferred solution for reforming financial systems in societies where the political environment suggests that activist policies are unlikely to succeed. Seeing only a limited role for governments in financial markets, this approach posits that governments should focus on policies that strengthen macroeconomic stability and the market-based provision of financial services through large-scale finance. Ensuring that banks can safely lend on financial resources, enabling companies in the formal sector to find the mix of equity and debt finance they need to grow, and implementing sophisticated tools for risk management rank high on the agenda of modernists (Honohan and Beck 2007, 9). The guiding principle is that the best practices of the advanced economies in developing countries should be imitated.

However, past experience demonstrates that the potential for building inclusive financial systems by solely following the modernist approach is limited. In Botswana, for instance, which has primarily followed a modernist approach since its independence, large gaps still exist in access to finance for the middle market, lower-income groups, agriculture, and industries depending on long-term finance (Boone, 2005; Harvey 1998; Jefferis 2007). The experience in other Sub-Saharan African countries is similar, and the increase in outreach during the modernist period has also fallen short of expectations (Beck, Fuchs, and Uy 2009; Nissanke 2001). African financial markets have remained highly fragmented with few effective linkages and little competition between market segments. This means the majority of the population is still outside the formal banking system, served only by microfinance institutions or informal arrangements.

Moreover, empirical evidence shows that a modernist approach also raises political economy problems and that inadequate governance

structures can undermine modernist policies. These difficulties are indicated by the problems of political capture in privatization processes or
revisions of capital adequacy requirements (Brownbridge, Harvey, and
Gockel 1998; Haggard and Lee 1993, 13–15; Lewis and Stein 1997).

For these reasons, it is now widely acknowledged that even countries
with an unfavorable political environment find it necessary to complement modernist approaches with deliberate interventions to broaden
access to finance, although the focus might shift away from government-
led solutions (Honohan and Beck 2007, see in particular pages 7–12).
Such interventions could be designed by groups that are removed from
internal political pressure—for example, donors or regional institutions
such as regional development banks.

However, what are the options for African policy makers trying to
work within unfavorable political environments?

- First, they could try to find ways of supporting the activist agenda of
  nonstate actors, such as social entrepreneurs, which are incentive-
  compatible for those actors in power.

- Second, it follows from the political economy analysis that policy makers and development practitioners should create a stable revenue base.
  It seems plausible that governments in fiscal crisis, lacking stable sources
  of revenue to finance public expenditure, are less likely to govern the
  financial sector in a way that contributes to broad-based private investment in the face of the incentive to use the financial sector as a source
  of finance for government.

- Third, and more generally, policy makers should incorporate the insights
  from research indicating that policies that target not only the poorest
  and least powerful groups but also the middle market are more likely
  to succeed. Defining a broad access agenda that includes middle-size
  enterprises that also lack access to investment resources helps to mobilize powerful supporters (Rajan 2006).

Finally, more recent research on the political economy of reform
suggests that improving existing or even establishing new second-best
institutions could be a promising way forward in countries with an
unfavorable political environment (Rodrik 2008). This body of literature challenges the notion that all developing countries should focus
on building up the best-practice (or first-best) institutions prevailing

in rich countries, such as efficient courts, private property rights, or bankruptcy laws. The key assumption is that the kind of institutions reformers should build should be contingent on the economic constraints and political realities of a specific country at a particular stage of development (Adler, Sage, and Woolock 2009; Gerschenkron 1962; Rodrik 2008). Since developing countries face different constraints and different political environments than rich countries, this may require adopting better-fitting second-best institutions, which differ from those prevailing in rich countries, as a transitional device. Second-best institutions might offer a more pragmatic way forward because they fit better with the economic and political realities in developing countries in the short term. In light of the difficulties African states face in implementing best-practice institutions, exploring the potential of second-best institutions such as relationship-lending, as opposed to rules-based lending, seems highly policy relevant (Biggs and Shah 2006). However, second-best institutions might involve social costs, arising in the case of relationship-lending for instance, from the provision of credit within exclusive credit networks. Therefore, determining the conditions under which second-best institutions can help build more inclusive financial systems in Sub-Saharan Africa remains an important question for research.

Figure 6.1 summarizes the reform strategies suggested for promoting access to finance in different political environments.

Figure 6.1   Strategies for Reform

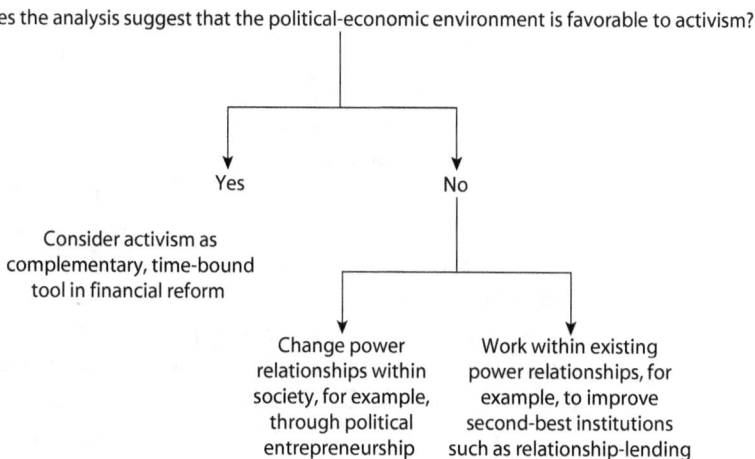

Does the analysis suggest that the political-economic environment is favorable to activism?

Yes → Consider activism as complementary, time-bound tool in financial reform

No → Change power relationships within society, for example, through political entrepreneurship / Work within existing power relationships, for example, to improve second-best institutions such as relationship-lending

Source: Author.

Conclusion

There is strong empirical evidence that access to finance for private investment is essential for enterprise development and economic growth. Financial systems in Sub-Saharan Africa have remained highly exclusive, however. This exclusivity is primarily the result of market failures that make the provision of financial services to lower-income groups and SMEs prohibitively costly or, because of an uncompetitive market environment, unattractive. While market failures provide an argument for activism (defined as deliberate government interventions to promote access to finance), experience with activism has been mixed at best. However, even though activism does not guarantee an increase in broad-based productive private investment, past experience—both in the developing and the developed world—suggests that achieving this goal without deliberate government interventions is difficult, if not impossible.[22] For this reason there is a renewed interest among development practitioners in determining the conditions under which activist government interventions in financial markets could serve as a tool to increase access to finance for productive investments.

It is now commonly acknowledged that the effectiveness of activism depends on politics, and there is a consensus that good governance is a precondition for government interventions to be successful. This chapter argues that although the current consensus on the potential of activism is a promising way forward, its policy implications are not quite clear. There is no fully developed positive approach of government activism and thus no framework that helps evaluating, ex ante, whether a government entity is likely to successfully assume an activist role. Without such ex ante predictors, development practitioners will find it difficult to prioritize reform policies and define the adequate role for government in a particular country; this could range from a modernist to a pro-market activist role. Moreover, without such a framework there is the risk of spending resources on policies that seek to increase financial access but are not likely to succeed and are unsustainable. This outcome could spread disenchantment with aid and leave African countries without the financial services they urgently need.

This chapter shows that political economy can provide a framework that helps to assess whether government interventions in a particular country have a chance to succeed. By focusing on endogenous policy choices, political economy allows the study of any policy as the outcome of a political decision-making process. Therefore political economy not only helps to predict the chances of success of an activist approach, but also draws policy implications for those countries currently not likely to have good enough governance to successfully pursue activist policies.

The existing literature on the political economy of finance suggests that the assumption of interdependencies between private and public agents should frame the political economy analysis. Existing work also shows the value of an approach that seeks to explain or predict financial policy choices through the analysis of coalitions of interests between private and public agents. In this way, the nature of a particular policy coalition and its power to determine financial policies seems to be particularly shaped by the historically produced organization of the private banking sector in relation to the state, and the revenue base of the state.

If the political economy analysis suggests that the political conditions are favorable, there are convincing arguments for supporting well-designed activist policies such as subsidies or tax incentives as temporary devices to complement modernist approaches. More often than not, however, the political environment is likely to be unfavorable, so governments must pursue strategies other than activism to encourage economic development. Political economy suggests two main strategies for advisors and policy makers in countries with an unfavorable environment. One possibility is to try to change the power relationships within society, for instance, through encouraging political entrepreneurship to empower financially excluded groups. The alternative possibility is to work within the political environment and, for example, improve the functioning of second-best institutions, such as relationship-lending.

These arguments entail a new approach for making decisions about spending resources to build inclusive financial systems by emphasizing the need to focus on what drives development and what is politically feasible. Taking such a pragmatic, but maybe more realistic, approach requires greater openness to second-best policies. While globally deemed first-best solutions such as property rights and efficient courts are crucial for financial development, they might be difficult and slow to establish in countries with an unfavorable political environment. In such countries a focus on the low-hanging fruit, such as fostering relationship-lending schemes or social entrepreneurship, might offer limited progress, but also a more promising way forward. In addition, through their effect on the political environment, second-best policies could increase the demand for first-best policies in the longer term.

Translating both implications—to revise financial reform strategies in accordance with the results of political economy analysis and also to be open to time-bound second-best (including activist) solutions—into policy is not straightforward. Very little research is available to build on that uses a political approach to explore issues of financial reform, and much of the research that does exist lacks operational relevance for the African context. Political economy has not yet received serious attention in the policy debate on financial reform, in spite of the rhetoric that insists it is necessary to go beyond the technicalities and address questions of political feasibility. Robinson (2009, 9) has received much support in policy circles for more generally pointing out that "the problem of under-development cannot be solved by economists coming up with better policies for poor countries to adopt or endlessly hoping for benevolent 'leadership'." It is time to take up the challenge and analyze more systematically how to propose financial policies in a way that they are chosen endogenously, and supported by those with political and economic power.

Notes

1. For an overview of the finance-growth nexus, see Levine, Loayza, and Beck 2000 or Beck, Demirgüç-Kunt, and Levine 2007.
2. Unless stated otherwise, the term *Africa* in this chapter refers to Sub-Saharan Africa.
3. Although there are a number of potential constraints to the expansion of firm credit in Africa (including the limited number of bankable projects), this chapter focuses on financial market failures because opinions tend to be highly polarized about the role of public action in addressing imperfect financial markets.
4. For an introduction to the terminology, see the World Bank report *Making Finance Work for Africa* by Honohan and Beck (2007, in particular pages 7–12).
5. The fact that setting up credit registries usually requires banks to share credit information about borrowers also helps to explain the slow progress in credit registry development in Sub-Saharan Africa.
6. The high degree of concentration in most of Africa's banking systems results partly from the small size of national markets. Honohan and Beck (2007, 41) report that the market share of the top three banks (concentration ratio) in each country averages 73 percent across 22 African countries, based on total assets in the latest year for which data are available. This figure compares with 60 percent for the world as a whole. The market dominance by a small number of banks points to considerable market power that—as will be explored in the section reviewing existing work/literature on the political economy of finance—is associated with substantial economic power and influence on political decision making.

7. For a more extensive discussion, see, for instance, Stiglitz and Weiss (1981).

8. An early discussion of this argument is provided by Bhagwati (1971).

9. The approach has been referred to as "modernist" because policies under this heading aimed at governing financial markets in the same manner as industrialized countries, focusing, for instance, on improving the macroeconomic environment and contractual and information frameworks in order to increase access to large-scale finance for formal enterprises (see, for instance, Honohan and Beck 2007, 7–12; Beck, Fuchs, and Uy 2009). Although the terms activism and modernism suggest a polarization into two highly contrasting and incompatible approaches to financial policy making, in most countries in the developing and the developed world activist and modernist approaches to financial reform complement each other today. Moreover, as Honohan and Beck (2007, 12) point out, "sometimes it is not immediately clear whether certain policies should best be considered modernist or activist." This chapter uses these terms because they have become important reference points in the debate on financial inclusion, analogue to the terms structuralist/interventionist and neoliberal/laissez faire in more general debates on the role of the state in the market.

10. A detailed account of the challenges arising from financial liberalization in Africa is provided, for instance, in the case study of Nigeria by Lewis and Stein (1997).

11. De la Torre, Gozzi, and Schmukler (2007) introduced the term *pro-market activism* in the access debate; the term has been picked up by others (see, for instance, Beck, Fuchs, and Uy 2009; De Luna-Martinez 2006; Ize, Pardo, and Zekri 2008). De la Torre, Gozzi, and Schmukler (2007) describe this new approach in detail, and many of the characteristics of activism presented in this chapter are based on their concept. This chapter adopts a broad definition of pro-market activism because, as outlined at the beginning of the section, activism is defined more broadly as the deliberate intervention to promote the outreach of financial services to groups of society which so far have been underserved. The term *pro-market* is used to contrast the current view with the market-replacing approach prevailing in the 1960s and 1970s.

12. Consumer protection has emerged as an important reform area complementary to the field of financial inclusion: efforts to expand financial inclusion in developing countries have allowed many new customers to access the formal banking system. Yet these new customers often have no experience in using banking services and lack an understanding of financial products, so they are more likely to pay excessively high interest rates and bank charges, and become overindebted.

13. One example is the initiative by a public-private alliance for financial inclusion, Banco de las Opportunidades, in Colombia. In their model, subsidies for

banks that open agents in rural areas are auctioned through a competitive process, with the winning bank receiving in the first year 100 percent of the subsidy, 50 percent in the second, and no subsidy in the third year.

14. For an account of the role of technocrats in economic policy making, see Criscuolo and Palmade (2008) and Winters (1996); specifically for finance, see MacIntyre (1993) or Cheng (1993).

15. Influential works include Bhagwati (1982); Brownbridge, Harvey, and Gockel (1998); Daumont, Le Galle, and Leroux. (2004); Haggard, Lee, and Maxfield (1993); and Nissanke (2001).

16. Fiscal economy posits that the structures of complex organizations such as states, and the strategies of their managers, are influenced by the location of their resources (see, for instance, Goldsheid 1958).

17. This argument is also at the core of resource dependency theory, a sociological theory of organizational behavior that suggests that the external resource needs of organizations and how and by whom they can be filled helps to explain organizational behavior (Pfeffer and Salancik 1978).

18. This argument can also be found in the growing body of work on the effects of oil and aid on governance on the one hand and of tax revenue on the other (Bräutigam, Fjeldstad, and Moore 2008).

19. For an account of how the organization of the private sector and the revenue base of the state determine central bank independence, and hence financial policy patterns in developing countries, see Maxfield (1994).

20. There are at least two reasons why electoral democracies might not necessarily have more inclusive financial systems. First, while the majority of voters in many developing countries are currently excluded from financial services, financial policy making does not necessarily reflect their preferences, because finance might be a topic that is removed from the sphere of political competition. Usually different parts of the state apparatus seek to fulfill the different and conflicting functions of the state. Some state organizations play leading roles within the clientelist spheres and cater to the electoral needs of the ruling parties, serving the majority of poor voters; others are more removed from political competition, as is often the case with central banks (Woodall 1996). If monetary agencies are removed from the political sphere, they are likely to prefer policies focusing on macroeconomic stability rather than policies seeking to encourage financial system deepening (Haggard and Maxfield 1993). The diversity of roles played by different state institutions also highlights the notion that states should not be regarded as unitary actors and that there are intra-state variations in the capacity and willingness to pursue particular policies. Second, the link between democracy and financial inclusion is problematic because in poor countries the institutional prerequisites for the effective representation of the preferences of financially excluded groups are often

missing. Excluded groups such as the SME sector and its employees are often weakly organized along institutional lines (Bräutigam, Rakner, and Taylor 2002), and "in patrimonial or personalistic regimes the potential numerical power of the votes of the poor is neutralised by their fragmentation among competing particularistic networks and interests" (Moore et al. 2003, 187), such as ethnic networks.

21. The phenomenon of "pockets of efficiency" illustrates that states vary, and that different state agencies have different interests and capacities, based on their political and economic support base. There is strong empirical evidence that even in countries with poor governance and weak public sectors, reform-oriented and well-functioning government entities do exist (Leonard 2008). In recent years the Central Bank of Nigeria seems to have emerged as such a pocket: compared to other developing countries, Nigeria ranks low in governance indicators such as corruption, rule of law, or government effectiveness (Kaufmann, Kraay, and Mastruzzi 2009). Yet, despite a weak overall institutional environment and government capacity, the Central Bank of Nigeria emerged as one of the most eager reformers in Sub-Saharan Africa, as indicated by the politically difficult consolidation of the banking sector in 2004/2005, corporate governance reforms in the banking sector in 2006 and 2009, or the ambitious Financial Sector Strategy 2020.

22. For a more general discussion of this argument with respect to agriculture, see Chang (2009).

References

Acemoglu, D., S. Johnson, and J. A. Robinson. 2001. "The Colonial Origins of Comparative Development: An Empirical Investigation." *American Economic Review* 91: 1369–401.

Adler, D., C. Sage, and M. Woolock. 2009. "Interim Institutions and the Development Process: Opening Spaces for Reform in Cambodia and Indonesia." Working Paper No. 86, Brooks World Poverty Institute, Manchester, U.K.

Alawode, A., M. Murgatroyd, S. Samen, D. McIsaac, C. Cuevas, A. Laurin, F. I. Wane, L. Chiquier, and M. Navarro-Martin. 2000. *Banking Institutions and Their Supervision: Nigeria Financial Sector Review* (Vol. 2), Washington, DC: World Bank.

Allen, F., E. Carletti, R. Cull, J. Qian, and L. W. Senbet. 2010. "The African Financial Development Gap." *EUI Working Papers*, ECO 2010/24, European University Institute, Florence, Italy.

Alliance for Financial Inclusion. 2010. "Consumer Protection: Levelling the Playing Field in Financial Inclusion." Policy Note, Alliance for Financial Inclusion, Bangkok.

Bankable Frontier Associates. 2009. *The Mzansi Bank Account Initiative in South Africa.* Johannesburg: FinMark Trust.

Bates, R. H., and D. Lien. 1985. "A Note on Taxation, Development, and Representative Government." *Politics & Society* 14: 53–70.

Beck, T., A. Demirgüç-Kunt, and R. Levine. 2007. "Finance, Inequality and the Poor." *Journal of Economic Growth* 12: 27–49.

Beck, T., M. Fuchs, and M. Uy. 2009. "Finance in Africa: Achievements and Challenges." In *The Africa Competitiveness Report 2009.* Geneva: World Economic Forum.

Benavente, J. M. 2006. "Programa de Crédito para la Microempresa Banco Estado." World Bank, Washington, DC.

Benavente, J. M., A. Galetovic, and R. Sanhueza. 2006. "Fogape: An Economic Analysis." Working Paper, Universidad de Chile, Departamento de Economía, Santiago.

Besley, T. 1994. "How Do Market Failures Justify Interventions in Rural Credit Markets?" *The World Bank Research Observer* 9: 27–47.

Bhagwati, J. N. 1971. "The Generalized Theory of Distortions and Welfare." In *Trade, Balance of Payments and Growth: Papers in International Economics in Honor of Charles P. Kindleberger,* ed. J. N. Bhagwati, R. Jones, R. Mundell, and J. Vanek, 69–90. Amsterdam, North-Holland.

———. 1982. "Directly Unproductive, Profit-Seeking (DUP) Activities." *The Journal of Political Economy* 90: 988–1002.

Biggs, T., and M. K. Shah. 2006. "African SMEs, Networks, and Manufacturing Performance." *Journal of Banking & Finance* 30: 3043–66.

Boone, C. 2005. "State, Capital, and the Politics of Banking Reform in Sub-Saharan Africa." *Comparative Politics* 37: 401–20.

Bräutigam, D., O. H. Fjeldstad, and M. Moore. 2008. *Taxation and State-Building in Developing Countries: Capacity and Consent.* Cambridge and New York: Cambridge University Press.

Bräutigam, D., L. Rakner, and S. Taylor. 2002. "Business Associations and Growth Coalitions in Sub-Saharan Africa." *The Journal of Modern African Studies* 40: 519–47.

Brownbridge, M. 1998a. "Financial Repression & Financial Reform in Uganda." In *Banking in Africa: The Impact of Financial Sector Reform Since Independence,* ed. M. Brownbridge, C. Harvey, and A. Fritz Gockel, 126–42. Oxford and Trenton, NJ: James Currey and Africa World Press.

———. 1998b. "Government Policies and Development of Banking in Kenya." In *Banking in Africa: The Impact of Financial Sector Reform Since Independence,* eds. M. Brownbridge, C. Harvey, and A. Fritz Gockel, 79–102. Oxford and Trenton, NJ: James Currey and Africa World Press.

Brownbridge, M., C. Harvey, and A. Fritz Gockel, eds. 1998. *Banking in Africa: The Impact of Financial Sector Reform Since Independence.* Oxford and Trenton, NJ: James Currey and Africa World Press.

Burgess, R., and R. Pande. 2005. "Do Rural Banks Matter? Evidence from the Indian Social Banking Experiment." *American Economic Review* 95: 780–95.

Candace, N., and W. Angela. 2008. "Financial Education in Kenya: Scoping Exercise Report." Financial Sector Deepening Kenya, Nairobi.

Chang, H. J. 2009. "Rethinking Public Policy in Agriculture: Lessons from History, Distant and Recent." *Journal of Peasant Studies* 36: 477–515.

Cheng, T.-J. 1993. "Guarding the Commanding Heights: The State as Banker in Taiwan." In *The Politics of Finance in Developing Countries*, ed. S. Haggard, C. H. Lee, and S. Maxfield, 55–92. Ithaca, NY: Cornell University Press.

Collier, P., and D. Rohner. 2008. "Democracy, Development, and Conflict." *Journal of the European Economic Association* 6: 531–40.

Criscuolo, A., and V. Palmade. 2008. "Reform Teams: How the Most Successful Reformers Organized Themselves." *Public Policy for the Private Sector* 318: 1–3.

Daumont, R., F. Le Galle, and F. Leroux. 2004. "Banking in Sub-Saharan Africa: What Went Wrong?" IMF Working Paper WP 04/55, International Monetary Fund, Washington, DC.

De la Torre, A., J. C. Gozzi, and S. L. Schmukler. 2007. "Innovative Experiences in Access to Finance: Market Friendly Roles for the Visible Hand." Policy Research Working Paper 4326, World Bank, Washington, DC.

De la Torre, A., M. S. Martínez Pería, and S. L. Schmukler. 2010. "Bank Involvement with SMEs: Beyond Relationship Lending." *Journal of Banking & Finance* 34: 2280–93.

De Luna-Martinez, J. 2006. "Access to Financial Services in Zambia." Policy Research Working Paper No. 4061, World Bank, Washington, DC.

Demirgüç-Kunt, A., T. Beck, and P. Honohan. 2008. *Finance for All? Policies and Pitfalls in Expanding Access.* Washington, DC: World Bank.

Evans, P. B., D. Rueschemeyer, and T. Skocpol. 1985. *Bringing the State Back In.* Cambridge: Cambridge University Press.

Frieden, J. A. 1991. *Debt, Development, and Democracy: Modern Political Economy and Latin America, 1965–1985.* Princeton, NJ: Princeton University Press.

Gerschenkron, A. 1962. *Economic Backwardness in Economic Perspective.* Cambridge, MA: Belknap Press of Harvard University Press.

Girma, S., and A. Shortland. 2008. "The Political Economy of Financial Development." *Oxford Economic Papers* 60: 567–96.

Goldsheid, R. 1958. "A Sociological Approach to Problems of Public Finance." In *Classics in Public Finance*, ed. R. A. Musgrave and A. T. Peacock, 202–13. New York: Macmillan.

Gordon, R., and W. Li. 2009. "Tax Structures in Developing Countries: Many Puzzles and a Possible Explanation." *Journal of Public Economics* 93: 855–66.

Haber, S., D. C. North, and B. R. Weingast, eds. 2008. *Political Institutions and Financial Development*. Stanford, CA: Stanford University Press.

Haggard, S., and C. H. Lee. 1993. "The Political Dimension of Finance in Economic Development." In *The Politics of Finance in Developing Countries*, ed. S. Haggard, C. H. Lee, and S. Maxfield, 3–22. Ithaca, NY: Cornell University Press.

Haggard, S., C. H. Lee, and S. Maxfield. 1993. *The Politics of Finance in Developing Countries*. Ithaca, NY: Cornell University Press.

Haggard, S., and S. Maxfield. 1993. "Political Explanations of Financial Policy in Developing Countries." In *The Politics of Finance in Developing Countries*, ed. S. Haggard, C. H. Lee, and S. Maxfield, 293–326. Ithaca, NY: Cornell University Press.

Hanson, J. A. 2003. "Banking in Developing Countries in the 1990s." Policy Research Working Paper 3168, World Bank, Washington, DC.

Harvey, C. 1998. "Banking Policy in Botswana: Orthodox but Untypical." In *Banking in Africa: The Impact of Financial Sector Reform Since Independence*, ed. M. Brownbridge, C. Harvey, and A. Fritz Gockel, 10–34. Oxford and Trenton, NJ: James Currey and Africa World Press.

Hausmann, R., D. Rodrik, and A. Velasco. 2007. "Growth Diagnostics." In *One Economics, Many Recipes: Globalization, Institutions, and Economic Growth*, ed. D. Rodrik, 56–84. Princeton and Oxford: Princeton University Press.

Honohan, P., and T. Beck. 2007. *Making Finance Work for Africa*. Washington, DC: World Bank.

Huang, Y. 2010. "Political Institutions and Financial Development: An Empirical Study." *World Development* 38 (12): 1667–77.

Ize, A., R. Pardo, and S. Zekri. 2008. "The Process of Financial Development: A Statistical View from the FSAP Program." Policy Research Working Paper 4626, World Bank, Washington, DC.

Jefferis, K. 2007. *Enhancing Access to Banking and Financial Services in Botswana, Gaborone*. Marshalltown and Gaborone: FinMark Trust and Econsult.

Kang, D. C. 2003. "Bad Loans to Good Friends: Money Politics and the Developmental State in South Korea." *International Organization* 56: 177–207.

Karl, T. L. 1997. *The Paradox of Plenty: Oil Booms and Petro-States.* Berkeley and Los Angeles: University of California Press.

Kaufmann, D., A. Kraay, and M. Mastruzzi. 2009. "Governance Matters VIII: Aggregate and Individual Governance Indicators, 1996–2008." Policy Research Working Paper 4978, World Bank, Washington, DC.

Keefer, P. 2007. *Beyond Legal Origin and Checks and Balances: Political Credibility, Citizen Information, and Financial Sector Development.* Washington, DC: World Bank.

Kosack, S. 2009. "Realising Education for All: Defining and Using the Political Will to Invest in Primary Education." *Comparative Education* 45: 495–523.

Krueger, A. O. 1993. *Political Economy of Policy Reform in Developing Countries.* Cambridge, MA: MIT Press.

La Porta, R., F. Lopez-De-Silanes, and A. Shleifer. 2002. "Government Ownership of Banks." *The Journal of Finance* 57: 265–301.

Leonard, D. K. 2008. "Where Are 'Pockets' of Effective Agencies Likely in Weak Governance States and Why? A Propositional Inventory." IDS Working Paper 306, Institute of Development Studies, Brighton.

Levine, R., N. Loayza, and T. Beck. 2000. "Financial Intermediation and Growth: Causality and Causes." *Journal of Monetary Economics* 46: 31–77.

Lewis, P., and H. Stein. 1997. "Shifting Fortunes: The Political Economy of Financial Liberalization in Nigeria." *World Development* 25: 5–22.

Lukauskas, A., and S. Minushkin. 2000. "Explaining Styles of Financial Market Opening in Chile, Mexico, South Korea, and Turkey." *International Studies Quarterly* 44: 695–723.

MacIntyre, A. J. 1993. "The Politics of Finance in Indonesia: Command, Confusion, and Competition." In *The Politics of Finance in Developing Countries,* ed. S. Haggard, C. H. Lee, and S. Maxfield, 123–64. Ithaca, NY: Cornell University Press.

Maxfield, S. 1990. *Governing Capital: International Finance and Mexican Politics.* Ithaca, NY: Cornell University Press.

———. 1994. "Financial Incentives and Central Bank Authority in Industrializing Nations." *World Politics* 46: 556–88.

Moncrieffe, J., and C. Luttrell. 2005. *An Analytical Framework for Understanding the Political Economy of Sectors and Policy Arenas.* London: Overseas Development Institute.

Moore, M. 1998. "Death without Taxes: Democracy, State Capacity, and Aid Dependence in the Fourth World." In *The Democratic Developmental State: Political and Institutional Design,* ed. M. Robinson and G. White, 84–121. Oxford: Oxford University Press.

————. 2001. *Types of Political Systems: A Practical Framework for DFID Staff* (Version 2). London: Department for International Development.

Moore, M., J. Leavy, P. Houtzager, and H. White. 2003. "Polity Qualities: How Governance Affects Poverty." In *Changing Paths: International Development and the New Politics of Inclusion*, ed. P. Houtzager and M. Moore, 167–203. Ann Arbor, MI: University of Michigan Press.

Moore, M., and H. Schmitz. 2008. "Idealism, Realism and the Investment Climate in Developing Countries." IDS Working Paper 307, Institute of Development Studies, Brighton.

Moss, T. J., G. Pettersson, N. van de Walle, and T. Floor. 2006. "An Aid-Institutions Paradox? A Review Essay on Aid Dependency and State Building in Sub-Saharan Africa." Working Paper No. 74, Center for Global Development, Washington, DC.

Mylenko, N. 2007. "Developing Credit Reporting in Africa: Opportunities and Challenges." *Access Finance Newsletter*. 19 (September).

Nissanke, M. K. 2001. "Financing Enterprise Development in Sub-Saharan Africa." *Cambridge Journal of Economics* 25: 343.

Noll, R. G. 1989. "Economic Perspectives on the Politics of Regulation." In *Handbook of Industrial Organization*, ed. R. Schmalensee and R. Willi, 1253–87. Amsterdam: Elsevier Science & Technology.

Nsereko, J. 1995. "Problems of Non-Performing Advances." *The Ugandan Banker* 3: 26–35.

Pagano, M., and P. Volpin. 2001. "The Political Economy of Finance." *Oxford Review of Economic Policy* 17: 502.

Pfeffer, J., and G. R. Salancik. 1978. *The External Control of Organisations: A Resource Dependence Perspective*. New York: Harper and Row.

Przeworski, A. 2000. *Democracy and Development: Political Institutions and Well-Being in the World, 1950–1990*. Cambridge: Cambridge University Press.

Rajan, R. 2006. "Separate and Unequal." *Finance and Development* 43: 56–57.

Rajan, R. G., and L. Zingales. 2003. "The Great Reversals: The Politics of Financial Development in the Twentieth Century." *Journal of Financial Economics* 69: 5–50.

Robinson, J. A. 2009. "Industrial Policy and Development: A Political Economy Perspective." Paper prepared for the 2009 World Bank Annual Bank Conference of Development Economics (ABCDE), Seoul, June 22–24.

Rodrik, D. 2008. "Second-Best Institutions." NBER Working Paper No. W14050, National Bureau of Economic Research, Cambridge, MA.

Rodrik, D., A. Subramanian, and F. Trebbi. 2004. "Institutions Rule: The Primacy of Institutions over Geography and Integration in Economic Development." *Journal of Economic Growth* 9: 131–65.

Sapp Mancini, A., M. Yee, and S. Jain. 2008. *SME Lending in Africa: Challenges, Current Trends and USAID Initiatives.* Washington, DC: USAID.

Skocpol, T. 1985. "Bringing the State Back In: Strategies of Analysis in Current Research." In *Bringing the State Back In,* ed. P. B. Evans, D. Rueschemeyer, and T. Skocpol, 3–43. Cambridge: Cambridge University Press.

Stiglitz, J. E., and M. Uy. 1996. "Financial Markets, Public Policy, and the East Asian Miracle." *The World Bank Research Observer* 11: 249.

Stiglitz, J. E., and A. Weiss. 1981. "Credit Rationing in Markets with Imperfect Information." *The American Economic Review* 71: 393–410.

Thomas, J. W., and M. S. Grindle. 1990. "After the Decision: Implementing Policy Reforms in Developing Countries." *World Development* 18: 1163–81.

Thurow, L. C. 1989. "Putting Capitalists Back into Capitalism." In *Unconventional Wisdom: Essays on Economics in Honor of John Kenneth Galbraith,* ed. S. Bowles, R. Edwards, and W. G. Shepherd, 189–204. Boston: Houghton Mifflin.

Tilly, C. 1992. *Coercion, Capital, and European States, AD 990–1992.* Cambridge, MA and Oxford, UK: Blackwell.

Townsend, R. M., and J. Yaron. 2001. "The Credit Risk-Contingency System of an Asian Development Bank." *Economic Perspectives* 25: 31–48.

Vittas, D., and Y. J. Cho. 1996. "Credit Policies: Lessons from Japan and Korea." *The World Bank Research Observer* 11: 277.

Winters, J. A. 1994. "Review: Power and the Control of Capital." *World Politics* 46: 419–52.

———. 1996. *Power in Motion: Capital and the Indonesian State.* Ithaca and London: Cornell University Press.

Wittman, D. 1989. "Why Democracies Produce Efficient Results." *The Journal of Political Economy* 97: 1395–424.

Woodall, B. 1996. *Japan under Construction: Corruption. Politics and Public Works.* Berkeley, CA: University of California Press.

World Bank. 1997. *World Development Report 1997: The State in a Changing World.* New York: Oxford University Press.

———. 2005. *World Development Report 2005: A Better Investment Climate for Everyone.* Washington, DC: World Bank.

———. 2007. *World Development Report 2008: Agriculture for Development.* Washington, DC: World Bank.

Yaron, J., M. D. Benjamin, and S. Charitonenko. 1998. "Promoting Efficient Rural Financial Intermediation." *The World Bank Research Observer* 13: 147.

Zysman, J. 1983. *Governments, Markets, and Growth: Financial Systems and the Politics of Industrial Change.* Ithaca, NY: Cornell University Press.

www.ingramcontent.com/pod-product-compliance
Lightning Source LLC
Chambersburg PA
CBHW061153220326
41599CB00025B/4464